BOONE COUNTY LIBRARY
2040 9100 544 919 7
S0-BAG-271
WITHDRAWN
Edith Head
1936
Stage and
Dressing room—
BOONE COUNTY PUBLIC LIBRARY
BURLINGTON, KY 41005
www.bcpl.org

EDITH HEAD

EDITH HEAD

THE FIFTY-YEAR CAREER OF HOLLYWOOD'S GREATEST COSTUME DESIGNER

Jay Jorgensen

Introduction by Academy Award-winning costume designer Sandy Powell

RUNNING PRESS
PHILADELPHIA • LONDON

LifeTime
Media

Grace Kelly on Oscar night 1955, in a dress and coat designed by Edith Head.

CONTENTS

For Walter Albrecht

LifeTime Media

A LifeTime Media Production
LifeTime Media, Inc.
352 Seventh Avenue, 7th Fl
New York, NY 10001
www.lifetimemedia.com

Neither LifeTime Media nor any of its goods or services are in any way affiliated with, associated with, sponsored by or approved by Lifetime networks, Lifetime television, or Lifetime Entertainment Services.

Printed in China

9 8 7 6 5 4 3 2 1
Digit on the right indicates the number of this printing

Library of Congress Control Number: 2010926483

ISBN 978-0-7624-3805-1

Designed by Roger Gorman/Reiner Design
Typography: Bodoni, Meta Plus and Trade Gothic

Running Press Book Publishers
2300 Chestnut Street
Philadelphia, PA 19103-4371

Visit us on the web!
www.runningpress.com

Shirley Ross in *The Big Broadcast of 1938*

"WHAT WE DO IS A CROSS BETWEEN MAGIC AND CAMOUFLAGE. WE ASK THE PUBLIC TO BELIEVE THAT EVERY TIME THEY SEE AN ACTRESS OR ACTOR THAT THEY ARE A DIFFERENT PERSON."

–Edith Head, 1958.

INTRODUCTION by Sandy Powell

EDITH HEAD CLAIMED SHE DIDN'T KNOW HOW TO SEW. THIS WASN'T TRUE—HER MOTHER TAUGHT HER WHEN SHE WAS YOUNG. SHE ONLY SAID SHE COULDN'T SO AS TO AVOID BEING ASKED TO DO SEWING DEMONSTRATIONS ON HER MANY TELEVISION APPEARANCES, OR AT LADIES' LUNCHEONS AND FASHION SHOWS. I ALSO LEARNED TO SEW AT AN EARLY AGE, AND BELIEVE IT IS ESSENTIAL FOR UNDERSTANDING THE DESIGN PROCESS.

Costume designers, like many others working in a creative field, are led to their vocation by a series of epiphanies. My first was seeing a show called *Flowers*, by *avant garde* dancer and choreographer Lindsay Kemp, in my teens. It reinforced my love of costume and theatricality. Although I look to contemporary fashion for inspiration, whether designing a modern or period film, I never wanted to be a *fashion* designer. To me it seemed too restricting. I was more interested in the idea of using clothes to bring characters to life in theatre or film, to make them believable as well as look good.

Under the Hollywood studio system, Edith Head was contracted to design as many films as the studio assigned to her, whether she wanted to or not. My experience of working in film has been very different. I'm fortunate in that I can choose my projects based on the scripts and directors with whom I'd like to work. But our careers began on a similar path. We both went to art school, and started working for little or no money.

Whenever I'm asked advice on becoming a costume designer I always say that practical experience is the most valuable asset—you just have to get out there and do it. Edith did just that.

Although the life of a costume designer may appear glamorous, it isn't. There is never enough time or money. Things can—and do—go wrong. Actors or directors can change their minds about a costume, sometimes moments before shooting, and a designer must quickly find an alternative. Schedules can suddenly change. A costume can get damaged. A costume designer must be resourceful and able to solve problems in an instant as any delay in shooting can cost hundreds of thousands of dollars.

Many actors have strong opinions about their character and what they should wear. There are egos and insecurities to deal with, changes of direction, and crises of confidence. About 80 percent of what a costume designer does is psychology; only 20 percent of it is art.

Nearly every costume designed for a film has a story behind its creation. While doing research for *The Young Victoria*, I was given access to the archives at Kensington Palace and allowed to see and touch some of Queen Victoria's gowns. Martin Scorsese once gave me an entire film to watch just to see the stripe on a collar.

This book isn't so much a biography of Edith Head, the woman, but more of a biography of the clothes that she designed. Here are some of their stories.

Sandy Powell
Academy Award-winning costume designer of *Shakespeare in Love, The Aviator,* and *The Young Victoria*

Edith examines fabrics in her salon at Paramount

CHAPTER ONE

THE EARLY YEARS

Edith (far right) and a group of friends are entertained by Anna Spare (top row, center)

Edith Claire Posenor, circa 1904.

EDITH HEAD WAS ONE OF HOLLYWOOD'S GREATEST DESIGNERS. AN AMAZING WOMAN WHO WORKED IN A FIELD THAT WAS DOMINATED BY MEN IN THE 1930S AND 1940S, SHE DESIGNED COSTUMES FOR MORE THAN 1,100 FILMS. CONSIDERED TO HAVE HAD ONE OF THE MOST PROLIFIC AND CELEBRATED CAREERS IN THE HISTORY OF MOTION PICTURES, SHE WAS NOMINATED FOR THIRTY-FIVE ACADEMY AWARDS AND WON EIGHT OF THEM.

Head was praised for her intelligence and diplomacy by co-workers and viewed as a plagiarist and publicity seeker by some other designers. For Edith Head, the character always came first. Edith Head was driven by her passion to create a second skin for actors and actresses. Her mission was to help them effectively serve the needs of the character. Additionally, she had to meet the needs of the entire film along with the demands of the directors and studio bosses with their numerous dictates, whims, and requirements. She was a talented artist who wanted to get it right for everyone.

Screen legend Bette Davis said of the designer: "Through the work of a fine costume designer, an actor or actress can *become* the character. We may rehearse our lines, our movements, and our expressions, but until we finally slip into the costumes does everything come together so that we actually *become* the character. If we are not comfortable in those clothes, if they do not project the character, the costume designer has failed us. Edith Head never failed."

Edith's childhood years were never up for discussion, even with friends. When interviewed, Edith always shared a few charming anecdotes, but never went into any detail. She would often purposely lie about her parents or mislead people about the cities in which she grew up, or even where she was born. Almost all of what is known about Edith's childhood is through the persistence of David Chierichetti, her friend and biographer, who, over time, was able to dig deeper into some of the more painful details of Edith's childhood. Edith's father, Max Posenor, emigrated from Prussia in 1876. He was one of the millions of Jews that came to the United States in the 1800s seeking better opportunities and to escape from religious persecution and political insurrections. Edith's mother, Anna Levy, was born in St. Louis, Missouri in 1874. There is no record of Max and Anna ever being married, though Chierichetti uncovered a 1900 census report in which Max listed himself as being married for five years. The couple lived in various cities in Southern California, including San Bernardino where their daughter Edith Claire Posenor was born on October 28, 1897. Max had opened a haberdashery, but it failed shortly after Edith's birth, and the family relocated to El Paso, Texas.

In the 1900 census, Max lists himself as living with Anna and Edith in El Paso. But a year later, Anna married Frank Spare, a mining engineer, in San Bernardino. There is no record of Anna divorcing Max, or Frank Spare adopting Edith, but as the couple moved from mining town to mining town, it was assumed by people that Edith was the couple's biological child.

In early photographs of a young Edith, she appears to be well cared for, despite the rough conditions that existed in mining camps during that period. In her autobiography *The Dress Doctor,* Edith describes how, even though the family was not very affluent, her mother always tried to make a nice home. Edith was well-dressed, and the family had enough income to be able to take a few trips across the country when Edith was five and eight.

The family moved around so much that later, Edith couldn't remember all the towns in which the family lived. But when writing *The*

(Right) Edith, sixth from left, while teaching at The Bishop's School, 1919. (Left) Edith on the porch of the family home in Searchlight, Nevada, circa 1905.

Dress Doctor, Edith focused on one particular photograph in her collection to describe her childhood — an image of a solitary Edith sitting on the porch of an unpainted house in Searchlight, Nevada. The isolation shown in the photograph of the young girl looking out onto the barren desert must have summed up Edith's feelings about her childhood better than any other for her. She said hated the desert and dreamed of big cities and having lots of playmates.

Edith's need for friends, imaginary or otherwise, can best be illustrated by the designer's description of how she found solace by making small figures out of the pliable greasewood that grew on the desert floor. She often threw tea parties with guests including, Tom, Edith's black cat, her white dog, Dina, dressed in doll clothes, and various other animals including burros, adorned with feathers, ribbons, and necklaces of crepe paper. Edith fashioned a table out of a cardboard packing box and a tablecloth from one of her mother's red-checked linen towels. She created a doll house out of old wooden boxes and furnished it with cigar boxes wrapped in scraps of old gloves, pulled from a sock bag in which she kept scraps of fabric she constantly collected. That scrap bag was, according to Edith, her most treasured possession.

Although Edith occasionally owned a doll, she often relied on some of the horned toads she found lying in the sand to dress up and play in her makeshift doll house. "I had no other children for playmates," Edith once said. "Naturally, all of my intensive imagination in child's play had to be connected into activities I could pursue alone. In later years, struggling as a dress designer, I used to tell myself, 'anyone who can dress a horn toad, can dress anything!' "

Surely one of the great tragedies which began in Edith's childhood was that some of her front teeth never grew in properly. Being taunted, in only the way children can be cruel, Edith was called "Beaver" by several of her classmates. Edith stopped smiling so that no one could see her teeth, making the already shy Edith even more introverted. Even years later, after her teeth were fixed, she rarely smiled.

Another childhood memory that Edith said contributed to her survival capabilities in Hollywood , involved her mother finding her

(left to right): Jean Arthur, Clara Bow, Jean Harlow and Leone Lane were the personification of young, modern women of the 1920's in *The Saturday Night Kid.* (Right) A portrait of Edith circa 1923, taken around the time she was being courted by Charles Head.

asleep on a wood pile with a rattlesnake coiled up sleeping next to her. Edith said she had no fear. Her theory was that if you left them alone, they would leave you alone.

THE BIG CITY BECKONS

In 1911, Edith finished elementary school in Redding, California. As Edith matured, Frank Spare's opportunities for work narrowed. Edith told David Chierichetti that the family ended up in some very unsavory locales in Mexico, where Edith and her mother were expected to cook and clean for the camp's occupants.

Anna Spare decided that mining camp life was not what she had envisioned for Edith or herself, and brought Edith to Los Angeles to attend high school in 1914. Though records do show that Edith had attended grade school, she would say later, "I lived in mining camps until I was ready to go to high school. I've never gone to grade school. I do not know the multiplication tables. I do not know the names of the captains of the fleet. I know nothing I should know." It was probably in Mexico that her education suffered the most, having to rely on only what her mother could teach her. But Edith learned to speak Spanish, and the experience was most likely the genesis of Edith's love of Mexican culture and heritage.

Edith and Anna moved in with Mittie Morgan, Anna's best friend, in downtown Los Angeles, and Edith began attending Los Angeles High School. Edith became very involved in extracurricular activities, including acting the lead in the school play. She now seemed to have the city life that she'd longed for back in Searchlight. Los Angeles was experiencing a huge migration of people who were arriving by the carload to work in the area's booming aircraft and film industries, to speculate in oil drilling, or to catch the religious fervor

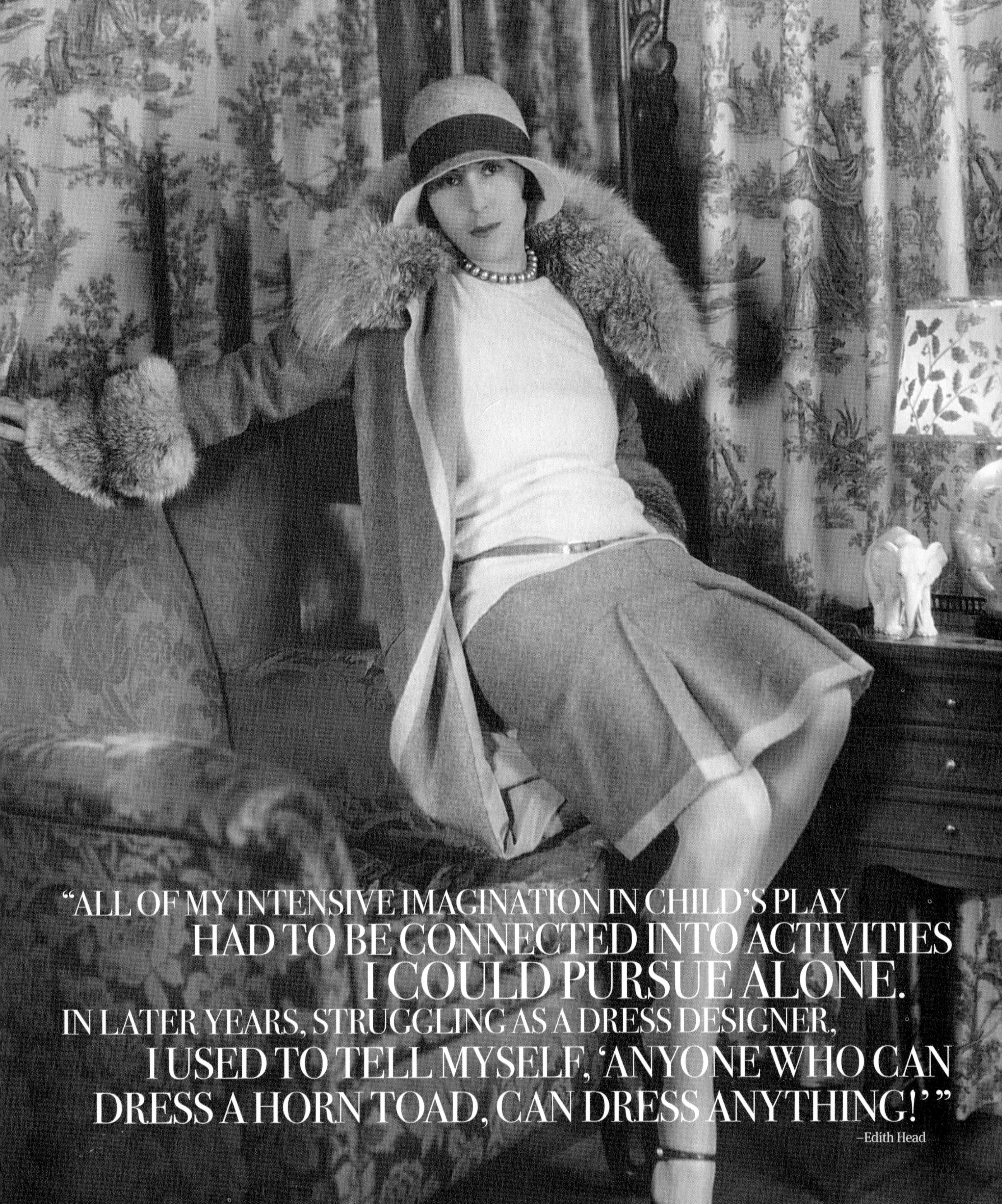

“ALL OF MY INTENSIVE IMAGINATION IN CHILD’S PLAY
HAD TO BE CONNECTED INTO ACTIVITIES
I COULD PURSUE ALONE.
IN LATER YEARS, STRUGGLING AS A DRESS DESIGNER,
I USED TO TELL MYSELF, ‘ANYONE WHO CAN
DRESS A HORN TOAD, CAN DRESS ANYTHING!’ ”

–Edith Head

of the charismatic minister Aimee Semple McPherson.

On April 6, 1917, the U.S. declared war on Germany and entered World War I. Though Southern California was not impacted greatly by the war, many of the area's young men were sent overseas to fight. After graduating from Los Angeles High School, Edith enrolled at the University of California at Berkeley to continue her education. She received her Bachelor of Arts degree in Letters and Sciences with honors in French in 1919. A year later she received a master's degree in romance languages from Stanford University. Returning to Los Angeles, Edith was fortunate to find a temporary job teaching French at the Bishop School in La Jolla, California. Still relatively new, the school had been founded in 1909 by The Right Reverend Joseph Horsfall Johnson, Bishop of Los Angeles. Most of the school's buildings were completed only a few years before Edith began teaching there. Edith's serious comportment probably helped her to fit right in with the school teachers at an upscale Catholic school. "I have a theory that once you've taught, you can do anything," Edith would say later.

When the teaching position ended in the summer of 1921, Edith Head found an even more exciting position — one that would introduce her to the personal world of some of Hollywood's most powerful figures. That September, she began teaching French and art at Hollywood School for Girls. The school was located on North La Brea Avenue, north of Hollywood Boulevard and south of Franklin Avenue. It was known for its "open air" concept in which its students could learn outdoors. The school became a favorite of motion picture personnel for their children. Even though it was primarily for girls, boys, including Douglas Fairbanks Jr. and Joel McCrea, attended.

Anna DeMille, sister-in-law of director Cecil B. DeMille was wary of sending her daughter Agnes (later a great choreographer), to public school, and enrolled her at The Hollywood School for Girls. Cecil B. DeMille then sent his daughters Cecilia and Katharine to the school. Field trips were given to the Famous Players-Lasky Studio on days when DeMille was filming a big scene, and both students and teachers went to observe.

In order to earn more money, Edith was also teaching art at the school; having exaggerated her qualifications, she was not particularly adept at the subject. To compensate, Edith enrolled in evening art classes at the Otis Art Institute, and would mold her own lessons for the girls on what she had learned the previous week in class. Edith continued her art studies at The Chouinard Art Institute, founded by painter Nelbert Murphy Chouinard, who had opened the school that year.

Betty Head, a classmate of Edith's at Chouinard, decided to play matchmaker between her brother Charles and Edith. Charles Head was a tall, handsome, personable young man with a job as a traveling salesman for The Super Refined Metals Company. Edith fell in love, and the pair courted in between the long empty spells when Charles was traveling for business. On July 25, 1923, they were married in Los Angeles and went on a honeymoon before Charles went back to his sales trips.

In 1919 World War I came to and end, bringing with it an era that was filled with new modern technologies such as cars, radios, and movies, all of which helped to make a break with the past. Architecture became more streamlined, jazz infused excitement into music, and a new breed of woman, the flapper, raised their hemlines above their knees, bobbed their hair and started smoking. Ironically, the 1920's also ushered in Prohibition, outlawing the selling of most alcohol in the United States. In response, clandestine clubs called speakeasies opened, where the alcohol flowed, patrons watched live floor shows and danced the night away. Speakeasy owners often bribed police to leave them alone or give them advance notice of raids.

Edith Head was just in her mid-20s, as Los Angeles became caught up in the Jazz Age. She bobbed her hair in the style of silent film star Colleen Moore. Photographs show her dressed fashionably for the day, despite her somewhat low pay as a teacher. Frank and Anna Spare were now living in Los Angeles, and Edith visited them during the long stretches of time when Charles was out of town. While she knew that Charles liked to drink, it was becoming more obvious to her that he had a problem with alcohol.

Edith with her first husband Charles Head, in 1923

CHAPTER TWO

THE DECEPTION WORKS

Edith (far right) assists at a fitting for actress Wynne Gibson (second from right) in 1933.

An early publicity photograph of Edith from 1928

AS THE SUMMER OF 1924 APPROACHED, EDITH NEEDED TO FIND A TEMPORARY WAY TO SUPPORT CHARLES AND HERSELF THROUGHOUT THE SUMMER WHEN SHE WOULD NOT BE TEACHING. EDITH SAW A CLASSIFIED AD IN THE *Los Angeles Times* THAT FAMOUS PLAYERS-LASKY STUDIO (WHICH WOULD EVENTUALLY BECOME PARAMOUNT), HAD AN OPENING FOR A SKETCH ARTIST WORKING UNDER HOWARD GREER, THE STUDIO'S CHIEF DESIGNER. GREER HAD COME TO THE STUDIO TO WORK FOR CLAIRE WEST ON CECIL B. DEMILLE'S *The Ten Commandments* (1923).

Prior to that, he had worked for Lucile (Lady Duff Gordon) in both her New York and Chicago salons, as well as for Paris designers Paul Poiret and Molyneux. At the time, he was designing for the studio's biggest stars including Bessie Love, Jetta Goudal, Pola Negri, and Anna Q. Nilsson.

Because Edith didn't feel her own work was adequate enough, she asked some of her classmates at Chouinard if she could borrow their drawings to show in her portfolio for her interview. She brought a selection of seascapes, landscapes, portraits and costume designs. Edith stopped short of actually saying the drawings were hers, and Greer complimented her on the versatility shown in the drawings, not realizing they had been created by several different artists. Edith never really expected to get the job, but she was hired on the spot and offered $40.00 a week.

When Howard Greer published his memoirs *Designing Male* in 1949, he described the interview and how he subsequently kept Edith on after her ruse was revealed:

"Today every studio would turn away fifty eager young designers daily who would gladly give a right arm for a beginner's job," Greer wrote, "but back in the early silent days one had to advertise for help. We placed an ad in the papers and a young girl, with a face like a pussy cat crossed with a Fujita drawing, appeared with a carpetbag full of sketches. There were architectural drawings, plans for interior decoration, magazine illustrations, and fashion designs. Struck dumb with admiration for anyone possessed of such diverse talents, I hired the gal on the spot. She came to work the next morning and looked out from under her bangs with the expression of a frightened terrier. She

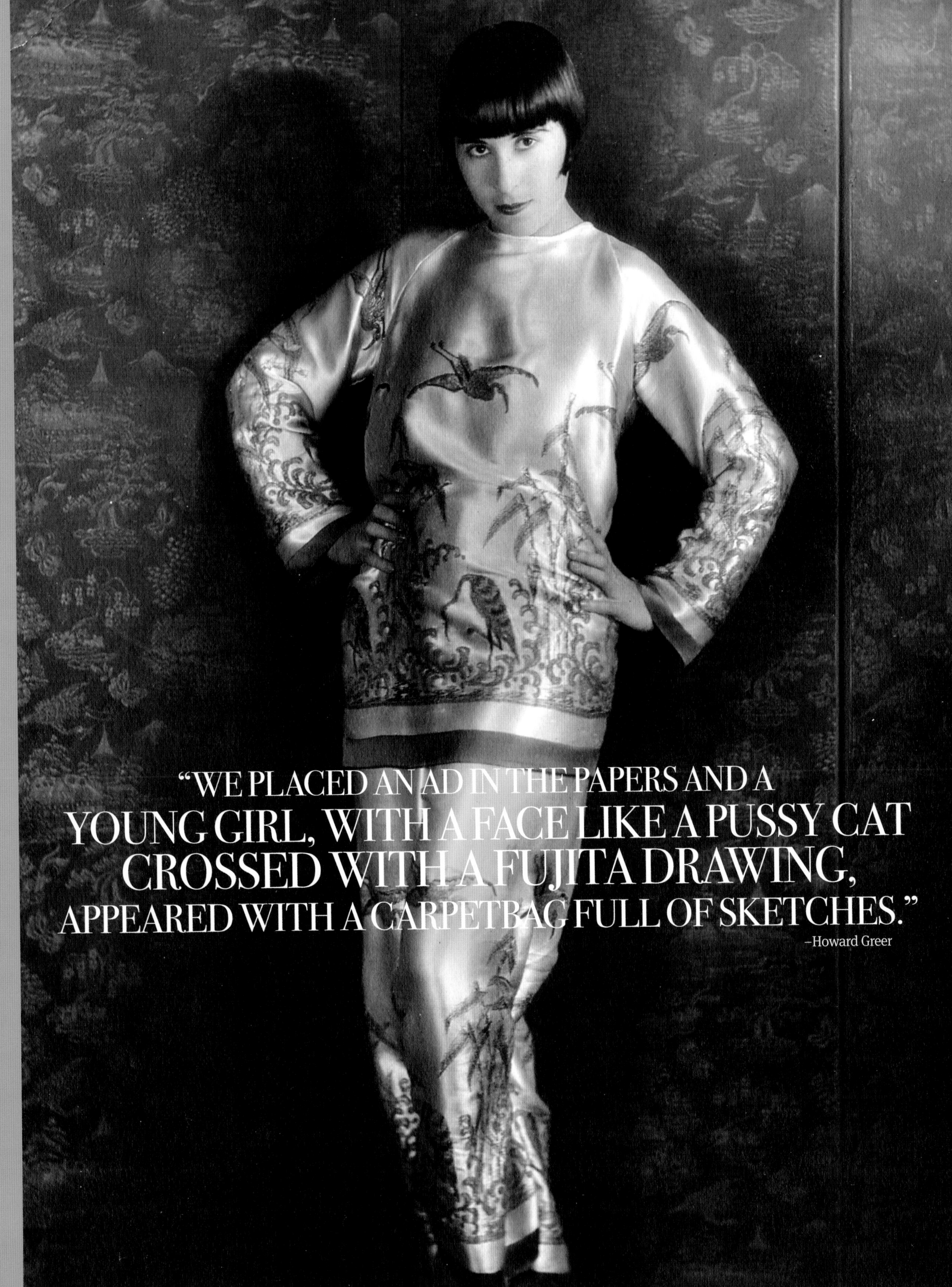

"WE PLACED AN AD IN THE PAPERS AND A YOUNG GIRL, WITH A FACE LIKE A PUSSY CAT CROSSED WITH A FUJITA DRAWING, APPEARED WITH A CARPETBAG FULL OF SKETCHES."

–Howard Greer

(Below) Designer Howard Greer greets one of his private clients in the 1920's (Right) A drawing by Edith, in the style of Howard Greer, for a dress for Geta Nissen in *The Wanderer.*

was anxious to please, but she was obviously ill at ease.

'Don't be upset,' I assured her. 'It won't take long to get onto the hang of things.'

'I'm not worried about 'that," she stammered, 'but I have the most awful confession to make! You see, when I was faced with my first interview, I was suddenly seized with panic! I was afraid that if I didn't have a lot of wonderful sketches, I'd never get the job.'

'But they were wonderful. All of them!'

'That's just it! They weren't any of them mine! I just went through the art school where I've been studying and picked up everybody's sketches I could lay my hands on!'

She might easily have saved her breath and her confession, for her own talents soon proved she was more than worthy for the job."

Years later, Edith would say "you know when you're very young, you have no sense of morality, I guess. I thought it was very amusing to get this big portfolio. It never occurred to me it was quite dishonest."

Edith's new salary was a considerable improvement over her old teacher's salary. She was put in a room in the costume department with twelve other sketch artists. Howard Greer taught her to draw in his style, so that when he presented his sketches to stars and producers, her sketches would be virtually indistinguishable from his own. "When I worked with a designer, I would sketch in their style, and I would more or less become indoctrinated to that type of designing," Edith said later.

Before the unionization of the film industry, the wardrobe workrooms at the studios allowed Edith to help wherever she was needed. Her Spanish skills made her indispensible to Greer, since she was able to communicate with the seamstresses and foreign stars, where he could not. "The only reason I survived to stay on his staff as a sketch girl was the fact that I had a background of speaking foreign languages," Edith said. "They were making foreign versions of films and I was the only one who could talk readily with the foreign stars. When I was asked to add a bustle or a hoop skirt, I knew exactly what they were talking about."

LIFE AT THE STUDIO

Howard Greer described the studio as a "sprawling conglomeration of sheds, barns and stages covering two city blocks that had not too long before been citrus groves and avocado ranches. Gray-painted buildings housed the moguls, writers, librarians, directors, auditors, bookkeepers, and technicians in cozy and democratic proximity. Boardwalks led from one office door to another there was no snobbery, no social inequality, and very little political chicanery during working hours.

"The area known as the Ladies Wardrobe was situated on the second floor of a concrete mausoleum on the northwest corner of the lot. On the ground floor was the Men's Wardrobe, easily identified by the strong and pungent male odor of well-worn shoes. shirts, and uniforms; while upstairs was the more refined and ladylike smell of tarnished metal, cloth, stale make-up, and scorched material on ironing boards. Several cramped cubicles served as offices, two slightly larger cubicles served as fitting rooms, a spacious stockroom was piled high with laces, brocades, and glittering embroideries, an enormous workroom housed the seamstresses, and a yawning cavity of a place held the completed, used, and discarded costumes."

"WHEN YOU'RE VERY YOUNG, YOU HAVE NO SENSE OF MORALITY, I GUESS. I THOUGHT IT WAS VERY AMUSING TO GET THIS BIG PORTFOLIO. IT NEVER OCCURRED TO ME IT WAS QUITE DISHONEST." –Edith Head

"TO THE IMMATURE MIND OF THE MOVIE FAN, IT WAS AN INSULT TO CLOTHE AN HEIRESS IN ANYTHING REMOTELY RESEMBLING THE COMMON-PLACE MODES OF OUR OWN WARDROBE."

–Howard Greer

(Right) **Travis Banton became Edith's mentor and she became his protector.** (Far right) **Edith's sketch for decorations for the elephants in *The Wanderer*.**

Paramount's stock wardrobe department consisted of about 50,000 costumes, including costumes from every time period and of every ethnicity. New costumes were added constantly as films were produced. Costume budgets for a star could be very elaborate. Within a year, a studio could spend $100,000 on costumes for Marion Davies or $150,000 on costumes for Gloria Swanson. Frank Richardson, who began at Paramount in 1924, and stayed for over fifty years, oversaw the business end of the costume department. He took a no-nonsense approach, and came to have a genuine respect for Edith, and she for him. He would come to her aid many times over the years when she needed a diplomatic solution to a problem.

Edith learned how to read a script and map out a wardrobe plot for a movie. A wardrobe plot would list the character and description of the costume and the sequence in which it was used. The costumer could check off which phase of production the costume was in. These included whether a sketch had been made and approved, if the outfit was being made or had been fitted, if jewelry, props and wigs had been made, if the outfit was ready to show to the director or producer, and if the outfit had final approval.

The film preparation time could run anywhere from two to eight weeks. A Cecil B. DeMille spectacular would take longer, from as little as fifteen months or up to three years. Depending on what was in production at the time, the department could have as few as eight people working or as many as fifty.

Designing for film was a radically different undertaking than simply designing ready-to-wear clothing. Howard Greer, who had worked in the best couture salons of the day, lamented the difference: "New York and Paris disdainfully looked down their noses at the dresses we designed in Hollywood. Well, maybe they *were* vulgar, but they *did* have imagination. If they were gaudy, they but reflected the absence of subtlety which characterized all early motion pictures. Overemphasis, as it applied to acting techniques and story treatments, was essential. If a lady in real life wore a train a yard long, her prototype in reel life wore it three yards long. If a duchess at the Court of St. James perched three feathers on her pompadour, the cinematic duchess perched six, just to be on the safe side. The most elegant Chanel dress of the early twenties was a wash-out on the screen. When you strip color and sound and the third-dimension from a moving object, you have to make up for the loss with dramatic black-and-white contrasts that enriched surfaces".

"In the same pagan spirit of overemphasis, we had to convince our eleven-year-old audience that the heroine was really rich, when the story demanded it. No halfway measures here! To the immature mind of the movie fan, it was an insult to clothe an heiress in anything remotely resembling the commonplace modes of our own wardrobe. So we sent her shopping in cloth-of-gold and sable, to cocktail parties in a blinding flash of embroidery, to evening affairs dressed, or undressed, to the teeth, and there could be no doubt that our girl was a rich man's wife or daughter. Clothes, we felt, were much more important than the story, and if an author or director dared demur, we fell back upon poetic license and pretended that some rich friend had *loaned* our heroine a dress for the occasion."

The studio maintained a large storage room with a multitude of fabrics available to the designers. "All the great fabric houses would send people here with their lines of fabric," Edith said. "And every studio, every designer would buy lace and satin and chiffon and Souffle, and the great fabrics from Switzerland, from Paris, from Rome, from all over. So we'd go into our little shop and say 'ah, there's that beautiful velvet, I'll do this cape.' We had these beautiful, fabulous brocades, the cut velvets, the hammered satin. Each studio also had these famous beaders, who made these jeweled dresses. Women would sit at these looms and sometimes take six to eight months to complete a dress."

A SLOW START

One of Edith's first assignments was painting polka-dots on six-foot butterfly wings for the silent version of *Peter Pan* (1924) starring Betty Bronson. While Edith wasn't always stimulated by the jobs given to her, she was driven to always do the best she could at whatever task or job she was attempting. People found her very likeable, and she fit in very well

Travis Banton oversees a fitting with actress
Betty Bronson in his salon at the studio, 1926

with the close-knit small studio family. If there was something she felt could be made better, she would use good-natured cajoling to get her way. Although Edith wasn't sure that she would stay in the wardrobe department permanently, the money was good, and she liked it enough to stay there until a better position might open up at the studio.

Things changed significantly for Edith when Travis Banton arrived at the costume department in 1925. Already an established designer in his own right, Banton was brought in for $150 per week by Howard Greer to design gowns for *The Dressmaker from Paris* (1925) with Leatrice Joy. Banton left behind his own salon in New York City, where he counted on clients such as Florez Ziegfeld for his famous Ziegfeld Follies costumes, as well as New York society ladies for his couture gowns. His reputation had been made when Mary Pickford selected one of his dresses to wear for her wedding to Douglas Fairbanks Sr.

with the studio over his elaborate budget. It was to be his last film for Paramount for six years.

Director Raoul Walsh also had to stop shooting his film *The Wanderer* (1925), when an elephant began eating a wreath made of flowers and fruits that Edith had designed for the animal to wear. "Nobody told me that elephants eat leaves" she said. "We had great blankets of flowers and grapes, and we made leglets of roses to go around the elephants' legs. The elephant just took up his trunk and ate practically everything." But Edith was getting a valuable lesson in pre-production planning that would serve her well in the years to come.

There was no rivalry between Greer and Banton. In fact, quite the opposite happened. "Much to every dressmaker's surprise, we got along famously together," Greer wrote. "Money was something new and almost unknown to both of us before, and the spending of it went to our

> "NOBODY TOLD ME THAT ELEPHANTS EAT LEAVES!"
>
> –Edith Head

heads." Along with buying elaborate furniture to furnish their new homes, Greer and Banton spent a lot of money and time going out on the town and getting drunk together. Just how much the men were drinking can be surmised in Greer's account of a typical night starting out on a transatlantic crossing by ship: "The night of your sailing began with a wave of bon voyage cocktail parties that washed you on to dinner at the Colony or twenty-one . . . the ship's bar wouldn't open until morning, but state rooms were rivers of champagne and bootleg Scotch and gin . . . as soon as you were able to crawl out of bed on the following morning, you staggered to the bar and tossed off a pick-me-up."

Banton and Greer began relying more on Edith for help with pro-jects. When Cecil B. DeMille rejected a sketch for a costume for Irene Rich in *The Golden Bed* (1925) as too ordinary, Edith sketched what she thought was a completely ridiculous riding habit of black velvet with gold kid riding boots. DeMille loved it and Greer offered Edith a real designing opportunity. For an elaborate candy ball sequence that DeMille had devised in *The Golden Bed*, Edith designed costumes using real chocolate and other candies attached to them. When the cameras rolled, the hot lights on the set began melting the chocolate, and production had to be halted. With all the offending real articles replaced, most of Edith's original costumes remained in the final film. But DeMille could not have been pleased, as there had already been major disputes

Edith also assisted Banton and Greer on the well-received *Are Parents People?* (1925), in which Betty Bronson sets out to keep her

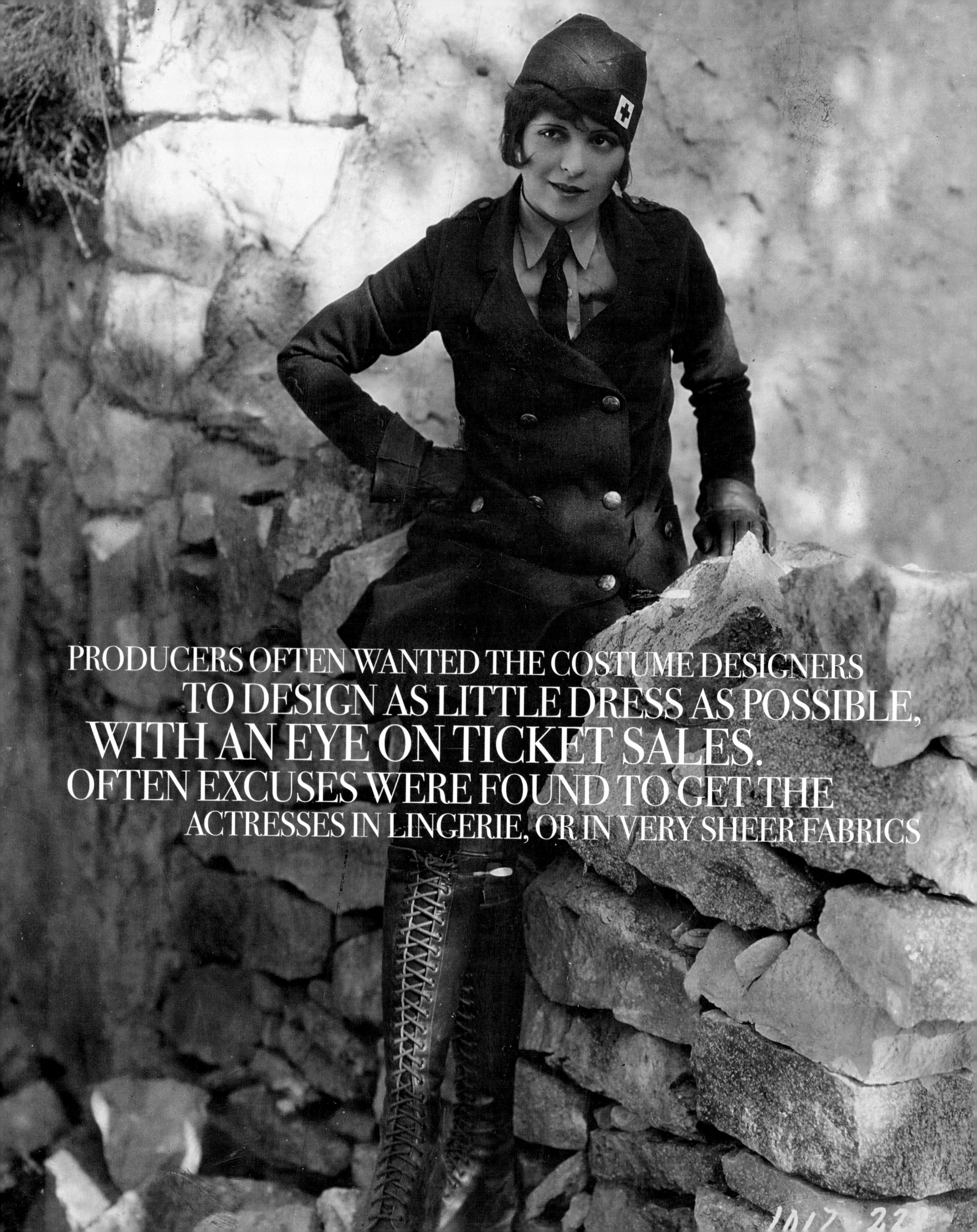

PRODUCERS OFTEN WANTED THE COSTUME DESIGNERS TO DESIGN AS LITTLE DRESS AS POSSIBLE, WITH AN EYE ON TICKET SALES. OFTEN EXCUSES WERE FOUND TO GET THE ACTRESSES IN LINGERIE, OR IN VERY SHEER FABRICS

(Left) Edith was given her first chance to design for a major star when Clara Bow made *Wings*. (Right) Edith on a picnic with (left to right) actor Richard Haydn and costume designers Howard Greer and Edward Stevenson.

parents from getting a divorce, and The *Trouble with Wives* (1925) starring Florence Vidor. Edith would dutifully return the worn items to stock after filming, or prepare the items for sale. "We used to sell the dresses the star wore in movies," Edith recounted later. "Theda Bara, Laura La Plante and all the others could buy suits and dresses styled especially for them at bargain prices. We also held annual sales open to the general public. Those were nerve-wracking events. Hundreds of Los Angeles women would invade the studio and scratch each others' eyes out in a mad battle to buy Pola Negri's negligee or Gloria Swanson's garters. We cut these out in self-defense."

More and more, Travis Banton seemed to be dominating the wardrobe department. Even Howard Greer had to admit that Banton possessed a greater flair for designing for film. More actresses began requesting to work with Banton, and Edith began to sketch in his style when doing drawings to present to producers and directors.

Edith assisted Banton on *Underworld* (1926), one of the first gangster films. Directed by Josef Von Sternberg, it told the story of the hoodlums born of the Prohibition era. Banton designed a fabulous flapper wardrobe for Evelyn Brent, playing the moll to George Bancroft's gangster. *Man Trap* (1926), a film starring Clara Bow, the studio's most popular star, was a problem, however. Banton and Clara couldn't quite see eye-to-eye about the actress' screen image. Still, the film about a married manicurist in a small town falling for a big-city visitor on vacation is considered one of Bow's best performances, perhaps because she was having an affair with Victor Fleming, the film's director at the time.

In what was known as the pre-code days in Hollywood, producers often wanted the costume designers to design as little dress as possible, with an eye on ticket sales. Often excuses were found to get the actresses in lingerie, or in very sheer fabrics. Sound was also being experimented with, to see if an audience, who previously were used to just musical accompaniment, would come to hear the new curiosity. John Barrymore's *Don Juan* (1926) was released with additional sound effects, as well as music.

When asked later if she was allowed to experiment with her designs during these years, Edith answered with an emphatic "no," going on to explain that "we would do thirty, forty, fifty pictures a year. That eventually meant that Banton and Greer would do just the stars. Then that meant I would do all the rest of the people, but those people

Edith learned to sketch in the style of Travis Banton. (Opposite) A design for actress Bebe Daniels, done in 1928.

were not necessarily designed for. Sometimes we dressed them out of stock or made-over clothes. In other words, I did the aunts, the grandmothers, the men. I did a lot of men things because they didn't like to do the men too much—what you call the background stuff. You try to keep the whole look of the picture together. You don't suddenly go out on your own and do something experimental."

THE FIRST BIG BREAK

Clara Bow had become the studio's top draw, perhaps even the biggest star in the industry. But one of the problems with silent female stars is that, once these pretty girls got to Hollywood, you could give them an exotic screen name and dress them up, but somehow they still couldn't shake the fact that they were mostly simple-minded Midwest girls from farms.

Clara Bow was the actress' real name, but one has to wonder how the vivacious young girl, who would come to personify the flapper era, ever survived her childhood. She was born in a tenement in Brooklyn to a schizophrenic mother and a physically abusive father. In New York, she entered "The Fame and Fortune Contest" as a teenager and won. When Clara told her mother that she was leaving for Hollywood, her mother tried to slash the girl's throat.

Clara usually played working-class girls, such as a shop girl in *It* (1927) leaving Banton very little room for doing anything glamorous for the star. And even the wardrobe he did design was usually accessorized by Clara with common touches like ankle bracelets and belts. Clara loved to put belts on everything because she felt it emphasized her waist. Even bathing suits had to have belts. Because Travis Banton couldn't take the fights that he foresaw would occur if he was to work with Clara on an upcoming feature called *Wings* (1927), he turned the star over to Edith.

Clara Bow and Edith Head hit if off immediately. Unlike the stars that came from poor backgrounds who demanded the best designers of the studio to fortify their egos, Clara had no problem working with Banton's assistant. They were both young women of the flapper era, and Edith was the serious yin to Clara's vivacious yang.

Edith was naturally disappointed to learn that Clara would have to wear a regulation army uniform almost throughout the entirety of the

"I DID THE AUNTS, THE GRANDMOTHERS, THE MEN. I DID A LOT OF MEN THINGS BECAUSE THEY DIDN'T LIKE TO DO THE MEN TOO MUCH —WHAT YOU CALL THE BACKGROUND STUFF." –Edith Head

film. What Edith couldn't have known was the film was destined to be an instant classic. Since MGM had a huge smash on its hands in 1925 with the film *The Big Parade*, Paramount wanted to make its own war epic. The director, the young William Wellman, had been a pilot in World War I, and later a stunt pilot so he had both the expertise and enthusiasm for the project. The film *Wings* became the first film to win an Academy Award for Best Picture. Charles "Buddy" Rogers and Richard Arlen were cast as young pilots in training while Clara was cast as an ambulance driver and love interest for the two men. Cinematographer Harry Perry photographed all the flying sequences without using process shots.

Part of the dramatic impact of The *Big Parade* came from its use of ill-fitting uniforms and little or no make-up for the actors. And while no one wanted to have Clara Bow go without make-up in *Wings*, authenticity in her costume became very important. Edith had to stay on the set at all times when Clara was filming, to literally snatch the belts off of her costume. She could certainly empathize with Clara over the drab costume, but her mentors Greer and Banton had taught Edith that what was right for the character was what needed to come first.

Edith loved Clara's zest for life. The two women were very close in age, and became great friends. Edith even co-hosted the now infamous party that Clara Bow threw for the USC football team. Hollywood legend has Clara bedding the entire team during the party, but Edith's version of the story has the team actually leaving the party early because they had to be up early in the morning for training.

Though *Wings* was made in a process which added music and sound elements to film, it was still essentially a silent picture. However, in 1927 Warner Brothers Studio introduced a movie called *The Jazz Singer*, which was nearly a full-talking picture. The industry was about to be rocked off its comfortable silent pedestal, as everyone wondered what stars would survive once the public heard their real speaking voices.

Sound also presented new problems for wardrobe people. The crude microphones picked up every sound a costume made. Material had to be minimized to avoid rustling. Soft material had to be put on the soles of shoes and jewelry had to be sewn securely on to dresses to avoid clacking.

THE RISE OF BANTON

In December 1927, Howard Greer resigned from Paramount. He wrote later that, "Travis had grown in popularity with stars and directors and shown an amazing aptitude toward designing photogenic clothes. I have always felt that my clothes depended upon a third dimension. If I live another hundred years, I doubt whether I will develop a 'camera eye' and know, from its inception, whether an idea will live up to my expectations on celluloid. This wavering doubt in my brain grew into a real obsession, and I began to think that Mr. Lasky's axe might fall across my neck at the very next option. Now that I'd resigned myself to dress designing as a vocation, I wanted to do the best I could with it, and the idea of custom dressmaking for a private clientele absorbed me." Greer opened his own salon in Los Angeles to great success, and would make the occasional venture back into film design from time to time.

Travis Banton became the official head designer at Paramount, and Edith was now his full-time assistant. They collaborated on the gritty *Ladies of the Mob* (1928), with Clara Bow. Although the film still didn't give Edith a chance to dazzle audiences with fabulous clothing on the "It" girl, Edith was now fitting the waistlines on the dresses for Bow's character Yvonne, a young woman raised by criminals trying to keep Richard Arlen from committing a bank robbery. Clara no longer had to bring belts to the set.

To capitalize on the success of *Wings*, the studio put *The Legion of the Condemned* (1928) into production. The film reunited *Wings* director William Wellman and screenwriter John Monk Sanders for another film about aviation. Instead of Clara Bow as a nurse, this time Edith was given Fay Wray as a paratrooper. Once again this didn't require a tremendous amount of creativity for clothes, however, Fay

Wray was given one lovely white dress for her romantic scenes with Gary Cooper. For the action scenes, the studio incorporated some of the daring aerial footage left over from *Wings*, and the film had a respectable showing at the box office.

Banton was coming to rely more on Edith to costume secondary characters for all the "A" and "B" films produced by the studio. The men's costumes were typically pulled from stock for period pictures or bought from stores, if contemporary. Some actors were even required to wear their own clothes. But, if something special was needed, Edith would step in. She was learning a great deal from watching Banton work. He was a master of using textures, and of trimming gowns in fur. Studio chief Adolph Zukor had once been a furrier and had requested that the wardrobe department use fur as often as possible to help the industry. "We had a formula for designing, which was 'make it look as trick, as bizarre, as unusual as you possibly can," Edith said. "Be sure it doesn't look like something you can buy in a store. Be sure that people will gasp when they see it.' "

Edith worked with Clara Bow again on *The Saturday Night Kid* (1929). Clara played a salesgirl in love with a clerk, whose sister (Jean Arthur) was trying to steal her beau. Playing another salesgirl was a young Jean Harlow, for whom Edith designed a dress of satin. The look was so stunning on Harlow, Edith was worried that Clara might feel somewhat upstaged. "But Clara couldn't have cared less," Edith said. "She thought Jean looked gorgeous and didn't mind her looking gorgeous." Edith took some pride in being the first person to recognize how white satin would emphasize Jean's natural gifts, and seemed to be rather proud that the look was adapted during the actress' tenure at Metro-Goldwyn-Mayer.

"BE SURE IT DOESN'T LOOK LIKE SOMETHING YOU CAN BUY IN A STORE. BE SURE THAT PEOPLE WILL GASP WHEN THEY SEE IT." –Edith Head

As gracious as Clara had been when Edith was assigned to dress her, Edith did not have that same luxury when working with actress Lupe Velez on the film *Wolf Song* (1929). Though Lupe had only been in the United States for two years from her native Mexico, the Latin beauty had already made a big impact opposite Douglas Fairbanks in *The Gaucho* (1927). In *Wolf Song*, Lupe played Lola, a beautiful Mexican girl from a wealthy family, and starred opposite her real-life lover Gary Cooper as Sam Lash. Edith's elaborate costumes for Velez prompted one of Edith's funniest reviews. For a love scene with Cooper, Edith put Lupe in a white lace wedding gown with an impossibly full skirt, which overwhelmed the five-foot-tall actress. It was so full, Cooper could hardly get near her to make love. One critic cracked, "if there hadn't been so much dress, there could have been more scene." Edith was undaunted. If Velez liked the dress, that was what mattered.

The great gains that had been made in the stock market through the Roaring Twenties, began declining throughout the summer of 1929. Investor anxiety came to a head on October 29th, otherwise known as "Black Tuesday." Overextended investors flooded the market with sell orders. Widespread panic ensued as telephone lines and the ticker tape system, on which investors relied for information, were overwhelmed. The Dow Jones Industrial average fell thirty-eight points to 260. This was only the first of many events that triggered one of the worst economic crises of modern times.

As the Depression progressed, so did the public's desire to

Real-life lovers Eleanore Whitney and Johnny Downs were costumed by Edith for *College Holiday*

escape it. "Talkies" had revolutionized the industry and the era of escapist fare had arrived. Nowhere was that more evident than in the costume departments of the major studios. If a woman couldn't afford a designer gown costing hundreds of dollars, she could at least pay a quarter to admire one in the movies, and studio designers were more than happy to oblige.

Metro-Goldwyn-Mayer had hired a young designer named Adrian Adolph Greenburg, known as "Adrian," to design costumes for its roster of stars at the time, including Greta Garbo, Joan Crawford, Kay Johnson and Norma Shearer. Adrian had been discovered by Rudolph Valentiono's wife Natacha Rambova, and had been brought to Hollywood to work for them. He became the head costumer for Cecil B. DeMille's studio during DeMille's absence from Paramount, and moved to the MGM lot when DeMille did. Adrian's designs were steeped in dramatic fantasy, and he spared no expense in creating them. Edith would call his designs for Joan Crawford in *Letty Lynton* (1932), "the greatest influence on fashion in film history." Many of the costume designers coming up through the ranks of the studios about this time would be influential in Hollywood costume design for at least another thirty years, including Walter Plunkett at RKO and Orry-Kelly at Warner Brothers.

Travis Banton was keeping pace on lavish films like *The Vagabond King* (1930) and *Monte Carlo*, (1930), both starring Jeanette MacDonald. Hollywood was beginning to influence the world of fashion as much as Paris. But the gloomy economic picture of the country had cast a more conservative pall over women's clothing. As the stock market fell, so did the hem lines on women's skirts. Films that had been readied the year before now looked dated.

A BLEAK OUTLOOK

Paramount suffered financial setbacks during the Great Depression, and layoffs were common in the wardrobe department as films went in and out of production. Charles Head was now spending more time in Los Angeles as the Depression had slowed his business. His drinking was becoming increasingly worse. Edith responded to these problems by extending her work load, and staying later and later at the studio. Throughout 1930, she worked on a string of minor Paramount films, including *Along Came Youth* with Frances Dee, *Follow the Leader* with Ginger Rogers, *Only the Brave* with Mary Brian and *The Santa Fe Trail* with Rosita Moreno.

Despite still being married to Charles Head, Edith had two romances in the early 1930's that each resulted in engagements. Edith's biographer David Chierichetti revealed one of these men to be Bayard Veiller, a Paramount writer and associate producer, whose attentions toward Edith resulted in her being assigned to three of his films. The affair may also have helped Edith secure her first contract with Paramount in 1931 for $175 per week. The identity of the second man has never been determined.

If movies were giving the public over-the-top fantasy, Edith wanted the women of the world to have a little reality that they could use in their own wardrobes as well. Though eventually actress Carole Lombard would graduate to some of the most beautiful gowns Travis Banton would ever design, the simple designs she could wear so well while playing a secretary, were a revelation to Edith. Since many of the actresses Edith had seen in Hollywood wore wardrobes on-screen and off that a typical woman could neither attain nor wear daily, Carole showed

"IF THERE HADN'T BEEN SO MUCH DRESS, THERE COULD HAVE BEEN MORE SCENE." –Film Critic

Edith how a star could stimulate fashion. Women could copy the look of Carole Lombard as a secretary, and be just as beguiling.

Reality was something that suffered in film costume, especially in the Westerns, or "horse operas" as they called them then, for which Edith was designing. "I did a picture once where one of the actresses was crossing the prairie from the *East to The Gold Rush* in a prairie schooner," Edith said. "We had a buffalo stampede, three Indian attacks, and a prairie fire. And every morning the heroine comes out with white ruffles, and her hair done up in curls, and nobody cared about it because the public accepted motion pictures as fantasy and an amusement. We used to give them low-necked dresses with the bosom hanging out, and I'd say 'but, you know, they didn't wear low-necked dresses in the old days.' And I was told 'my dear Edith, if everybody had worn high-necked dresses, you wouldn't have been here today. There would've been no sex.' "

In 1932, Paramount, always a studio to turn a profit, was operating at a deficit of $15 million. Edith's contract was renewed, but her salary was cut by $25.00 per week. Edith worked on Rouben Mamoulian's charming *Love Me Tonight* (1932) with Jeanette MacDonald as a princess and Maurice Chevalier as a Parisian tailor. Richard Rogers and Lorenz wrote the music for the film and introduced the standard Isn't it Romantic?

Edith also dressed background characters on Cecil B. DeMille's returning venture to Paramount, the epic *The Sign of the Cross* (1932) with Frederic March and Claudette Colbert. Mitchell Leisen, who had been working as DeMille's art director on such productions as *Madame Satan* (1930) and *The Squaw Man* (1931) took over designing the major costumes on the epic. Leisen designed body-baring art deco-inspired gowns dripping with jewelry for Colbert that caused the kind of titillation that DeMille loved to give audiences in his biblical epics.

Edith was experiencing some frustration at not being able to work at her potential. She told a story in her book *The Dress Doctor*, to illustrate her unhappiness. Late one afternoon, after Travis Banton had left the studio for the day, Marlene Dietrich walked into the department looking for him. The actress' hands were full of gossamer white feathers that Banton was using for a hat that he had designed for her. Dietrich felt the hat could be better, and Edith and Marlene spent the evening reworking it. Though Edith rarely talked about her satisfaction with her job with anyone, let alone one of the studio's stars, she said she confided to Marlene that she wasn't very happy and was afraid she would be stuck designing "horse operas" for the rest of her days. Edith said Marlene took Edith's birth date to her own astrologer and brought back her horoscope that read: "Better times are coming."

Edith said she never forgot the interest the actress had taken in her, and years later extolled Dietrich's virtue as a true friend she could trust. Edith became known for exaggerating a story for its best effect, and sometimes even contradicted herself totally later. When an interviewer asked Edith about the Dietrich story in the 1970s, she asked him, "where did you get that?"

Whether the Dietrich story is true or not, better times were indeed ahead for Edith. The following year. Edith's salary was reinstated to $175 per week. While working on *Cradle Song* (1933), she met the art director Wiard "Bill" Ihnen, and the two began a flirtation. The film was based on Gregorio Martinez Sierra's classic Spanish play, and Edith and Wiard found a common bond in their love of Spanish art and architecture.

Ihnen viewed working at the studio as a way to finance his two passions, painting and women. Ihnen was quite the ladies' man and when he had some money in his pocket, he preferred traveling to Mexico to paint, leaving behind, at least temporarily, what he viewed as the creative restrictions imposed by the studio. Though Edith was still committed to Charles through marriage and to Bayard Veiller through her engagement promise, Ihnen still found ways to stay in touch with Edith, even after leaving Paramount for Twentieth Century-Fox.

Edith cultivated good working relationships with the actresses for whom she worked. She became more self-assured in her knowledge

"I'D SAY 'BUT, YOU KNOW, THEY DIDN'T WEAR LOW-NECKED DRESSES IN THE OLD DAYS.' AND I WAS TOLD 'MY DEAR EDITH, IF EVERYBODY HAD WORN HIGH-NECKED DRESSES, YOU WOULDN'T HAVE BEEN HERE TODAY. THERE WOULD'VE BEEN NO SEX.'"

–Edith Head

Edith at her sketch board in 1936

Designing for Mae West (here with Cary Grant) for *She Done Him Wrong* gave Edith her first high-profile job designing glamorous gowns

of what would or wouldn't translate well to the screen and what would most flatter an actress' figure. She was still learning the psychology of how to deal with actresses, directors and producers. Nancy Carroll was a popular Paramount star, who was known for her temperament. During a fitting with Edith for *The Woman Accused* (1933), the two disagreed so strongly on a dress that Carroll ripped it off and stamped on it. Edith relented and made Carroll another dress, but made up her mind at that point to never impose her will strongly on an actress. "You can lead a horse to water and you can even make it drink, but you can't make actresses wear what they don't want to wear," Edith said.

Edith began making multiple sketches for the same scene, and allowing an actress to choose which she liked best. Making multiple sketches wasn't a new idea to Edith. She had done it for Howard Greer in the early days to give him options to present to directors. But Edith felt that if an actress was brought in on the creative process, there would be fewer objections later.

For *White Woman* (1933), Charles Laughton played Horace H. Prin, a plantation owner who marries Judith Denning (Carole Lombard), only to reveal his cruel nature once he takes her to his rubber plantation in Malaysia. Edith credited Charles Laughton with teaching her the value of research and how a costume helps an actor inhabit a role. Laughton requested the costume department make him elaborately embroidered vests to wear in the film. Laughton had worked out the psychological implications of these vests to the character, and how they would set him apart from the other planters.

BETTER TIMES ARRIVE

The biggest break in Edith's career to that point came in a 5' 1" package, embellished with curves. Mae West had just had a huge hit on Broadway in 1928 with *Diamond Lil*, a show she both wrote and in which she starred. She was signed to Paramount in 1931 to turn the play into a film, and even though the Production Code had not yet been enacted, Will Hays of the Motion Pictures Producers and Distributors Association was gaining more power to censor what could and couldn't be shown on screen. It took two years to bring the play to the screen as *She Done Him Wrong* (1933) with West now playing Lady Lou, a New York singer and nightclub owner with a dangerous ex-beau. Cast opposite Mae was a young Cary Grant in his third major film role.

Travis Banton was on one of his yearly excursions to Europe to view the collections and to order fabric when *She Done Him Wrong* went into production. The costume design responsibilities were turned over to Edith. Even though Mae was not yet a film star, she was still a big celebrity who had been testing the limits of decency with her plays in New York. This was Edith's first chance to shine with a wardrobe of sumptuous gowns, created entirely by her and with full screen credit. Edith said later she was relieved to be free of the gingham and calico fabrics she was so used to having to use in the westerns.

Edith found Mae articulate and full of self-confidence. Mae had created a style for herself that utilized the best of what she had to offer, and had no desire to follow the fashion of the day. She was a throwback to the belles of the 1890s, but with the sexual bravado of a 1920s flapper,

"MAKE THE CLOTHES LOOSE ENOUGH TO PROVE I'M A LADY, BUT TIGHT ENOUGH TO SHOW 'EM I'M A WOMAN."

–Mae West

Edith poses for a publicity photograph in 1936

"MAE WEST TAUGHT ME WHAT A WOMAN CAN DO WITH A FORMAT."

–Edith Head

conveyed through sly innuendo. The film may be most well-known as the first time a film audience heard Mae utter her famous line, "why don't you come up sometime and see me?"

Mae had wrestled with the censors in New York, but Hollywood would have to be different. Film was too costly to be re-shot if a scene was found to be objectionable. But Mae also had control over her own material, and would go head-to-head with the writers if there was anything that displeased her. Everything had to be planned out to make sure the audience was titillated, while the censors could not make any objections.

Mae West's full-figure offered the perfect proportions for the period gowns. She explained to Edith the formula that she felt worked the best for her, and Edith had no desire to make any changes. "Make the clothes loose enough to prove I'm a lady, but tight enough to show 'em I'm a woman," Mae told Edith. Mae preferred soft fabrics such as satin and velvet that felt good against her skin, telling Edith "I love fabrics I can feel, honey; so do men." The more rhinestones, lace or ostrich feathers that could be embroidered on the gowns, the better. Edith traveled to Cawston's Ostrich farm out in South Pasadena to order the feathers personally.

Even though *Diamond Lil*, was no longer the title, jewelry was still an essential. Mae told Edith,: "without diamonds, honey, I'd feel undressed." So Edith showed Mae pictures of period jewelry. "Fine Honey," Mae said, "just make the stones bigger." In one scene, Mae requested Edith make a particularly eye-catching gown, since the actress had very little dialogue in the scene, but still wanted all eyes to stay on her. Edith gave Mae her wish, designing a gown with six swallows, outlined in brilliants, flying across the bodice from the left-hand waistline to the right shoulder.

Edith wrote in *The Dress Doctor*, "Mae West taught me what a woman can do with a format." Shortly after the release of the film, the Paris designer Elsa Schiaparelli introduced materials into her collections influenced by Edith's designs for Mae, including feathered hats and boas, and an emphasis on the hourglass figure.

Public outcry over the sensational Hollywood scandals of the 1920s, including the manslaughter trial of Roscoe "Fatty" Arbuckle and the murder of director William Desmond Taylor, led to the creation of the Motion Pictures Producers and Distributors Association in 1922. The association was headed by Will Hays, who, in 1927, had compiled a list of subjects he felt movie studios would be wise to avoid. The ensuing economic downturn had forced the studios to provide racier fare to entice ticket buyers into the cinema, and Hays lacked any real power to enforce his restrictions. That all changed in 1934 when The Catholic League of

One of the rare occasions Edith used a bold print on a dress was for Anna May Wong in *Dangerous to Know.*

Decency was formed in direct response to Warner Brothers' *Baby Face* (1933) and Mae West's *I' m No Angel* (1933), and boycotts and blacklists were threatened throughout the film industry.

An amendment to Will Hays' code established the Production Code, which required all films released on or after July 1, 1934 to obtain a certificate of approval prior to being released. Provisions of the code included: nakedness and suggestive dances were prohibited, scenes of passion were not to be introduced when not essential to the plot; and the treatment of vulgar subjects, including prostitution and surgical operations, were to be "subject to the dictates of good taste."

The question of just whose good taste the Code was referring to was not clearly defined, and designers and costumers found themselves scrambling to interpret to the Code. The diaphanous see-through fabrics used by designers and low-cut, flesh-exposing gowns were now a thing of the past. One mistake could cost a studio tens of thousands of dollars in reshooting fees or halted production, and often did. "The censorship thing was very funny. You could have a girl in a room with a white slip, and that was all right. But you couldn't have lace on it because that was sexy. But it was much more fun in those days," Edith would say.

Besides the grandmothers and maids, Edith also had to design for the children. *Little Miss Marker* (1934) was yet another B-film to which Edith was assigned. Along with designing clothes for its star Dorothy Dell, Edith also designed clothes for the little girl who had been loaned from Twentieth-Century-Fox to play the daughter of a delinquent client of a bookie. Edith remembered that the fittings with Shirley Temple, who was accompanied by her mother Gertrude, were very pleasant affairs. Unfortunately, she could not always make that claim about many child actresses and their stage mothers.

But nobody could have known that this film was going to rocket Shirley Temple to fame. Within two years, the little girl would be the top box-office attraction, beating out Clark Gable and Bing Crosby. Unfortunately, Dorothy Dell, the film's star and the woman who Paramount was giving the big publicity build-up, was killed in a traffic accident just as the film was released.

David Holt, another child star with whom Edith would work that year, was billed later as "the male Shirley Temple." He would go on to song writing success with Johnny Mercer and Sammy Cahn. David Holt played a young boy being adopted by a comedian, played by Lee Tracy and a singer, played by Helen Morgan in *You Belong to Me* (1934). Only seven at the time, the young actor was making on average, five films a year. When asked in an interview later, what was the age of a person she preferred to design for, Edith answered, "I like them best at the age when everything I make for them is wonderful and they have no ideas of their own. The younger, the better, I guess."

Edith's salary was raised to $200 per week in 1934; she was given a trip to study what New York designers were doing at the time. Travis Banton was losing interest in doing interviews to promote the gowns in Paramount's films, so Edith began getting the assignments. The publicity department requested Paramount's contract photographer John Engstead, who was already a good friend to Edith, to take her first publicity photographs. Reluctantly, Edith posed for him without her glasses.

Edith got her first taste of life in front of the camera, appearing as herself in the short film *Hollywood Extra Girl* (1935), produced by the studio to promote Cecil B. DeMille's new film *The Crusades* (1935). The scripted documentary followed two actresses, played by Suzanne Emery and Ann Sheridan. Emery reports to Central Casting to work on T*he Crusades* as a Christian slave girl, and ostensibly this will lead her on the path to stardom. Emery never made another film. Ann Sheridan, however, worked with Edith later that year on *Car 99* (1935) and later found stardom under contract to Warner Brothers.

Edith, Travis, and designer Natalie Visart had spent a good part of 1934 working on the drawings and costumes for *The Crusades*. As was typical with a DeMille film, the behind-the-scenes goings-on could be as dramatic as anything on screen. The costume budget was cut to

Edith gave Shirley Ross a gown covered in glittering sequins for The Big Broadcast of 1938.

CONFUSION REIGNED SO MUCH DURING PRE-PRODUCTION OF *WITHOUT REGRET* (1935) STARRING ELISSA LANDI, THAT PRODUCER HAROLD HURLEY HAD TO SEND A MEMO ASKING EVERYONE TO STOP "INTERFERING WITH MISS HEAD'S DECISIONS."

$100,000, which was still an enormous sum at the time. DeMille sent memos to Frank Richardson complaining that a representative from the wardrobe department was not on the set at all times to coordinate with his department. Problems arose, such as a costly reshoot, when a bit too much of an actress was seen onscreen because dress shields weren't used in her costume.

Edith's duties in the department were increasing as more and very diverse films were sent into production. *The Big Broadcast of 1936* (1935), was a musical starring Gracie Allen, and George Burns; *The Lives of a Bengal Lancer* (1935) was an action film starring Gary Cooper; and *Ruggles of Red Gap* (1935) was a comedy starring Charles Laughton. Edith was still only receiving credits on films for which she was assigned the main star, and those were still few and far between.

THE CRACKS BEGIN TO SHOW

As Banton's drinking worsened, he came to rely on Edith to run the department during his frequent absences. Adele Balkan had been brought in to the department in 1934 as a sketch artist, but just as Edith had done, she helped out wherever she could. Edith appreciated having the authority when Banton was gone, but not at the expense of possibly losing him as her boss. Edith had no reason to believe that if Banton lost his job, she would be his automatic replacement. Chances were good that another high-profile couturier would be hired, and they would most likely bring in their own assistant. Already able to sketch like Banton, Edith passed off her own sketches as Banton's, to producers and directors. When she could find him at home in the morning, she would even drive him to work and ply him with coffee.

But even with Banton out frequently, there was no such thing as complete autonomy for Edith. Frequent squabbles between creative departments often led to an impasse until someone with authority could step in. Confusion reigned so much during pre-production of *Without Regret* (1935) starring Elissa Landi, that producer Harold Hurley had to send a memo asking everyone to stop "interfering with Miss Head's decisions."

Although Edith had the inevitable "horse operas" to dress in 1936 including *The Texas Rangers* starring Fred MacMurray and Jean Parker, she was finally given a slate of films with good design opportu-

LAMOUR'S DARK COLORING AND EXOTIC LOOKS WERE JUST WHAT THE SARONG NEEDED, AND SHE WAS SIGNED TO A CONTRACT WITH PARAMOUNT.

Edith used satin to make a sarong that adequately hugged Dorothy Lamour's curves in *Her Jungle Love.*

nities. *Rhythm on the Range* (1936) was a musical set in the West and introduced the hits "I'm an Old Cowhand," sung in the film by Bing Crosby and "Mr. Paganini" sung by Martha Raye. Edith designed a suit for Raye with a fitted waist that was attractive, but whose skirt allowed for plenty of the movement for which Raye was famous.

College Holiday (1936) also starred Raye, with Jack Benny, Marsha Hunt, and Gracie Allen. What there was of a plot, centered on a eugenics nut trying to bring beautiful college students together to mate to create perfect children. The classic Greek togas and sarongs the students wore provided plenty of sex, while Marsha Hunt's wardrobe provided plenty of glamour. For Hunt, Edith designed a brown wool skirt topped by a brown and white check jacket and box coat with patch pockets; and a rose red linen dress with lacings and a belt frog of white cord. For the "The Sweetheart Waltz" number, in which Hunt danced with Leif Ericson, Edith designed a beautiful gown of white organdy with ruffled sleeves and a row of buttons down Hunt's back. They were all perfectly beautiful and could have been worn by any college student that season. However, the suit of gray Kasha trimmed in platinum fox that Hunt also wore, may have been out of the reach for the typical college student of the period.

Hunt wore a daffodil tulle gown with gold sequins on the skirt and waistband from *College Holiday*, to the various parties and theatres in Washington D.C., and finally to the White House for all of the events associated with President Roosevelt's birthday ball. Hunt recalled that at each venue there was a crush of fans, and she could barely get through the throngs of excited people. The dress "barely lasted the rigors of the night and never recovered from its wounds," she wrote in her book *The Way We Wore*.

In 1933, Paramount had a respectable hit with a B-film called *King of the Jungle* starring Olympic swimming champion Larry "Buster" Crabbe as a jungle man captured by a circus owner and brought to the United States. Three years later, Studi, Chief Adolph Zukor, developed the cheesecake version, eventually titled *The Jungle Princess* (1936). Escapism to the movies became not only a national passion, but almost essential, and a film set in Malaysia took Americans as far away from their problems as possible.

Edith designed the sarong for the princess to wear before the film was even cast, and each aspiring princess was paraded through Edith's salon, given the sarong to put on, and sent downstairs to make a screen test. About 200 girls had tested before a young band singer and former Miss New Orleans named Dorothy Lamour was brought in. Lamour had a minor role as a coed in *College Holiday*.

Lamour's dark coloring and exotic looks were just what the sarong needed, and she was signed to a contract with Paramount. In the film, civilization would come to Ulah, the jungle princess, in the form of handsome Christopher Powell (Ray Milland), who she nurses back to health after a tiger attack.

The sarong was not an authentic sarong, which would have been worn below the waist leaving the actress' breasts bare and the censors in a rage. Nor was the fabric even authentic. The original cotton fabric didn't hug Lamour's curves at all, so Edith had satin crepe fabric screen printed with an island print of her own design. But when the sarong got wet, the fabric became slippery. The knots that had been tied to hold the sarong onto Dorothy's figure slipped, causing the actress a little embarrassment until Edith found a solution. Dorothy was sewn into the costume, and wore a pair of panties in matching fabric so there would be no more indiscreet moments for the young actress. Nonetheless, Edith still had to endure letter after letter to the studio by well-meaning fans explaining to her how an authentic sarong was worn, and that they were actually made of tapa cloth.

Because Lamour was a little short in the waist and a little broad in the hips, Edith planned how the sarong would be photographed with the cameraman. In *The Dress Doctor*, Edith told how Dorothy's bust had to be filled out with bust padding because Lamour had not been entirely truth-

Even though Edith would receive credit on an entire film, often the men's wardrobe was purchased or designed by the men's wardrobe department. Gile Steele's design for Henry Wilcoxon in *Souls at Sea* was credited to Edith.

ful about her age at her audition, and continued to blossom. While Lamour had mature looks above the sarong line, below was something else. But Lamour was twenty-one when she began filming and insisted later that Edith's story was strictly for publicity, and that she never needed any pads.

The low-budget film was an incredible financial success and gave Edith her first great publicity as a designer. Sarongs and sarong-inspired wear began being manufactured and sold in stores across the country. In addition Edith forged a great friendship with the young Lamour who would begin to wield more power at the studio as her star rose. The studio would find plenty of scripts over the next ten years that would keep Lamour wearing sarongs, and Edith designing them.

With *True Confession* (1937), Carole Lombard ended her contract with Paramount and departed for RKO. Edith and Carole had developed a close friendship over the previous few years, as Carole waited in the wardrobe department for the tardy Banton to show up for her appointments. Edith been given an opportunity to design for Lombard, in the thriller *Supernatural* (1933). Edith loved her fittings with Carole. By now, Edith had watched Travis work with Lombard so often, she knew exactly what would please the star and could help Banton achieve "The Lombard look" with ease. Carole's colorful vocabulary littered with four-letter words kept things lively and people laughing at the fittings. The costume department staff also enjoyed working with the actress, so Edith didn't have to do any cajoling to get the staff motivated for help, as she did with a star that was disliked.

In *The Dress Doctor*, Edith said she learned a great deal from the relationship between Banton and Lombard as to how important a designer is to an actress, and to the women in the audience who were influenced by what the star wears. Edith had been designing so many period clothes that she said she had never quite known the excitement a designer feels when their clotheshorse is in perfect step with modern fashion, until she worked with Lombard.

This Way Please (1937) was Betty Grable's first starring role. In

EDITH HAD THE INEVITABLE "HORSE OPERAS" TO DRESS IN 1936 INCLUDING *THE TEXAS RANGERS*

Forlorn River starring Larry "Buster" Crabbe, June Martel and Harvey Stephens was exactly the kind of film on which Edith grew tired of working.

the film, she played a young theater usher with dreams of stardom, opposite Buddy Rogers. Though the film was criticized for a low-budget look, Edith designed a white chiffon gown solidly embroidered with crystal beads for Grable, that was every bit as stunning as the gowns Banton had designed for Lombard. The gown featured a high molded bodice with a slim skirt descending into a train and a wide panel of beaded chiffon that crossed from one shoulder to the other. The film wasn't a hit, but Grable didn't have to worry. She was just about two years away from major stardom.

Edith also began her association with Shirley Ross when she worked on the film *Waikiki Wedding* (1937). Ross had been performing in musical theater and cabarets in Los Angeles, before being scooped up by MGM in the early 1930s. The studio had her singing in nightclubs in a string of films, most notably *Happy New Year in San Francisco* (1936) with Clark Gable. An attractive woman, although not overtly glamourous, Ross was easy to cast opposite some of Paramount's biggest musical and comedy actors such as Bob Hope and Bing Crosby. Edith was able to design crisp, tailored suits for Shirley, some with tropical flowers. For a white fringe evening gown, Edith copied the design of the hula grass skirt around the waistline and put silken white fringe over a slip of white crepe across Shirley's torso. Edith draped the gown with a lei of fresh white gardenias.

Edith developed a stable of young female stars that trusted her. Her technique of collaboration with an actress served her well. Even when the studio insisted that an actress have no say in her wardrobe, Edith would still try to find out what the actresses liked and incorporate those details into her sketches. One of those actresses making a splash at this time was Gail Patrick. When Travis Banton was loaned out to design Carole Lombard's wardrobe for *My Man Godfrey* (1936), Edith was loaned out as well to design the wardrobe for Gail Patrick. Edith designed a beautiful silk powder blue evening gown with puffed sleeves and a belt of blue stones for Patrick to wear as the spoiled, treacherous Cornelia Bullock. Edith worked with Patrick on films including *Mississippi* (1935) and *The*

"AT THAT MOMENT I MADE UP MY MIND TO LET EDITH DESIGN MY WARDROBE FROM THAT DAY FORWARD." –Barbara Stanwyck

Big Broadcast of 1936 (1935), and would continue with John Meade's *Woman* (1937), *Artists and Models* (1937), *Dangerous to Know* (1938) and *Mad About Music* (1938). Years later, Patrick would serve as a producer on the television show Perry Mason.

"Who would dream that a couple of broken-down suits which I was to wear in my role as a poor girl in *Internes Can' t Take Money* would change my viewpoint? So uninspiring were those costume requirements that Travis Banton sent his assistant Edith Head, to do my wardrobe," Barbara Stanwyck wrote of her first encounter with Edith in *Movieland* magazine. *Internes Can' t Take Money* (1937) was the very first film to introduce the character of Dr. Kildare to film audiences. Up until that time, Stanwyck had played in a string of melodramas and westerns, usually with little or no opportunity for fashion. *Internes* would be no different really, but the relationship that formed between Edith and Barbara would be career-altering for both of them, creating a lasting bond.

"She came in bubbling with enthusiasm," Stanwyck wrote of Edith. "She was a 'dress girl,' that is, she expressed her rebellion against the current mannish suits by wearing simple dresses. Tiny, with coal-black straight hair contrasting with her white skin, Edith reminded me of a Fujita drawing. She wanted the two suits I was to wear to be more feminine than the current vogue. Not that Edith doesn't always consider the story first, but she wanted the suits to do something for me. And they did! I acquired a thorough respect and liking for Edith Head."

Stanwyck always maintained severe, tailored clothes in her personal wardrobe, but at the premiere of *Stella Dallas* (1937), her self-image took a hard knock. "The studio, as usual, had additional police guards stationed around the theater to protect stars from fans' over-enthusiasm," Barbara wrote. "I arrived with Robert Taylor as my escort, and his cheering fans broke the barriers and surged around us. In the melee, an officer assumed I was a fan who had grabbed Bob's arm. He yanked me away. Not until Bob started swinging, was I released. Not at all abashed, the officer said 'she doesn't look like a movie star to me!' Deflation replaced elation. At that moment I made up my mind to let Edith design my wardrobe from that day forward."

Internes Can't Take Money began a long partnership for Edith and actress Barbara Stanwyck.

CHAPTER THREE

THE REIGN BEGINS

The publicity department at Paramount groomed Edith more and more to help the studio's films get into the press

L PATRICK

Gail Patrick, shown here in John Meade's *Woman*, was one of the actresses on the Paramount lot whose trust Edith earned

EDITH'S LOYALTY TO TRAVIS BANTON COULD ONLY BE MATCHED BY HER DESIRE TO KEEP THE DEPARTMENT RUNNING SMOOTHLY DURING HIS ABSENCES CAUSED BY HIS DRINKING. IN MARCH 1938, PARAMOUNT BEGAN NEGOTIATING TRAVIS' NEW CONTRACT FOR THE UPCOMING YEAR. AS MUCH AS EDITH HAD TRIED TO COVER, THE STUDIO WAS WELL AWARE OF WHAT WAS HAPPENING WITH BANTON'S LATENESS AND ABSENCES.

They were willing to keep Travis on, but with no increase to his previous year's salary. Travis balked, and the studio released him from his contract early. "I was probably more influenced by Travis Banton than any designer in the world," Edith would say of her mentor. "I think his design was so pure and ungimmicky. His design was pure and simple, classic."

At first, Paramount couldn't decide how to handle the loss of Banton. Should they look for a designer of Travis' stature with which to replace him, or promote Edith? Designer Ernst Dryden had been working at the studio since the previous year, and was considered along with several other famous designers. But as Edith continued to run the department smoothly with the help of Adele Balkan, economics prevailed and Edith was promoted to the head of the department. Although Edith's salary was raised to $400 per week, it was significantly less than the $1,200 per week that Banton was making. Edith was given the standard designer contract which allowed Paramount the right to license her name and her designs.

Edith had been doing more and more publicity since the mid-1930s, but was still not yet exactly what fashion columnists might expect in a designer. Patricia Morison began acting at Paramount just as Edith was taking over the costume department and remembers, "There was nothing about her that was movies or show business. She was a rather withdrawn person. She sometimes talked to you and averted her eyes. With me she was good. A lot of people said maybe she was cold, but there was nothing cold about her. It was tough in the business she was in."

"She was not an Adrian or any one of those flamboyant designers who wanted their name on everything. She was a serious designer and she had certain signatures, like the waist line of a dress would be

Edith's sketch for Dorothy Lamour in *The Big Broadcast of 1938.* (Opposite): Edith with director Mitchell Leisen and actress Mary Boland on the set of *Artists and Models Abroad.*

high in the front and go down in the back. You could always tell an Edith Head from her idea of line. I think in her films, the clothes fit the film and the characters so beautifully. There was not a lot of flamboyance. It's not Adrian, who was the big talent, yes, but he sold Adrian. She, in many ways, sold the character."

MGM was having hit after hit with musicals like *The Great Ziegfeld* (1936) and its series of Jeanette MacDonald-Nelson Eddy operettas; Paramount increased its production of musicals to keep pace. Edith could no longer complain about a lack of opportunities for spectacular designs.

The Big Broadcast of 1938 (1938) is probably most notable for Bob Hope's film debut and the introduction of the song "Thanks for the Memory," sung by Hope and Shirley Ross. Directed by Mitchell Leisen, the plot involved a race between two gigantic ships, with one staging an all-star radio show. The film also starred Dorothy Lamour and W.C. Fields in his last film for Paramount. In the movie, Shirley Ross wears a stunning two-piece gown covered entirely in sequins that rivals anything created by Adrian at MGM. Leisen most likely had the creative vision for the gown, as he would often overtake the design of his films from Edith. Frank Richardson wrote in a memo that "Mr. Leisen (having been a designer) comes to the wardrobe department, makes patterns, changes Edith Head's designs and supervises fittings. Really Mr. Leisen becomes the designer, and Edith Head the sketch girl on his dressy productions." The movie was very successful, despite its ridiculous plot. The studio quickly followed it with *Thanks for the Memory* (1938), also starring Hope and Ross, which Edith worked on as well.

Mad About Music (1938) would be the only film that Edith would work on featuring a young singing star named Deanna Durbin, whose immense popularity would be credited with saving Universal International Studio. In the film, Deanna plays a young woman at a girls' school in Switzerland who has fabricated letters from her imaginary adventurer father. Edith shared costume credit with Universal's Vera West on the film, who most likely designed all of Deanna's outfits, with Edith costuming Gail Patrick, who played Deanna's mother.

College Swing (1938) starred George Burns, Gracie Allen, Martha Raye and two up-and-coming musical stars Betty Grable and John Payne. Even Grable's real-life husband Jackie Coogan got in on the action. Gracie Allen played Gracie Alden, who inherits a small-town school and hires vaudeville performers as professors. Grable was put in tailored form-fitting dresses, and an ice blue gown was purchased at a department store for one of her scenes.

Artists and Models Abroad (1938) starred Jack Benny as Buck Boswell, a down-on-his-luck band leader stuck in Paris with his all-girl

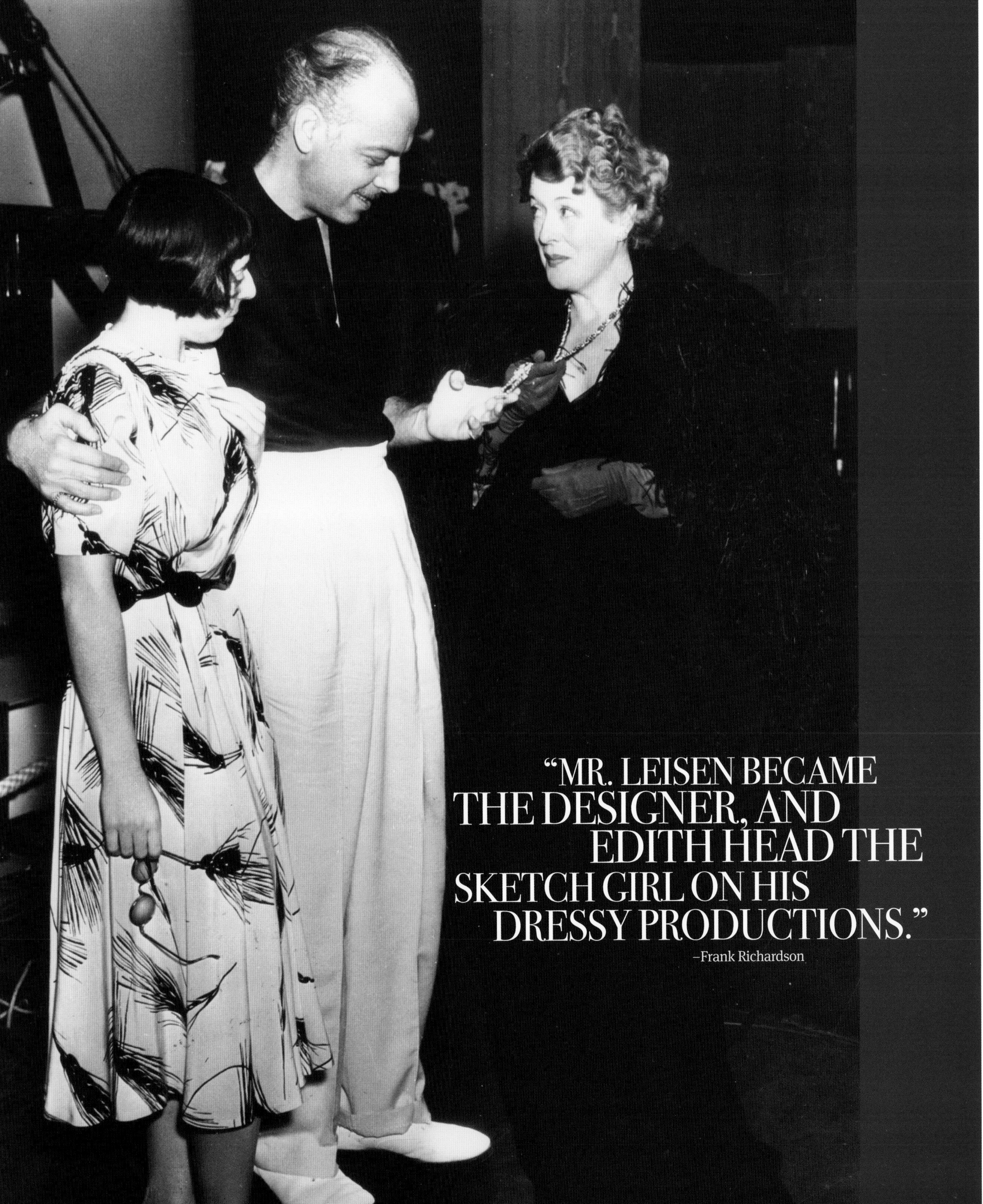

"MR. LEISEN BECAME THE DESIGNER, AND EDITH HEAD THE SKETCH GIRL ON HIS DRESSY PRODUCTIONS."

–Frank Richardson

BUYING CLOTHES FROM PARIS TO POPULATE A FILM WARDROBE WAS A PRACTICE NEARLY AS OLD AS THE MOVIES THEMSELVES.

Joan Bennett in a gown selected by Edith for *Artists and Models Abroad.*

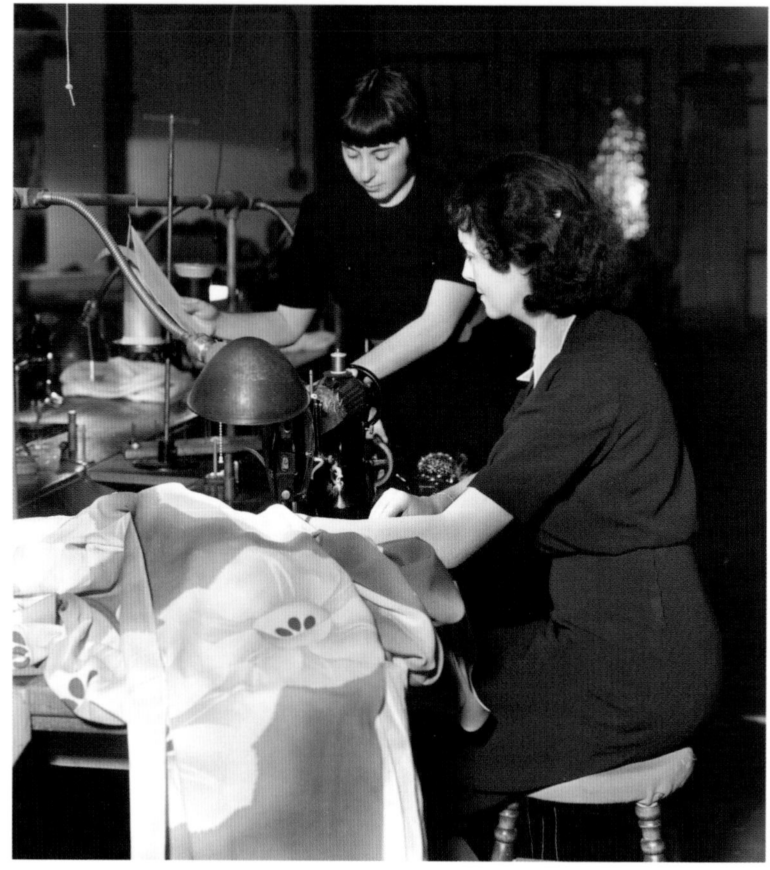

troupe. When Buck gets a job for his girls modeling at the Palace of Feminine Arts at the Paris International Exposition, it gives a great opportunity to showcase some fabulous fashions in a twelve-minute fashion show sequence. Actual Paris couture gowns were brought in for the show. This practice would often cause confusion in Edith's career regarding credits, though it was hardly limited to Edith or Paramount.

Buying clothes from Paris to populate a film wardrobe was a practice nearly as old as the movies themselves. Silent film stars like Gloria Swanson would wear gowns from designers such as Paul Poiret, which were shipped to the studio, or just purchased by the actresses themselves while in Paris. Studios that were only contracted to put their own designers' names on a film completely overlooked the fact that not all the designs were created in-house. In *Angel* (1937), Marlene Dietrich wears a Chinese brocade jacket and navy blue double silk jersey skirt created by the French designer Alix exclusively for her, but the dress is credited to Travis Banton in the film.

Paramount, not being a studio to fight a formula, re-paired Ray Milland and Dorothy Lamour (again in more sarongs) in *Her Jungle Love* (1938). It was another smash, giving the audience a chance to see the beautiful Lamour in Technicolor. Dorothy played Tura, a jungle girl who rescues two men from a typhoon, and is then expected by a tribe to pay with her life for befriending the hated white men. The film came complete with an earthquake and a love triangle between Lamour, Milland, and Virginia Vale.

In *Dangerous to Know* (1938), Anna May Wong plays Lan Ying (a role she originated on Broadway), the spurned mistress to racketeer Steve Recka (Akim Tamiroff). Publicists filled the fashion pages with Wong in Edith's slinky white crepe gown with long sleeves, a high neckline and molded bodice and jacket with a leaf motif in contrast to her traditional Chinese robes. Anna Me Wong's style also had a profound influence on Edith. Noticing the hairstyle that Wong wore in the early 1930s, flat bangs with a chignon at the back, Edith copied the look around this time when she was experimenting with hairstyles, and kept it for the rest of her life.

To publicize *Spawn of the North* (1938), photographs of Dorothy Lamour were released wearing a dramatic Spanish-influenced black lace gown with a strapless bodice. Atop her head, Edith designed a modern version of the mantilla, and draped it over her head, falling softly to her shoulders. For Lamour's personal wardrobe that year, Edith designed a "Sarongown," inspired by the native sarongs that

(Opposite) **Edith and seamstress Mary Northover work on a variation of the popular sarong that could be worn in the evening.**

(This page) **The "sarongown" as the dress came to be known, is modeled by Dorothy Lamour**

NOW THAT HER POSITION AT THE STUDIO SEEMED TO BE ESTABLISHED, EDITH FINALLY DECIDED TO DIVORCE CHARLES HEAD.

(left to right) **Howard Greer, Edith and Travis Banton at Paramount**

Dorothy wore in films. Edith used an imported Tahitian crepe with a flame-colored background and an exotic print of huge white magnolias. She added a cape cut in toga fashion from white crepe, and lined with flame-colored crepe. The gown was a huge hit with the public. Manufacturers had already been adapting versions of the sarong for loungewear.

Security in her employment and personal life had always been of the utmost importance to Edith. Now that her position at the studio seemed to be established, Edith finally decided to divorce Charles Head. David Chrierechetti noted in his biography of Edith, that her romance with Bayard Veileer was most likely the reason. Charles Head's fate after divorcing Edith is a mystery, but by the time *The Dress Doctor* was published in 1962, Charles had apparently died. Edith purposely does not mention their divorce, and the reader is left to assume that she was widowed. One of the few comments Edith ever made publicly about her relationship with Charles was that "it was an affair of the intellect."

A BUMPY, BUT FRESH START

1939 is a magic number to both film critics and fans — the year that is generally considered the artistic apex of the Hollywood Studio system and the "Golden Era" of motion pictures. Two of the most popular films of all time, *Gone With the Wind* and *The Wizard of Oz* were released that year, as well as *Stagecoach*, with John Wayne, *Drums Along the Mohawk*, *Mr. Smith Goes to Washington*, the Greta Garbo comedy *Ninotchka*, *Gunga Din* with Cary Grant and *The Little Princess*, considered Shirley Temple's finest film. For glamour, it was hard to top Adrian's designs for MGM's *The Women*, set against a backdrop of New York's high society and starring three actresses who knew a few things about wearing clothes: Norma Shearer, Joan Crawford, and Rosalind Russell.

That year, however, Paramount, didn't release many films that left a lasting memory. Its golden period was still about ten years away. But *Beau Geste* (1939) with Gary Cooper was highly regarded by

"MISS COLBERT CONSIDERS EDITH HEAD AN ART STUDENT, AND HAS NO FAITH IN HER DESIGNING ABILITY." –Frank Richardson

Though things appear calm in this publicity photograph of Edith with Claudette Colbert for *Zaza*, tensions ran high over the costumes for the film.

critics; as was Cecil B. DeMille's *Union Pacific* (1939) and there was certainly magic in the Mitchell Leisen-directed *Midnight* (1939) starring Claudette Colbert.

Edith's first full year as a designer got off to a rocky start. Her relationship with her stable of "B" actresses seemed to not change at all after Banton left. Stars like Gail Patrick, Shirley Ross, and Frances Farmer still relied on Edith's judgment and good taste. But a few of the bigger stars who had been dressed by Banton, were not pleased to now be turned over to his former assistant. The most vocal of these was Claudette Colbert, whom Edith was dressing in *Zaza* (1939).

Not helping the matter was a rumor being spread by Hedda Hopper, who was then acting at Paramount, that Edith had a hand in getting Travis fired. What went on behind the scenes can probably best be summed up in the words of Frank Richardson, who sent a memo to Fred Leahy in 1940 recommending that Colbert's clothing be made outside of the studio, rather than have Edith design it for an upcoming feature.

"Miss Colbert considers Edith Head an art student, has no faith in her designing ability. This means (as has happened before) continual changing of this line and that and more shopping while Miss Colbert experiments with her own ideas," wrote Richardson. "The dress becomes so disorganized and worn out after so many changes that it becomes necessary to build a new one. Miss Colbert was a dressmaker herself in France, before the screen discovered her." Colbert began using Irene Lentz, a designer for the Ladies Custom Salon at Bullocks Wilshire. "She could have just as easily asked for Travis Banton," David Chierichetti says, "so I don't know ultimately how loyal she was to him."

Banton found work at Twentieth Century-Fox, and Edith told Chierichetti that she was so anxious that he keep his job, she would wake him up and drive him to Fox before she had to be at Paramount in the morning. All of the idle talk about her usurping Banton's position put Edith on guard, and she responded by becoming more reserved around the other employees in the costume department.

As part of her new contract, Edith was sent to Paris, as Howard Greer and Travis Banton had been sent in prior years. Greer and Banton gave Edith pages of advice of things to do in Paris. She traveled with Lillian Farley, wife of the head of the Paramount office in Paris, who was working for *Harper's Bazaar*. Even though Parisian designers had been working on Hollywood films for years, often the collaborations were not happy ones. So Edith, feeling like she had little clout as Paramount's designer, let Lillian take her through all of the collections. Edith met designers such as Alix, Schiaparelli, and Balenciaga and bought at least one item from all of the collections. She was stunned when the customs official in New York told her that she owed hundreds of dollars in import duties, and the Paramount office in New York had to come to her rescue.

When asked later if her trips to Paris affected her designs for contemporary clothes, Edith replied "not a bit, because what is shown in Paris today is a dead duck tomorrow. I cannot do what's contemporary. If they were doing a certain type of thing in Paris, and then I came back and did it in pictures, within eight to twelve months when the picture came out, it would be a passé look."

EDITH AT WORK

(Above left) **Mary Martin demonstrates how her look in *The Great Victor Herbert* can be adapted for day wear.** (Above) **One of Edith's sketches for Martin in the film.**

EDITH DECORATED HER SALON ON THE SECOND FLOOR OF THE WARDROBE BUILDING with pale silver gray carpets and walls; she used French provincial furniture covered in silver leaf to make it look like French fashion salon. She installed a large mirror with doors on each side that could swing, to allow several views of a dress at one time. Lights were installed to reflect into the mirrors, so that when the mirrored doors at the far ends swung together, the rest of the room could not be seen. This helped Edith and the actress concentrate on how the clothes looked under harsh lighting. Little dressmaker forms were placed around the room on tables. Working under Edith was a staff that included four expert fitters, and drapers, beaders, finishers, and cutters, each of them with a staff of their own.

The workflow remained the same as it had under Banton. A technician was assigned to each picture to research costumes in the large research library. Pictures and stories from the period were then brought to Edith. She would select the best costumes with lines that would adapt to the modern figure. Then Edith would make her sketches "giving full play to my imagination with one eye on the budget allowance," she said. She would select fabric from the huge supply store, which was constantly augmented by salesmen bringing in new fabric. The sketches, with material attached, went to the producer, director, and star for approval. Edith would ask the camera men and art directors to approve the sketch for color and lighting, and to make sure the fabric didn't clash. If the movie was in color, the technical advisor saw them for color, harmony, and contrast. Edith would then give the sketch to wardrobe, where expert cutters and fitters executed the design. Each star had a dummy of their figure made and the dresses were built on those. Edith usually required a maximum of three personal fittings as well. Then, if there was budget, a camera test would be made for the final approvals.

Edith began wearing the uniform for which she would become known (and later berated), the tailor-made suits in monotone colors. Edith said she didn't want the stars looking at her figure while she was trying to analyze theirs. She wanted to fall into the background and let the actor or actress only see themselves in the reflection of her mirrors. Edith adopted the blue eyeglasses that would eventually become her trademark at this time. Looking through blue glass at an object or fabric would help costume designers, cinematographers, and art directors understand how an object would look when photographed in black-and-white.

By now, Edith had learned there was a rhythm to most meetings about costumes with actresses. Before meeting Edith, most actresses would already have a preconceived notion of what they could or couldn't wear. Some actresses even had colors that had meaning to them, such as green for good luck. But the first meeting was almost always very cordial—too cordial. Edith said she wished the actresses would just really tell her what they wanted, but often they would just say something like, "I'm so glad you're doing the clothes. I'll leave everything in your hands." The second meeting, when the sketches were shown, was where the actress' true wishes really came out. Some exceptions Edith would find included Bette Davis and Katharine Hepburn, both busy women, who had very clear ideas about what worked for them or for the character they were portraying.,

"I believe you should allow an actor or actress to discuss and criticize and say, 'I cannot wear this costume because I cannot do this' and I always do that before I go on set. Occasionally you get a bitch who does it to you on set, but not very often," Edith said. She truly felt that dressing an actress in something she didn't like or in which she didn't feel comfortable could hamper her performance. For fittings, Edith always hoped the actresses would come in made up, with their hair done to help show the costume in the best possible way. She hated it when actresses would come to fittings with their hair in curlers, pin curls, or a bandana.

Gail Patrick and Edith pose for an idealized version of a costume consultation.

"I BELIEVE YOU SHOULD ALLOW AN ACTOR OR ACTRESS TO DISCUSS AND CRITICIZE."

–Edith Head

STUDIO POLITICS

The closest fashion film Edith had to design in 1939 to rival Adrian's *The Women* was *Café Society*. The film starred Madeleine Carroll, one of Hitchcock's original cool blondes, who had appeared in his *The 39 Steps* (1935). Madeleine was at the height of her popularity and was one of the highest-paid actresses at the studio. She was also used to being dressed by the best couturiers in Europe, and Edith said Madeleine taught her that "the snobbery of fashion is a potent weapon." But with the recent trip to Paris under her belt, Edith was able to meet Madeleine on her own fashion playing field, naming the designers of the suit, hat, and jewels that the star wore to the fitting.

The story of the film involved a wealthy publicity hound (Carroll) who marries a reporter (Fred MacMurray) on a bet. Edith loved designing the clothes for the film because it was a dress picture and she designed what she described as "big, bouffant, off the shoulder evening gowns, utterly feminine and princess-looking." Edith costumed Shirley Ross in a slim-lined gown of gold lamé with an all-over sequin highlight, with a long-sleeved bolero and a transparent flesh bodice. Edith added a gold hair ornament studded with emeralds.

On the opposite spectrum of sophisticated clothing came *The Great Victor Herbert* (1939), starring Mary Martin and Walter Connolly, about the prolific operetta composer. Edith said of working with Martin, "I had her for a couple of the frilliest pictures ever . . . in which she was all but smothered in tulle, pantalets, ruffles and curls."

Edith went all out with Mary's wardrobe, which included several extraordinary designs including, an evening gown of blue tulle edged in silver, with nosegays of sweetheart roses and forget-me-nots, accented with pale blue opera gloves and a flowered fan; a tailored suit of French blue broadcloth with sleeves and collar trimmed in mink, with a picture hat of blue velvet and silk, accented by deep red velvet posies with chin-streamers to match; a skirt of blue viscose taffeta with circular flounces, topped by a blouse of pink mousselline with Val lace insertions

"THE SECOND MEETING, WHEN THE SKETCHES WERE SHOWN,
WAS WHERE THE ACTRESS'

Above, left to right: **Dorothy Lamour in *Tropic Holiday*; Edith and Dorothy consult on wardrobe for the film; The matador costume worn by Martha Raye in *Tropic Holiday* was based on Rudolph Valentino's "suit of lights" in Blood and Sand; Edith's original sketch for the costume.**

TRUE WISHES REALLY CAME OUT."

–Edith Head

The Great Victor Herbert is an example of how Paramount never properly utilized the talents of Mary Martin. The actress was never comfortable in the lightweight roles which the studio required her to play.

and beading with "baby" black velvet ribbons; and a negligee of flowered rose challis, trimmed in ruching of rose taffeta with an under slip of pink taffeta with a deep accordion-pleated flounce. The princess lines and corseted effect of the waistline and the rounded bust and hip line that Edith used were all authentic trademarks of that era. Martin's hair, done by Paramount's Marie Livingstone, was also kept authentic to the period.

The studio only seemed interested in Martin appearing in saccharin-sweet roles, and the actress was constantly going to battle to be given better scripts. She had already had a great success on Broadway singing *My Heart Belongs to Daddy,* but the studio could never find a script that utilized the best of Martin's talents. They had a similar problem with Patricia Morison, who they had found in New York singing in a musical opposite Alfred Drake. Morison had striking features and beautiful long dark hair. Paramount felt they had found a new Dorothy Lamour.

For Morison's film, *The Magnificent Fraud* (1939), the actress and Edith were first brought together for publicity's sake. Morison had worked in New York making $10 a week as a sketch artist, and when she told this to the Paramount publicity people, they decided to have Morison work up some sketches for her own wardrobe and photograph her with Edith.

"We really collaborated on the designs. I don't take any credit, but we did them together," Morison says. "I trusted Edith completely. And the gowns she did for *The Magnificent Fraud* were spectacular. I played this wealthy lady, and the clothes fit the body so beautifully. You could move in them. She had a knack for what to do with the human body.

"Edith's wardrobe didn't stand out, because it was part of the film. They were very much the character. While I loved wearing flamboyant gorgeous things, when you wore Edith's designs, you felt like you had lived in them. I don't think she ever overstepped, or was even to be tempted. I think being shy, she was not one to push herself on people."

Edith created an entire wardrobe for Morison of only black-and-white designs, which complemented Morison's creamy white skin and long brown hair. "During the filming, there was one gown that she did that was white with black flowers and had a peasant neckline," Morison says. "There was a close-up, a love scene with Lloyd Nolan that was beautifully photographed. A note came from the censor that my bosom was too obvious. We had to shoot the whole thing over. Luckily, Edith didn't have to re-work the neck line, they only had to change the lighting. But we were laughing our heads off."

"EDITH'S WARDROBE DIDN'T STAND OUT, BECAUSE IT WAS PART OF THE FILM. THEY WERE VERY MUCH THE CHARACTER."

–Patricia Morison

Edith, producer Harlan Thompson and Patricia Morison look over sketches of Morison's costume ideas for the film.

Man About Town (1939), cast Jack Benny as a theatre producer in love with the star of his show (Dorothy Lamour). For Dorothy, Edith designed a spring street dress of dark red with embroidered white beaded wings, worn with a white felt hat and white gloves, and a three-piece suit of black wool embroidered with shiny black raffia. On the long coat, Edith added reveres of blue fox, and accented the entire ensemble with a muffler of solid black Raffia and a black jersey hat with a wimple.

Invitation to Happiness (1939), paired Fred MacMurray as a boxer, who falls for the daughter of one of his wealthy backers (Irene Dunne). Dunne was a talented singer, and possessed one of the best senses for comedic timing in the screwball comedies being made in the 1930's. She also wore clothes incredibly well, as evidenced in the magnificent wardrobe that had been designed for her by Robert Kalloch in *The Awful Truth* (1937). For *Invitation to Happiness*, taking place in 1927, Edith used authentic detail of the period on Dunne's three-piece beige Kasha suit with a short, straight skirt, beltless over-blouse of matching crepe with a tied neckline and covered buttons. Edith added a full, short cape of the period trimmed with Nutria and a matching felt cloche hat. True to the time period when all accessories had to match, Dunne's perforated street shoes, bag and gloves were all made of the same beige leather.

Edith designed for Madeleine Carroll again in *Honeymoon in Bali* (1939). Carroll played a New York department store executive, giving Edith plenty of opportunities for terrific clothes including a Victorian gown of Bianchini's bright sapphire blue faille that featured an extreme décolletage above a fitted bodice with Edith's famous dropped waistline. Edith used a narrow clip of sapphire and diamond stones to highlight the neckline.

The production of forty to fifty films a year at Paramount caused Frank Richardson to bring in Oleg Cassini as an additional designer to the wardrobe department. Cassini got the job based on a strong portfolio of sketches, which he had stayed up creating the entire night before his

Below left: **Isa Miranda in *Hotel Imperial*.** Below right: **Anna May Wong in *King of Chinatown*.**

Opposite: **Edith in 1939, the year she succeeded Travis Banton at Paramount.**

"SHE SPOKE A CURIOUS LANGUAGE, A CROSS BETWEEN HOLLYWOODESE AND FASHIONESE"

–Oleg Cassini

Edith's sketch for Dorothy Lamour in *Man About Town.* Opposite: Edith checks a measurement with actress Osa Massen

interview. In his book *My Own Fashion*, Cassini described what it was like for him to work with Edith Head, "she spoke a curious language, a cross between Hollywoodese and fashionese (I was learning that there were many languages in America, most of which were ways to say nothing while sounding expert). She could really sell her ideas to producers. 'This will shoot very well, very rich . . . you can tell this girl is wealthy, but not ruthless. She has good taste. You can just see her polite Southern background, can't you?' "

Cassini wrote that he learned the visual tricks a designer must know when working in films. For instance, with actresses like Madeleine Carroll who could appear heavier on camera, he would use soft fabrics in dark shades on top, and a tight elasticized black matte waist for contrast to achieve a slimming effect; for black-and-white films, a touch of white around the neck made the face photograph better; dresses made in off-white or off-black could appear muddy on camera, but dresses of true black absorbed too much light and dresses of true white reflected too much light.

Cassini said he believed that Edith thought that he would use his masculine charms to convince the more powerful actresses at Paramount to use him as their designer instead of her. "But when I had lunch with someone like Madeleine Carroll," he wrote, "work was nowhere at the top of my agenda, and that is something Edith Head would never understand. Though she was married, work was the only item on hers. She arrived at daybreak each morning and was the last one to leave at night."

The outbreak of war in Europe caused some fabrics to become scarce. Silk supplies from Japan were cut off, and lamé, which was made from fine spun metal at the time, was another casualty. Dorothy Lamour's famous silk sarongs had to be made of rayon.

Edith's close professional relationship with Barbara Stanwyck still couldn't stop Mitchell Leisen's interference into the actress' costumes when he directed *Remember the Night* (1940). Stanwyck starred in the film as a shoplifter on trial who stays at the home of the judge who is prosecuting her during the holidays. Though much has been written about how Edith transformed Stanwyck in the following year's *The Lady Eve* (1941), Edith began using her trick of building skirts high on the waist to compensate for Stanwyck's figure problems on this film. One such design was a suit employing a circular effect, with extra fullness in the front. For the suit, Edith created a collarless, long-sleeved bolero that was short-waisted and had a zippered treatment. The skirt had a narrow pigskin belt whose color matched the hand-knit sweater underneath. Edith topped the ensemble off with a hat of two-toned green grosgrain ribbon across the forehead.

When Paramount made *The Road to Singapore* (1940) it was

"A NOTE CAME FROM THE CENSOR THAT MY BOSOM WAS TOO OBVIOUS. WE HAD TO SHOOT THE WHOLE THING OVER."

–Patricia Morison

not intended to be the first of a series of films. But the magical casting of Bob Hope, Bing Crosby and Dorothy Lamour together, left the public wanting more. The studio had originally considered casting Jack Oakie and Fred MacMurray in the film about two playboys fleeing their misadventures with girlfriends. As always, Lamour played the dark eyed beauty of an exotic land, and Edith, who usually shied away from using prints in film, felt most comfortable using them in an arena like this.

For the *Road* pictures, Edith would get her research on the wardrobes worn in the locales of the pictures, and then work up her sketches based on samples brought in from Western Costume, a costume rental house located just outside of the Paramount lot. Authenticity was not always as important as getting a laugh, and sometimes the more ridiculous a costume was, the better. Authentic locales and even the features of the natives of whatever country in which the story was taking place, never seemed to be an issue for the producers. But you could always be sure that the women were seductively dressed. For co-star Judith Barrett, Edith designed a billowing gown that swirled out below a bodice inspired by a basque sweater, that was embellished with ropes of golden braid embroidery.

Safari (1940) teamed Madeleine Carroll and Douglas Fairbanks Jr. in an homage to MGM's *Red Dust* (1932). Carroll played Linda Stewart, whose millionaire fiancée employs Jim Logan (Fairbanks) as a guide for a jungle hunting trip. As with many films of this nature, even when the heroine is out in the middle of jungle, her clothes are always crisp and clean. The always stylish Carroll looked elegant in a Jungle brown gabardine regulation safari costume that Edith designed for her, with straight-tailored slacks, a single-breasted jacket with four "bellows" pockets and a neckerchief of scarlet and cream tie-silk. Edith also designed a crisp heavy white linen suit with a flared skirt and one-button jacket that nipped in at the waistline, and a shirt of navy Irish linen embroidered in stripes of white. Edith topped the ensemble off with a casual white panama hat.

Opposite: **Edith used two-toned blue silk jersey for this dinner dress for Muriel Angelus in *Safari* and added a "stomacher" of handwrought silver scroll across the mid-section.** Above: **Edith's sketch of a white linen suit for Lillian Cornell in *A Night at Earl Carroll's*.**

Barbara Stanwyck credited Edith's ingenuity with correcting the actress' figure problems visually, thus allowing Stanwyck to be considered for more glamorous roles in films such as *The Lady Eve* (opposite) and *Ball of Fire* (right).

Edith was always quite verbal about how she resented the way Paulette Goddard would parade her fabulous jewel collection in front of the seamstresses in the wardrobe department, some of whom were only earning about one dollar an hour. Edith often had to ask her employees to work throughout the night to have clothes ready for morning shoots. By most accounts, Edith was very empathetic to the women who worked under her, and they were very loyal to her. But even when Edith didn't particularly like a star off-screen, if the script called for beautiful designs, Edith made them beautiful. *For Ghost Breakers* (1940), Goddard wore a jaw-dropping evening gown with an open midriff, made of heavy white crepe emblazoned with gold discs. The slim skirt was held to the hips by a belt of the gold disks. To accessorize it, Edith added a voluminous handkerchief scattered with gold discs, a solid gold evening bag and white crepe sandals.

Occasionally Edith would be asked to work on films that were out of her usual range.The science-fiction film *Dr. Cyclops* (1940) was even a bit of an oddity for Paramount. It was directed by Ernest B. Schoedsack, one of the brilliant minds who brought the original *King Kong* (1933) to the screen. The film is also notable because it was the first science fiction film made in the three-strip Technicolor process. Edith never talked about her contribution to this film, perhaps because she felt the wardrobe was too ordinary, or because a good portion was pulled from stock to accommodate the film's small budget. But Janice Logan's unusual print dress with puffed sleeves is certainly notable, as is the concept of the group of humans who are shrunk by the mad doctor, having to resort to toga-like ensembles to stay clothed in their small state. The film has achieved a great cult status among science-fiction fans, and critics consider the role of the title character to be Albert Dekker's best performance.

A SURPRISE WEDDING

A romance that had been brewing for years between Edith and art director Wiard Ihnenn finally took a more serious turn. Both of them had been committed to other people when they worked on *Cradle Song* together, but Wiard had kept in touch with Edith after leaving Paramount to take a position at Twentieth-Century Fox. David Chierichetti said Ihnen would find pretenses to call Edith and ask her advice on his wardrobe or what kind of corsage to purchase for a date. When Ihnen proposed, Edith

Edith's imagination was allowed to flourish in costuming Dorothy Lamour for *The Road to Morocco* (this page and opposite), as long as some of the costumes allowed for Lamour's bare midriff to show.

This was Edith's favorite photo of herself, perhaps partly because animals had been a big part of her childhood when friends were hard to come by.

wasn't even sure he was serious. Even as they left for Las Vegas on a chartered plane in September of 1940, with friends Vic Calderon and Betty Freeby, Edith still wasn't sure they would come back married. But they did. Among the telegrams of congratulations Edith received was one from director Edward H. Griffith, the director with whom she was working on the film *Virginia* (1941), saying, "Well you cute little fox you — my warmest congratulations to you both."

The Ihnens settled into Edith's house on Doheny Drive. They filled the home with their collection of Mexican art and Bill's collection of authentic antique cannons. Edith preferred French provincial furniture, such as the kind she had chosen for her salon at the studio, and her bedrooms were always decorated in that style. Bill was very content around the house, and spent his time off from the studio at his easel painting. Edith expressed her creativity at home in the kitchen. She said once, "I don't think I'm one of the greatest costume designers in the world, but I am one of the greatest cooks."

"I DON'T THINK I'M ONE OF THE GREATEST COSTUME DESIGNERS IN THE WORLD, BUT I AM ONE OF THE GREATEST COOKS."

–Edith Head

Paramount re-teamed Fred MacMurray and Madeleine Carroll in *Virginia*, about a Southern beauty trying to sell her homestead. The movie was to be shot on location in Howardsville and Albemarle County in Virginia, and Edith had fitted all the clothes in Los Angeles. With the start of the shoot less than a week away, Paramount decided to switch the film from black-and-white to Technicolor. Due to the saturated levels of color that Technicolor employed, most of the wardrobe had to be remade. Carroll booked a hurried flight to New York from England, where she had been staying, and Edith met her there. Edith brought trunks of clothes with her and hired Madeleine's favorite fitter from Hattie Carnegie to assist them. Within three days, all the clothes were done. The bridal gown that Madeleine wore in the film was merchandised and *Vogue* ran a photo of it. It was Edith's first recognition in a fashion magazine.

While making *Kiss the Boys Goodbye* (1941), Mary Martin continued her battle with the studio over the roles she was being offered. Mary would invent euphemisms to describe the clothes in which she was being fitted. Edith said later "she was being given whipped-cream clothes for hot-fudge pictures, when all she wanted was plain vanilla." After about three more years of musicals, Mary returned to Broadway, and never worked under contract to a studio again.

For *The Lady Eve* (1941), Barbara Stanwyck had a dual role of a titled English woman and a lady cardsharp out to take advantage of an unsophisticated millionaire (Henry Fonda). Edith designed dual wardrobes to suit both of Stanwyck's characters. As the gambler, Edith went with a black-and-white color scheme, and experimented with Spanish influences in the designs. For the noblewoman, Edith used softer, finer fabrics.

Edith recounted a story of Barbara trying on the evening gown of black crepe, which employed a high cummerbund, and a short jacket with black glitter; the actress was apparently surprised by how flattering the dress was to her figure from the side. Stanwyck had always had a problem fitting what she considered her long waist and low-slung rear-end. By bringing the waist of the dress up higher and

Opposite: The simple, elegant wedding gown Edith designed for Barbara Stanwyck in *The Lady Eve.* Right: Edith used pink and green to mimic the color of a watermelon on the long tunic jacket she designed for Mary Martin in *Kiss the Boys Goodbye.*

widening the waistband in the front and narrowing it in the back, Edith solved Barbara's figure problem with illusion. Edith had accomplished this on the previous year's *Remember the Night*, but the synergy of Edith's Latin-American-inspired designs and the cultural embracing of Latin music, made fashion columnists re-evaluate Stanwyck as a woman to watch. It also changed the way Stanwyck was perceived in the film industry. "Once you've felt the pleasure of introducing clothes which set a new fashion trend, you become much more conscious of fash-

stay behind. Everybody asks what is the worst time you ever had? Really, it's not been with people, but mostly animals." In the end, the idea was abandoned.

After filming wrapped, Stanwyck gifted Edith with a machine used by milliners for sewing hats. It resembled a sewing machine, but was smaller. Edith began adding to her collection when she would scour flea markets on her travels. They occupied a table in her salon, and became just as identifiable to the actresses who spent time there, as Edith's collection of Oscars that she would later win.

WHEN IHNEN PROPOSED, EDITH WASN'T EVEN SURE HE WAS SERIOUS. EVEN AS THEY LEFT FOR LAS VEGAS ON A CHARTERED PLANE IN SEPTEMBER OF 1940, WITH FRIENDS VIC CALDERON AND BETTY FREEBY, EDITH STILL WASN'T SURE THEY WOULD COME BACK MARRIED.

ion," Stanwyck said. Now Barbara didn't always have to play earnest working girls, and could be cast in dress films. Barbara continued to work with Edith throughout her career, even having Edith's design services written into her contract when she could, while being loaned out to another studio.

If Edith scored a success with Stanwyck , she struck out with Emma the snake. Director Preston Strurges had written a snake into the credit sequence for *The Lady Eve*, to play on the theme of Eve in the title. He asked Edith to design a diamond necklace for Emma to wear. "A snake is all in one piece, and they wanted us to design a little necklace with a bow on it. And every time she would wiggle off, the bow would

Another gift that Edith received from Stanwyck, was the encouragement to finally have her teeth fixed. Barbara had asked Edith why she never smiled, and Edith revealed her missing front teeth to her. Being an actress, Stanwyck was acutely aware of the need to correct a physical flaw like that, and the ease with which it could be done. Stanwyck recommended a dentist to Edith and convinced her to have her teeth fixed. It was a great relief to Edith. Later, she said that she wondered herself why it had taken her so long to do it. But even after doing so, Edith still chose to smile rarely, and almost never for photographs.

One Night in Lisbon (1941), re-teamed Madeleine Carroll and Fred MacMurray in a reworking of John Van Druten's play *There's*

"ONCE YOU'VE FELT THE PLEASURE OF INTRODUCING CLOTHES WHICH SET A NEW FASHION TREND, YOU BECOME MUCH MORE CONSCIOUS OF FASHION."

–Barbara Stanwyck

Barbara Stanwyck had to be both predatory and alluring in her role as a cardsharp in *The Lady Eve*

Left: **Edith and Wiard at their home on Doheny Drive in Beverly Hills.** Opposite: **Edith used gold braid to accent a gown for Stanwyck in *The Lady Eve*.**

Always Juliet. For Carroll, Edith designed a violet crepe dinner suit, with a jacket featuring a deep peplum. Two bunches of beaded violets in the floral colors were embroidered on the dress, and Edith slit the slim skirt in the front to allow for freedom of movement. Critics felt the film couldn't decide if it was a sophisticated romantic film or a wacky comedy, and it didn't catch on with audiences.

Edith was loaned to Samuel Goldwyn when Barbara Stanwyck was cast in *Ball of Fire* (1941). In an imaginative re-telling of *Snow White and the Seven Dwarfs*, Stanwyck played Sugarpuss O'Shea, a nightclub singer who hides out from the police with a group of professors. For Sugarpuss' nightclub outfit, Edith created a glittering bustier that had chiffon sleeves with sequined stripes from shoulder to wrist. Stanwyck's ankle-length skirt was hung with sequined fringe to make the most of the actress' legs.

Aloma of the South Seas (1941) was responsible for some bad blood in the wardrobe department. Edith received credit on the film, even though Oleg Cassini had done all the major designing. Because Cassini's agent had forgotten to negotiate screen credit in his contract with Paramount, the studio refused to put his name on the film. The movie was a re-make of the 1928 film of the same name, and Dorothy Lamour was cast as Aloma, the exotic beauty who is romanced by Jon Hall. In a bid for sarong equality, Cassini also put Hall in them as well. Oleg recounted a story later about how he chose to discuss "manly" things with Hall, as his fitter measured the area around Hall's groin.

HOLLYWOOD AT WAR

AS THE WAR IN EUROPE PROGRESSED, the rental fees abroad for films starring Greta Garbo, which MGM relied on heavily, all but vanished. The studio requested that costume designer Adrian "deglamorize" Garbo to make her more accessible to American audiences. Against his better judgment, he complied, and their next film, *Two-Faced Woman* (1941), was an embarrassing flop for both the designer and actress. Greta Garbo announced her retirement from films after its release, and Adrian also tendered his resignation. "When the glamour ends for Garbo, it also ends for me," Adrian said. "She has created a type. If you destroy that illusion, you destroy her. When Garbo walked out of the studio, glamour went with her, and so did I." The man that most studio designers looked to as the measure of excellence, was now gone from the industry.

On December 7, 1941, aircraft and midget submarines attacked the United States fleet at Pearl Harbor, Hawaii. More than. 2,350 men and women were killed, and twenty-one ships were severely damaged. The United States, which had been abstaining from entering the war in Europe, officially entered World War II.

One of the first Hollywood casualties of war came unexpectedly on January 16, 1942, and touched Edith profoundly. Carole Lombard, returning to California with her mother from a war bond rally in her home state of Indiana, was killed in airplane crash near Las Vegas. Those in Hollywood who had loved Carole and her husband Clark Gable, joined him in mourning her. She was only thirty-three years old. There were many sacrifices still to be made. Edith's husband Wiard later joined the Army to work as a camouflage expert.

The U.S. War Production Board (WPB) issued a regulation governing the manufacture of clothing, known as Limitation Order L-85. This was mainly focused at the women's apparel industry to conserve the amount of fabric, labor, facilities, and machinery expended in the creation of garments. Voluntary restrictions had already been in place since the outbreak of the war in Europe, and the government hoped that the average consumer would not notice the difference in the garments available after the ruling. But the changes were quick and profound. Straight lines replaced what had once been pleats in a dress or a ruffle on a cuff.

Hollywood was expected to go along with all of the restrictions as an example to women that clothes could still be fashionable, while conserving resources. Though the L-85 ruling did limit some creativity, it forced costume designers to have more ingenuity to get things accomplished. One of the first casualties for Edith was Dorothy Lamour's wardrobe in *The Road to Morocco* (1942). Edith substituted cottons for exotic fabrics and had some of the costumes hand-painted. However, on screen, the costumes are superior to some of the later *Road* pictures made after the war. When giving advice to columnists about upcoming fashion trends, Edith always kept the limitation of L-85 in mind. There was no other choice for her. One bright spot was that the pattern industry saw a surge in sales, as home sewing became the norm, and women altered and re-worked garments they already owned.

When Paramount was looking to trim payroll, Edith convinced them that she was able to handle all the design responsibilities on her own, and placed Oleg Cassini's neck squarely on the chopping block. "She wanted everybody, she wanted every picture," Cassini said. "She would like me to have a car accident, fall, and disappear. That was Hollywood. There was only room for a few. You had to come out and win, otherwise you were out. Once you lost your job as a designer, it may have taken you tenyears to get another one." But ultimately, Cassini resigned when he showed up for a date at a young lady's home, only to be met at the door by Henry Ginsburg, who was the man in charge of making the staffing cuts at Paramount.

Paramount's cuts didn't spare Edith's good friend, the photographer John Engstead. He had been responsible for some of the studio's most memorable publicity photographs of Carole Lombard, Claudette Colbert and Marlene Dietrich, as well as some of Edith herself. Engstead was hired by *Harper's Bazaar* to do advertising and portrait work, and eventually became a freelance photographer. He stayed close to Edith for the rest of her life, and often photographed many of the stars in their close-knit circle, including Anne Baxter and her family.

Paramount's biggest star to emerge in the war years was a 4' 11" ?" bundle of dynamite with the alluring name of Veronica Lake. She was nicknamed "The Peek-a-boo Girl" after the hairstyle she wore, which covered the right side of her forehead and her right eye. Veronica had only been living in Hollywood a few years when success found her in *I Wanted Wings* (1941), designed by Oleg Cassini. He was surprised upon his initial costume consultation to realize that Lake was pregnant. Edith did Veronica's next film, *Sullivan's Travels* (1941) for director Preston Sturges. Hiding Lake's pregnancy became a bigger challenge by this point. Edith put her in baggy hobo clothes and Preston would position her behind objects, and together they were able to trick the eye.

Edith cited Veronica as an example of how a woman can totally transform herself through styling. Veronica's real personality was in direct opposition to the wisecracking and seductive persona created for her by the studio. She eschewed any display of overt sexuality, and hated posing for cheesecake photographs. Edith said the real Veronica liked to wear tweeds, flat heels, and her hair pulled back. During their fittings, when Veronica had to leave her real self at the door and slip into the slinky gowns and negligees that Edith had designed, she would say to Edith "pardon me while I put on my other head."

Above: Veronica Lake on the set of *This Gun For Hire* with Alan Ladd.

Right: Ginger Rogers dressed as a little girl for *The Major and the Minor.*

Edith would recycle clothes from other projects for use in films and publicity stills. Here, a dress with a seahorse motif originally designed for Kay Linaker, is re-purposed for Veronica Lake.

"WHEN THE GLAMOUR ENDS FOR GARBO, IT ALSO ENDS FOR ME," ADRIAN SAID. "SHE HAS CREATED A TYPE. IF YOU DESTROY THAT ILLUSION, YOU DESTROY HER."

I Married a Witch (1941) was a screwball romantic comedy that paired Lake as a 17th-century witch who comes to the 20th-century and falls in love with a mortal, played by Frederic March. The film was the basis for the 1960s television show *Bewitched*. Lake and March did not get along at all during the filming, and Lake hid a forty pound weight under her costume for a scene in which March had to carry her. After that, March began referring to the film as "I Married a Bitch." *This Gun for Hire* (1942) with Alan Ladd as a professional killer, solidified the actor's reputation as a star. Veronica played a cabaret performer, allowing Edith to give her an evening gown of sparkling lamé, and a fishing costume of shiny black fabric, for her stage appearances.

Patricia Morison had originally been cast in *The Glass Key* (1942) opposite Alan Ladd. "The night before I was to start shooting," Morison says, "I was in wardrobe with Edith fitting the costumes, when word came down that they were taking me out of the picture. Veronica Lake was going to be in it. They told me,'We've decided you're not really a leading lady.' Edith and I cried together." In the same way that Mary Martin had to return to Broadway for her real talents to shine, so it was with Morison. After about six more years in Hollywood, she returned to New York, eventually triumphing in the original Broadway cast of *Kiss Me Kate.*

*The Major and the Mino*r (1942) marked Billy Wilder's directorial debut in the United States. Ginger Rogers was cast as Susan Applegate, a world-weary beauty who pretends to be twelve-year-old "Su-Su" Applegate to save money on train fare to get from New York to her home town. The big trick for Edith in this film was that Ginger had to transform from the adult Susan to "Su Su" almost on camera. For the initial costume consultation, Edith had an eighteen-inch doll fabricated with Ginger's likeness to show Ginger, director Billy Wilder, and producer Arthur Hornblow, Jr. the steps of the transformation of the costume.

"I designed a traveling suit with straight lines, a rather longish pleated skirt and a smart belted jacket with lapels that opened clear to the waistline, showing a deep V of blouse; in the neck of the blouse is a polka-dot ascot," Edith explained. "Ginger would wear a simple broad-brimmed hat, slightly drooping, with tailored gray bow in front; plain pumps, medium-heeled."

"Ginger took her hat, flipped up the brim, ripped the bow, and let the ribbon hang down in streamers. She fastened the silk shirt up at the neck and made the ascot into a big pussy-cat bow under her chin. The belted jacket was unbelted and buttoned up to the bow. She tucked her skirt in until it came just below the knees, using the jacket belt around the waist to pull it up."

Ray Milland played opposite Ginger as Major Philip Kirby, an Army major who brings "Su-Su" to the military academy at which he teaches. Though he can't quite figure it out, Kirby is drawn to the twelve-year-old in an adult fashion. "The censors didn't notice" said Wilder, "but we got away with situations sexier than Lolita."

In *The Great Man's Lady* (1942), Barbara Stanwyck played a 109-year-old woman recounting her pioneer days, and her quest alongside her husband for the discovery of oil. Paramount's research depart-

"PARDON ME WHILE I PUT ON MY OTHER HEAD."

–Veronica Lake

Though Veronica Lake personally preferred clothes of a more simple nature, there is no denying she knew how to wear more elaborate gowns for films such as *I Married a Witch* (opposite page) and *Sullivan's Travels* (left).

ment turned up a painting of a noted woman of the early west wearing a black velvet dress embroidered with diamond birds. Edith copied it for Stanwyck, and it beacme their favorite piece in the film. When some studio executives suggested that the dress would look better without the birds, Stanwyck decided to appeal to their budget-conscious minds. "If the birds go, the dress goes," Stanwyck told them. Rather than spend the money on the creation of a new dress, the executives relented and the dress stayed.

When Dorothy Lamour announced her impending engagement to advertising executive William Ross Howard III, she asked Edith to design her wedding dress. It was the second marriage for Lamour, and Edith designed a blue gown with a sweetheart neckline and blue sleeves. The couple were married on April 7, 1943. Ross was serving as a lieutenant in the Army, and in between films, Lamour would rent an apartment near where he was stationed. Edith would even travel to visit them occasionally. The marriage lasted until Howard's death in 1978.

Paramount bought the rights to Ernest Hemmingway's best-selling novel, *For Whom the Bell Tolls* (1943) for $150,000, and cast Gary Copper and Vera Zorina in the leads. Ingrid Bergman had been so taken with the book, she waged a campaign for the part of Maria and begged producer David O. Selznick to lend her to Paramount. Even though Zorina had already had her hair trimmed for the role and begun shooting, the part was awarded to Bergman. When Ingrid was told she would have to cut her hair, she replied "to get that part, I'd cut my head off!"

Part of Selznick's agreement with Paramount was that he would have approval over Bergman's wardrobe. The film, set against a background of the Spanish civil war in the 1930s, called for no fashion for Bergman's character. Edith pulled some simple, well-worn clothes from stock that looked of the period, and Bergman approved them. However, Selznick insisted that new clothes were required for his star and that nothing could be pulled from stock. Edith made up some sketches, which Selznick approved, and new clothes were constructed. Edith found it amusing when the fabric had to be aged and distressed to make the new clothes look just like the old clothes that Selznick had rejected. The film missed the great critical acclaim it should have received, due to Paramount's unwillingness to adhere to the book's Spanish Civil War detail. But audiences found great chemistry between

Part of Barbara Stanwyck's contracts for loan-outs to other studios included the use of Edith's services, for films like *Flesh and Fantasy.*

Cooper and Bergman, as did Hemmingway, who said he envisioned them in the parts when he was writing the original book.

Edith was loaned to RKO to design Ginger Rogers' wardrobe for *Tender Comrade* (1943), in which the actress played a defense plant worker. Renie Conley, who had once assisted Edith at Paramount, was now the head designer at RKO, and did the remaining cast. One bright spot in the wardrobe was a charming cotton pinafore-inspired gown, which Jo Jones (Rogers) wears to a party. The film was later used as evidence by the House Un-American Activities Committee, who suspected director Edward Dmytryk and writer Dalton Trumbo of being communists. Despite the presence of the right-wing Ginger Rogers and multiple pro-American speeches, the committee tried to show that the communal living situation of Jo and three other women (whose husbands were also off at war) in the film was an attempt to brainwash Americans with communist propaganda.

When *Lady in the Dark* (1944), was brought to the screen, Ginger Rogers was cast as Liza Elliott, the editor of *Allure*, a prestigious fashion magazine. Elliott is a sexually frustrated woman who lives out her fantasies in daydreams and seeks the help of a psychoanalyst to determine their cause. The project had a great pedigree, with a book by Moss Hart, music by Kurt Weill and lyrics by Ira Gershwin, and Gertrude Lawrence playing the lead on Broadway three years before.

Director Mitchell Leisen was given a budget estimated between $150,000-$200,000 to execute Rogers' costumes. He collaborated on the designs with Edith and Raoul Pène Du Bois, a Broadway designer who had come to Paramount in 1941. Edith had learned after years of working with Leisen to simply try to execute his vision on a film, and Du Bois had to learn the same lesson. Initially, Edith wasn't even supposed to be working on the project, and Rogers' clothes were to be designed by the New York couturier Valentina. When Ginger rejected Valentina's designs, Edith was asked to step in because of her good working relationship with the actress.

There is almost no doubt that left to only her own devices, the budget-conscious and conservative Edith would have never come up with the dress that is considered by many to be the most expensive costume ever designed for a film. But Leisen was always asking Edith to push herself creatively, and under his supervision, a gown was designed that was encrusted entirely of faux rubies and emeralds in a paisley design, lined in mink, with a matching jacket, also lined in mink. At the time, it was estimated to cost around $35,000, with $15,000 being spent on the mink alone. When building the dress, Edith covered the floor of her salon with mink skins and she and Leisen selected the most photogenic ones.

When Rogers tried the gown on, the faux stones proved to be too heavy for her to dance the routine that had been choreographed for the show-stopping Saga of Jenny. A second gown was created with sequins in the same paisley pattern. Both gowns are seen on screen. The dress with the stones is seen in close-up as Ginger unpacks it and wears it to the nightclub, and the sequined version is seen in the dance number. The gown with the faux stones was later donated to the Smithsonian Institution and kept on display for several years; Edith used the sequined version in her fashion shows that would be developed later.

Du Bois' experience working on the film was not a happy one. Used to working with more autonomy on Broadway, he had to adjust to the more collaborative Hollywood process, which was especially essential on a Leisen film. Madame Barbara Karinska, who had been working with Paramount to execute costumes since 1942, sometimes would change Dubois' designs during the making of the pieces. The confusion over the credits as to who actually designed what on the film also caused some consternation with all of those involved. The mink dress received enormous publicity, with Edith taking full credit for it. At the time Leisen preferred that people not know his level of involvement in the costumes. Du Bois' contributions seemed to be almost entirely overlooked. He designed two more films at Paramount before his contract

Edith was amused when she had to create new distressed clothing for Ingrid Bergman in *For Whom the Bell Tolls* that looked just like the worn clothing she could have pulled from the stock wardrobe for the actress.

"TO GET THAT PART, I'D CUT MY HEAD OFF!"

–Ingrid Bergman

People who only saw Edith wear black, beige and gray at the studio would be surprised to learn that she loved to wear bright, vibrant colors at home

Opposite page and below: **Ginger Rogers played a defense plant worker during World War II in** ***Tender Comrade.***

expired in 1945, whereupon he returned to designing for Broadway productions.

Edith was loaned again, this time to Selznick International, when Ginger Rogers was cast in *I' ll Be Seeing You* (1944), a sentimental film with a touch of melancholy, Ginger played a woman serving a prison sentence who meets a shell shocked soldier (Joseph Cotten) on a Christmas furlough to visit her family. Interestingly, for two films that Ginger made in the year following, *Heartbeat* (1946) and *Magnificent Doll*, the designers would be Edith's mentors Howard Greer and Travis Banton respectively.

Edith's joy at Wiard winning his first Oscar for art direction for the film *Wilson* (1944) was tempered by her disappointment at being named to columnist Hedda Hopper's list of worst-dressed women in Hollywood that year. Since taking over from Banton, Edith purposely had been limiting her wardrobe at the office to suits of black, beige, and gray, to ensure that actresses would not be distracted from their own reflection in the mirror during fittings. Edith's consolation for that sacrifice had always been that when she went home, she could wear bright colors, including the Mexican-influenced dresses, in which she felt most comfortable.

Many of the actors and actresses with whom Edith worked offered sympathy to Edith and felt it unfair that Hopper would criticize someone not in the public eye. Hopper, on the other hand, felt that if Edith was offering fashion advice in newspaper columns to other women, she should at least use a little of her own advice in her working wardrobe. "Stars don't like to look past the mirror and see a designer in a brightly colored dress," Edith said. "When I'm at the studio, I'm always little Edith in the dark glasses and the little beige suit. That's how I've survived."

Frank Richardson hired Mary Kay Dodson to help in the overburdened wardrobe department on *Duffy' s Tavern* (1945) and *Murder, He Says* (1945). Dodson was a striking beauty, who had been a model at Bullock's Wilshire Department Store. Edith felt, much like she did with Oleg Cassini, that Dodson may be requested more for films based on her sex appeal. Only this time, it wouldn't be by the actresses, it would be by the directors and producers.

A STAR ON THE HORIZON

Edith recognized the value that producers' put on the publicity she generated for a film for which she did the designs. Her ace in the hole was a fledgling radio show being started on CBS by Art Linkletter. Called *House Party*, the daytime show dispensed information from all sorts of experts in their fields to the average American housewife, with Linkletter serving as host. For fashion, Linkletter opted to have a motion picture designer, rather than a New York couturier, to explain how the typical American woman could make herself more attractive. When Edith's name came up for consideration, Paramount sent her to talk to Linkletter, who remembers "I'd never met her before. And she came into my office and I thought 'oh my, what are we going to do with this quiet, shy, reticent little woman wearing very unglamorous clothes and glasses and kind of a dull hat?' She had her head down when she talked to you."

Below: Ginger Rogers' gown of mink and faux rubies and emeralds for *Lady in the Dark* is one of the most expensive costumes ever designed for a film. Opposite page: the version of the *Lady in the Dark* gown which Edith used for her fashion shows.

The show was filmed in front of a live audience and Edith was expected to give the same sort of practical advice that she had been giving to newspaper and movie magazine editors for years. Linkletter would walk Edith down the aisle of the studio and the audience members would stand up and ask for advice on their look. Edith would have to describe to the audience at home what her in-person guinea pig was wearing and how she would improve their look. Of course, simplifying a look was always a hallmark of Edith's fashion philosophy, and that was something every woman could do on any budget. Not buying clothes that are too tight, using color as an accessory, choosing the appropriate clothing for the activity you are doing, were all things to which every woman could relate. Edith needed to be quick and blunt, but not hurtful. It was a delicate tightrope to walk.

Edith was terrified at first. Linkletter literally held her hand through the experience, and before each show he would give Edith tips on how to improve her performance. As she became more relaxed, she was able to loosen her style with the audience and speak more like a friend giving advice, rather than a costume designer. Edith also offered fashion advice to any of the listeners at home willing to send in a full-length photo of themselves to her. Thousands of letters and photos poured in. The requests for interviews from magazine and newspaper editors also increased, as their readers became more and more aware of Edith Head, designer to the stars. Edith would stay on *House Party* for its entire 15-year run, including the show's transition to television.

For Masquerade in Mexico (1945), director Mitchell Leisen remade his own film *Midnight* (1939), with Dorothy Lamour in the role Claudette Colbert had handled so adeptly. Critics didn't care much for the direction or the re-worked story that now had Angel O'Reilly (Lamour), a stranded showgirl in Mexico, hired by a jealous husband to lure a bullfighter away from his infatuated wife. However, Lamour felt that this was one of the best film wardrobes ever created for her. Once again, Leisen collaborated with Edith on the costumes, including a stunning black lace dress over nude soufflé that Leisen said had to be held up with "rubber cement, tape, and everything else" to keep the dress from running afoul of the censors. Lamour was just relieved that there wasn't a sarong in sight, and the clothes gave Lamour's image a boost toward a new level of elegance.

By 1945, Veronica Lake's career had peaked. During the war, Lake had been asked to revamp her hairstyle from the "peek-a-boo" style to something that would be safer for her fans that worked in the war industry to emulate. But her new style never caught on with the public, and to her co-stars and the studio, she was becoming more difficult to work with. A divorce and the death of an infant son lead Veronica to start drinking, and her contract was not renewed in 1948. In a 1970

Opposite: **Barbara Stanwyck has murder on her mind in *Double Indemnity.*** This page: **Loretta Young, one of the screen's great fashionistas in *And Now Tomorrow.***

interview she said, "I've reached a point in my life where it's the little things that matter. I was always a rebel and probably could have gotten much farther had I changed my attitude. But when you think about it, I got pretty far without changing attitudes. I'm happier with that."

Paramount was grooming now its new star, the blonde and bubbly singer Betty Hutton. Hutton had been performing since the age of thirteen and had already made an impression in a string of Paramount films including *Star Spangled Rhythm* (1942) and the screwball comedy *The Miracle of Morgan's Creek* (1944). The film *Incendiary Blonde* (1945), based on the life of Texas Guinan, a silent film and Broadway star, showed that Hutton's star had arrived. With the show business backdrop, Edith was able to create some beautiful period gowns for Hutton. Though Edith rarely used harsh criticism for any star, it is interesting to note that she described Betty Hutton's fittings in *The Dress Doctor* as almost manic-depressive. She found Betty a "restless, mercurial person who is always very up or very down." Betty would bring along sometimes as many as twelve friends to a fitting, which Edith allowed grudgingly, because she felt that Betty was at her best with an audience.

The Stork Club (1945) allowed Edith a chance to design more serious fashion for Betty. Betty played Judy Peabody, a hat check girl at the famous nightclub who saves a millionaire (Barry Fitzgerald) from drowning. The millionaire repays the favor by setting Judy up in a luxury apartment and giving her a charge card at a department store. As Edith had taught Barbara Stanwyck the importance of incorporating fashion in her personal life, so she did with Betty Hutton while working on this film.

When David O. Selznick loaned Ingrid Bergman to RKO to make *The Bells of St. Mary's* (1945), Ingrid requested Edith to be loaned to design her nun's habit. *The Bells of St. Mary's* was the sequel to the previous year's *Going My Way*, and Bing Crosby reprised his role as Father O'Malley. *Going My Way* had been produced by Paramount, and it was unusual for a rival studio like RKO to produce a sequel. Since no one was interested in offending the Catholic Church during the production, a Catholic priest was brought on to the set as a special advisor. For her research into the nun's costume for Ingrid Bergman, Edith visited the Mother Superior at Immaculate Heart in Los Angeles. She designed a habit similar in feel to the traditional one, but different enough that it represented no particular order.

The Oscars were held the night before principal photography was to begin, and both Bing Crosby and director Leo McCarey (who was also directing the sequel) won for *Going My Way*. In an odd coincidence, Ingrid Bergman won Best Actress for *Gaslight* (1944). In her acceptance speech, Bergman told the audience "I'm glad I won, because tomorrow morning, I start shooting the sequel to *Going My Way* with Bing Crosby and Leo McCarey, and I was afraid that if I didn't have an Oscar, they wouldn't speak to me."

"STARS DON'T LIKE TO LOOK PAST THE MIRROR AND SEE A DESIGNER IN A BRIGHTLY COLORED DRESS," EDITH SAID. "WHEN I'M AT THE STUDIO, I'M ALWAYS LITTLE EDITH IN THE DARK GLASSES AND THE LITTLE BEIGE SUIT. THAT'S HOW I'VE SURVIVED."

Because of a heavy workload, Edith turned to sketch artists and assistants more and more. However, for publicity photographs, she would often return to the drafting table

David O. Selznick loaned Jennifer Jones and Joseph Cotten to Paramount for *Love Letters* (1945). Jones played Singleton, an amnesia victim who has murdered her husband. Cotton played a friend of the husband, who had ghost written letters for him to send to her. Jennifer Jones preferred not to make any final decisions on her costumes, instead leaving the decisions to David O. Selznick, her husband at the time, and producer Hal Wallis. Selznick wasn't a problem for Edith, but Wallis nixed a wedding dress that Edith had designed, which was her favorite dress in the picture. Wallis told Edith that he found the dress too conventional and pretty for such a brooding film. "Oh, the clothes that are never born! Sometimes they die before they are even born," Edith lamented later. "That's the tragic thing about designing. You never can tell what will happen to a dress. You work and work over a costume. At last it works out just right. Then they decide on a close-up, or maybe the leading man puts his arm around the star's neck. You never see the dress at all, maybe just the neckline. That's heartbreaking."

Another disappointment that year was that a book Edith worked on with the editors of *Look* magazine about fashion, never made it to print. The book was to be entirely fashion advice for the modern woman, though *Look* sent its photographer Dorothy Taylor to photograph actresses Jinx Falkenburg, Olivia De Havilland, Veronica Lake, Diana Lynn, Barbara Britton, Lizabeth Scott and Shirley Temple to illustrate the book. *What Are You Going to Wear?* contained recommendations for outfits for formal and informal parties, shopping, lunching, and even cleaning the house. Unfortunately, the project was halted before it was completed.

Edith had now done two films with the beautiful Ingrid Bergman, but still hadn't designed one high fashion ensemble or gown for her. All that changed when Ingrid requested Edith be loaned for *Notorious* (1946), directed by Alfred Hitchcock and co-starring Cary Grant. Selznick had sold *Notorious* to RKO, along with the package

Opposite: *The Stork Club* was Betty Hutton's first high-fashion film, and gave the star a new appreciation for clothes. Below: Edith visits Dorothy Lamour on the set at Paramount.

of Hitchcock, Bergman and Grant for $800,000, to help finance his production of *Duel in the Sun* (1946). Ingrid played Alicia Huberman, the daughter of a late German spy, who is recruited by T.R. Devlin (Grant), an agent of the U.S. government, to spy on some of her father's Nazi friends in South America. It was Edith's first time working with Hitchcock, who was famous for making the clothes in his film an integral part to the characters portrayed on screen.

Hitchcock would put the clothing directives in the script itself, so that when Edith asked him what kind of clothes he wanted, he said "I really don't care, whatever the script says." Edith would take her cues from the script and make designs from the suggestions. "It was not the easiest job," Edith said after the film's release. "Hitchcock is a director who dominates every single scene of his pictures, even to fashion. The job was tricky. The clothes couldn't be smart in the ordinary sense. They had to avoid the fussy and the extreme. And they had to be right for her (Bergman). Some women need accessories galore—jewels, furs, feathers, silly hats—to look glamorous—all the things she hates. She looks marvelous in plain things—a smock, or a blouse and shirt, or a schoolgirl's tailored dressing gown. Her clothes must have simplicity, skillful design and practically no ornamentation. This is elegance in the subtlest sense."

Edith had to find a formula that would make Alicia elegant enough to attract the attention of Devlin and Alexander Sebastian (Claude Rains), yet still believable as a spy. Hitchcock had specified a palette of all black-and-white clothes. In the second scene in the film, Bergman is hosting a small cocktail party, and her clothing is one of the best examples of how Edith and Hitchcock collaborated for maximum impact on film. Bergman was filmed partially against the dark silhouette of the back of Cary Grant's head, and the viewer's eye is continually drawn to Bergman, who is dressed in an ensemble with a zebra print top embellished with black sequins, and baring Ingrid's midriff. It was vital to Edith that Bergman have an impact at the beginning of the film, and the actress did not disappoint.

In *To Each His Own* (1946), Olivia de Havilland played Josephine Norris, a small-town girl who has an illegitimate son with a pilot during WW I. After she gives her son up for adoption, she regrets it. During their separation, Olivia's character builds a successful cosmetics business, and becomes a rich woman. Years later, she is reunited with him during WW II.

The film was de Havilland's return to the screen after a two-year legal battle with Warner Brothers over the lengths of studio contracts. The challenge for the production was how to age Olivia, then only twenty-nine, into a mature woman aging gracefully. "Paramount's make-up department wasn't exactly sure how to turn me into a woman of forty or forty-five, until I found a series of pictures of Winston Churchill in a magazine," de Havilland said when the film was released. "These portraits showed him as a young man and also as he grew older, wiser and more experienced.

"Bill Woods, my make-up man on the film, studied the pictures and used them as models when he made me up. I deliberately gained weight. I drank malted milks and ate special foods, rested as I could and actually put on fifteen pounds while the picture was in production."

Edith's interest in unusual jewelry began with a gift of a gold bracelet with antique coins, given to her by Barbara Stanwyck.

Edith added padding to de Havilland's figure and then added a tightly laced corset and pulled in the padding. Edith felt this was the best way to suggest that Olivia's character was still a well-dressed wealthy woman, but that her youth had faded. The camera man arranged the lighting to make Olivia's shoulders look heavier. Under Mitchell Leisen's direction, Olivia de Havilland won an Oscar for Best Actress for the film. It was the first Oscar award in that category for a Paramount film. Ginger Rogers, who had turned the part down, said "It seemed Olivia knew a good thing when she saw it. Perhaps Olivia should thank me for such poor judgment."

Edith had been loaned to Warner Brothers in 1943 to design Barbara Stanwyck's wardrobe for *My Reputation*, but due to a backlog of Warner productions, the film was not released until 1946. Stanwyck played Jessica Drummond, a widow who is trying to find love again in the arms of Major Scott Landis (George Brent), but becomes the subject of town gossip. *My Reputation* suffered a bit with timeliness, since it had been made and set during wartime. But luckily, because Edith would often keep faddish details to a minimum, Stanwyck's wardrobe did not look as dated as it could have to audiences.

California (1946) was Barbara Stanwyck's first Technicolor film. Set against the backdrop of the fight for statehood for California, Barbara played Lily Bishop, a gambling queen with a shady past. Stanwyck had twenty-two changes of costume in the film, and Edith copied her wardrobe from authentic museum pieces of the period. *The Bride Wore Boots* (1946) featured Stanwyck as Sally Warren, a horse lover married to a bookish historian (Robert Cummings), who doesn't have the same affection for the animals. Edith managed to keep Stanwyck's wardrobe feminine, despite the plot, using colored ribbons sewn cross-bar fashion on a white linen overskirt, that topped a black-and-white slack suit underneath. For a satin gown and chiffon negligee, Edith repeated insets of lace down the negligee and center panel of the gown.

The Strange Love of Martha Ivers (1946) cast Barbara Stanwyck as the title character, a wicked heiress responsible for the death of her autocratic aunt. The film is notable as the first screen appearance for Kirk Douglas, as Stanwyck's husband, and the second appearance for producer Hal Wallis' discovery Lizabeth Scott as a drifter. For one outfit in the film, Edith's overly cautious approval process for the wardrobe didn't save her. "I was supposed to design a beautiful and expensive evening gown for Miss Stanwyck, and I did it with sequins," Edith said. "My troubles began on this gown when Kirk Douglas who plays Barbara's husband, tries to shoot her. The director, Lewis Milestone, wanted to hold the suspense by having Douglas, who has Miss Stanwyck in his arms, bring the gun up slowly to Barbara's back before shooting. The camera man's job was to "pan" the gun in a close-up. The lights, however, glittered on the sequins so that the bright flashes hid the gun and spoiled the effect. So I had to do a rush job and whip up a new gown, this time in dull beads that wouldn't reflect the light."

When Raymond Chandler sold his unfinished story *The Blue Dahlia* (1946) to Paramount, he also sold his services as screenwriter, with the understanding the script would be finished before the start of production date. Chandler faltered and production began without a completed screenplay. Edith's challenge was to design clothes for Veronica Lake and Doris Dowling for a film that was being written as it was shot. Edith put Dowling in a sleek low-cut pair of gold lamé lounging pajamas and matching gold slippers and described her as "the best dressed

Though there had been a return to using more fabric in clothes since the end of L-85, skirt lines were still very straight. The Joan Crawford large-shoulder-look was still in evidence throughout 1946, and Lake's black-and-white wardrobe bore all the hallmarks of what every *film noir* fan would hope. For Veronica, Edith designed a collarless cardigan suit of black Kasha bound in black braid, accessorized with a black suede belt and shoes. The screenplay was finished by Chandler just as the end-of-production approached and turned out to be a great success. The film's title inspired the nickname "The Black Dahlia" for Elizabeth Short, a young

This page: **Edith attends a party for Betty Hutton (seated in center).** Opposite top: **Edith kept the wardrobe simple for Ingrid Bergman in *Notorious*, so that her character would be believable as a spy.** Opposite bottom: **Edith attends to Ingrid Bergman's dress form in the workroom.**

"YOU NEVER CAN TELL WHAT WILL HAPPEN TO A DRESS. YOU WORK AND WORK OVER A COSTUME. AT LAST IT WORKS OUT JUST RIGHT. THEN THEY DECIDE ON A CLOSE-UP, OR MAYBE THE LEADING MAN PUTS HIS ARM AROUND THE STAR'S NECK. YOU NEVER SEE THE DRESS AT ALL, MAYBE JUST THE NECKLINE. THAT'S HEARTBREAKING." –Edith Head

Ingrid
Bergman

Clothing for Olivia De Havilland in *To Each His Own* had to span from the 1920's (opposite), when her character was a young woman, to the character's middle-age (left).

woman who was found murdered in Los Angeles in 1947.

Edith's personal projects in 1946 included designing the wardrobe for Zasu Pitts in a touring theatre production of *Cordelia*, in which the actress played Cordelia Tuttle, a spinster raising two children in a New England fishing village. When Betty Hutton announced she was pregnant that year, she asked Edith to design her maternity wardrobe. Edith decided to design it along ballet lines, with high waists and flaring skirts. Among the pieces Edith designed for Hutton were a dress with an apron skirt of black taffeta that tied in the back and a butcher boy jacket that Hutton could wear over a skirt or slacks.

FASHION NEWS

In January 1947, Edith traveled to New York City to preside as commentator for a fashion show at The Waldorf Astoria to showcase fashions she had designed for *The Perfect Marriage* (1947), starring Loretta Young. Thirty-three of Edith's costumes were showcased, including others she had designed for Joan Fontaine, Betty Hutton, Dorothy Lamour and Olivia de Havilland. It was perfect publicity tie-in for a film that relied so heavily on fashion. In the film, Loretta Young plays a magazine editor who is drifting apart from her husband, played by David Niven, after ten years of marriage.

The film had already been getting a lot of attention in the fashion press because of the interest that Loretta Young's clothes generated. The August 12, 1946 issue of *Life* magazine featured Loretta on the cover in pajamas that Edith had designed for the film, and the article inside featured the nightgowns that Loretta wore in the film. The most widely publicized outfits included a gown with a skirt of slim white jersey with a huge overskirt embroidered with gold, red and green sequins in a paisley pattern, that could double as a cape.

A sleeveless poncho coat was designed that was embroidered with Loretta's character's name "Maggie" on it in gold thread. It was worn over a simple black dress with high cowl neckline and circular inserts in the front of the skirt. Loretta Young ordered one for herself from Edith for her personal wardrobe with "Loretta" embroidered on it.

For Virginia Field, as the other woman, Edith designed a two-piece champagne beige wool jersey dress accented with small fourteen-karat gold safety pin studs and a large gold safety pin lapel piece. Edith accessorized the dress with long gloves of champagne beige silk jersey. In another scene, Field wore a long torso coat and skirt in ink blue lightweight wool. Her ink blue blouse had white polka dots centered with ink red sequins. Again, Edith accented the outfit with

Opposite: Edith based the gowns for Barbara Stanwyck in *California* on real period pieces, which she found in museums. Below: A wardrobe department test photo for Stanwyck in *The Two Mrs. Carrolls.*

matching accessories including blue fabric gloves that had polka dotted palms to match the blouse, navy blue calf pumps, a shoulder strap bag and a blue beret. The gold key, studded with diamonds and rubies, which Field wore as a watch fob, was a wedding anniversary present from her real-life husband Paul Douglas. All was not easy on the set between Young and Field during the making of the film. Field said she found Young's syrupy sweet personality was just a façade, and Field went home crying on several occasions.

Edith was loaned to RKO to costume Loretta again for *The Farmer's Daughter* (1947). The project had originally been purchased by David O. Selznick, who planned to use it as a starring vehicle for Ingrid Bergman. When Ingrid declined the role, Selznick sold the rights to RKO. Young played a Swedish girl working as a domestic for a senator, who is unwittingly thrust into politics. For Loretta, Edith designed an oatmeal-colored wool Bolero dress, with a saddle leather belt studded with gold stars with a gold medallion buckle. Edith accessorized the ensemble with hand-sewn doeskin gloves, a heavy gold link choker and earrings, and a spring bonnet. The film was wildly popular and won Loretta Young a Best Actress Oscar that year.

The fifth in the series of *Road* films, *The Road to Rio* (1947), cast Bob Hope and Bing Crosby as two musicians sailing to Rio de Janeiro to avoid an arson charge. On the ship they meet Lucia Maria de Andrade (Dorothy Lamour), who has been hypnotized by her evil aunt (Gale Sondergaard) to marry a man she doesn't love. Lamour had twelve costume changes, with a Latin-American motif in modern styling.

The show-stopping gown for Lamour was a dinner gown of heavily beaded material draped softly in front and split almost to the knee. A heart was cut out of the breast plate, and embroidered across the front of the bodice. As though piercing the cut-out heart, Edith designed an arrow which dripped several ruby red beads down one side of the bodice and skirt. The Latin influence was seen in Lamour's black lace poncho, which she wore over white crepe lounging pajamas with wide legs, accessorized with a wrapped belt. For Dorothy's wedding dress, Edith used a molded bodice and modified Polonaise drape silhouette in satin. Edith kept Gale Sondergaard's silhouette very slim and used striking fabrics such as lamé and brocade for her formal wear.

Pearl White, one of the biggest silent screen stars during the period of 1914-1920 was the subject of *The Perils of Pauline* (1947) starring Betty Hutton as White. Edith copied old costumes that had been worn by White in her silent films for historical accuracy. But the filmmakers did take liberties with the facts of White's life, and the famous scene where Hutton is tied to railroad tracks in the path of an oncoming train never actually happened in a Pearl White film, but rather in a Keystone comedy. Edith's wardrobe for Hutton included a plaid sports outfit of jumper, a "natty" tweed Norfolk sports jacket over a middy blouse, a floppy "tam" beret; and a suit dress of rose beige brocade trimmed with rust satin with a lace jabot, topped by a hat dripping with ostrich feathers.

Lizabeth Scott had just finished *Dead Reckoning* (1947) for Warner Brothers, with Humphrey Bogart, when she began *Desert Fury*

PRODUCTION BEGAN WITHOUT A COMPLETED SCREENPLAY. EDITH'S CHALLENGE WAS TO DESIGN CLOTHES FOR VERONICA LAKE AND DORIS DOWLING FOR A FILM THAT WAS BEING WRITTEN AS IT WAS SHOT.

(1947). Scott's stardom seemed assured, and there was great interest in what the actress was wearing. Edith developed a palette for the film, set against a desert backdrop of soft, muted and neutral tones with Edith feeling that the soft shades of gray and beige showed up best. Scott played Paula Haller, the rebellious daughter of Fritzi Haller (Mary Astor), a wealthy Nevada casino owner. Paula is pursued romantically by policeman Tom Hanson (Burt Lancaster), and gangster Eddie Bendix (John Hodiak).

Edith's numerous designs for Scott included an ivory linen resort dress with a leather belt with gold jewelry accent; a raw silk suit with slit pockets on jacket and skirt; a hooded coat of yellow wool with slit pockets and dolman sleeves with turn-back cuffs; an evening dress of white silk with gold nail-head trim; natural linen slacks with red silk shirt, with a purse and sandals of natural-colored raffia; a shirt-maker dress of champagne beige silk with push-up sleeves with a narrow cuff; and a cocoa brown dress with big round white bib collar, with wide cuffs that ended loose on three-quarter sleeves, accessorized with a white hat and gloves and a bracelet of antique gold coins.

No matter how great the wardrobe, problems with the script seemed to confound both audiences and critics. As Bendix professed his love for Paula, his sidekick (Wendell Corey) was intimated as his homosexual lover. A review in Washington, D.C.'s *Pathfinder* said "Lizabeth Scott is a handsome clothes-horse for Edith Head's western wardrobe, but her deadpan acting gives little depth or reality to her part. Neither Mary Astor nor Lancaster seems to know whether to be nice or villainous.

"To further confuse the issue, there are veiled psychological references to the relationship between the gangster and his sidekick (Wendell Corey). Hodiak, like the rest of the cast, appears bewildered—as if he were thinking 'I hope the audience understands this better than I do.' They don't."

Photoplay Magazine decided to begin offering patterns for sale based on film designs and its first "Pattern of the Month" was a bolero suit worn by Scott in the film. It became the top-selling design that year, selling 8,298 patterns and was later carried by department stores.

Dorothy Lamour played the scheming Fay Rankin in *Wild Harvest* (1947), who plays upon the friendship between two wheat harvesters, Joe Madigan (Alan Ladd) and Jim Davis (Robert Preston). Edith put Lamour in siren black silk and satin dresses, some with midriffs of lace and fist-sized mesh. Edith referred to these dresses as "whistle dresses"—literally dresses so attention-getting, they get whistles. "Very bad taste, don't you know, the dress, not the whistles," Edith said at the time. "Men, poor ignorant things, don't know the difference."

During fittings for *Wild Harvest*, Dorothy asked Edith to accompany her to a designer's salon to help her select a final purchase of hats from a dozen she'd tried on the day before. Every time Dorothy tried on a hat, Edith shook her head "no." Finally, Dorothy suggested Edith

The press was always interested in what Loretta Young wore in her films, and Edith filled the papers with copy about *The Perfect Marriage.*

remove her dark glasses. "It's not my dark glasses," Edith told her, "it's simply that I hate hats."

In the 1940s, it was still taboo to mention an illness like cancer in a film, even when the heroine would be dying from the disease. In *The Other Love* (1947), the audience is told that concert pianist Karen Duncan (Barbara Stanwyck) is seriously ill and remanded to a Swiss sanitarium for her health, but not because she is suffering from tuberculosis. Edith had the unusual challenge of this film being set in 1948, two years later than she would be designing it. It was difficult enough for Edith to predict trends in the nine months to one year that it usually took from designing a film to its release, but styles could swing much further in two years.

Edith shared screen credit with Marion Herwood Keyes, who did the wardrobe for Barbara Stanwyck's co-stars Joan Loring, Natalie Shafer and Lenore Aubert. For Stanwyck, Edith designed a diverse wardrobe including an unusual play suit made of pure dye silk scarves in cerise, Kelly green, royal blue and black forming the handkerchief borders. The dress was made of thirty-six-inch silk squares. The skirt was comprised of four scarves shirred in the waistband. The jacket was one scarf, in which the border was appliquéd. The bra was made of the center of a scarf, and the shorts from two more. For day wear, Stanwyck wore a tailored suit of soft yellow flannel with bottle green tie that matched a bottle green skirt, and a sports dress of soft beige wool, worn with a turtle neck dickie. For evening, Edith created a Grecian dress of white chiffon draped across one shoulder, which wrapped around the bodice, and fell to a graceful, full skirt. For lounging, Stanwyck wore a heavy white silk robe with gold tassels set in squares outlined with gold beads.

Edith also designed the gown that Stanwyck would wear to the premiere of the film - a full black satin skirt with a turtle-necked blouse which was embroidered with gold sequins in a wheat design from the waist to the shoulders. Stanwyck was so happy with her wardrobe on the

Edith felt she did some of her best work for Joan Fontaine in *The Emperor Waltz* and was disappointed when she was passed over for an Oscar.

film that she gave Edith a gift that would jumpstart Edith's interest in unusual jewelry. "Time was when she wouldn't wear jewelry of any description," Stanwyck said. "I inveigled her into it when I gave her a gift of a heavy gold bracelet with antique gold coins attached. She was so intrigued, she had one made for me."

My Favorite Brunette (1947) was the first film produced by Hope Enterprises, Bob Hope's fledgling production company. Hope cast himself as Ronnie Jackson, a baby photographer and would-be private eye, romancing Carlotta Montay (Dorothy Lamour). There were plenty of great gags, including cameos by Bing Crosby as an executioner and Alan Ladd as a private detective.

Dorothy Lamour issued a "no more sarong" ultimatum to Paramount, which Edith worked around, giving the audience at least one garment that would bare some of Dorothy's flesh. Edith's solution was a white slip with a bare midriff at the back, which she played up by using jeweled embroidery against the white of the dress. At the front, the waist plunged down to a deep "V," and was unadorned. Edith also used the last of the studio's pre-war fourteen-karat gold-plated fabric, designing a stunning gold dress for Dorothy, that she accessorized with a belt of gold kid, embossed with South American gold coins and gold studs. At the time, the dress was estimated to have cost $2,500 to construct.

When Dorothy was loaned out for *On Our Merry Way* (1948) for producers Benedict Bogeaus and Burgess Meredith, she agreed to wear a sarong, but declared in the press this would be the last time she would wear the garment in a movie. Dorothy said: "From now on, it's going to be shorts, slacks and evening gowns." When Edith went to pull a sarong from stock, she discovered that all twenty-six sarongs she had made for Lamour in the *Jungle* and *Road* films, had been sent on Dorothy's war bond tours and were given as prizes for bond selling. Considering Lamour had sold more than $300 million worth of war bonds, Edith felt it was worth it to make a new sarong for her.

After Bette Davis parted ways with Orry-Kelly, her longtime costume designer, Edith came to the actress' aid in *Beyond the Forest.*

THE GREAT FASION SHAKE-UP

On February 12, 1947, Paris designer Christian Dior launched his first fashion collection for Spring-Summer 1947. The collection was characterized by Dior's use of a full-skirt falling at the ankles, a large bust and small waist, with each dress using twenty yards of luxurious fabric. Originally, the two lines were called "Corolla" and "Eight," but when *Harper' s Bazaar* editor-in-chief Carmel Snow saw them, she exclaimed "it's such a new look!" and Dior's New Look was christened.

At first, no one could be sure if the New Look would be a fad or would be there to stay. Hedda Hopper wrote in June of 1947 that "Edie Head doesn't believe that American women will wear French clothes, as the styles will destroy the appearance of their figures, make them look fantastic, and have their beaux whining 'what's wrong with women anyway? ' " Edith told another columnist "I certainly don't intend to put any Paramount stars in dust ruffles. Everybody seems to think that because someone in Paris says that long skirts should be long, they have to have them sweeping in the dust. It's a terrific battle, but we prefer them short."

By the following month, however, the writing was on the wall that the New Look was being embraced by Americans. On July 6, 1947, Carol Adams wrote in the Portland Oregon Journal, "In a little while, modern pictures that are one-year-old will look like period films. That's how great the changes are." Edith had to re-make the extras' dresses at Paramount to accommodate the New Look. 600 evening dresses, 400 day dresses and 450 suits in the Paramount wardrobe were re-tailored by cutting necklines to a boat shape, adding lace overskirts twelve-inches from the floor and pulling in the waists.

Edith learned a valuable lesson from the experience. If she couldn't exactly predict a fashion trend six months in advance, she would design something that sat somewhere in the middle of a current trend and where she thought it was going. Necklines, hemlines, collars, cuffs, jewelry—all of it would now sit at a mid-point between high and low, or large and small. The "safe" formula would later earn Edith criticism from other designers, but it also helped Edith's designs endure the test of time.

Fashion writers from all over the country wanted to know what Edith was doing about skirt lengths in the wake of the New Look. Edith's solution was to vary them throughout a film. For *Dream Girl* (1948), which was in production at the time, Betty Hutton's day clothes measured fourteen-inches from the floor, her suits were twelve-inches and evening gowns varied. For Veronica Lake in *Saigon* (1948), dresses were twelve-inches off the floor. Because Barbara Stanwyck and Dorothy Lamour always liked dresses a little shorter than the prevailing fashion, Edith made nothing longer than fourteen-inches from the floor for them.

Edith was one of just a handful of female executives working in the film industry, and was the only woman featured in an article about Paramount executives in a profile of the studio in the June 1947 issue of

EVERY TIME DOROTHY TRIED ON A HAT, EDITH SHOOK HER HEAD "NO." FINALLY, DOROTHY SUGGESTED EDITH REMOVE HER DARK GLASSES. "IT'S NOT MY DARK GLASSES," EDITH TOLD HER, "IT'S SIMPLY THAT I HATE HATS."

Because Edith smiled rarely, most of the public had no idea that she was a witty, charming woman who enjoyed to socialize.

Look magazine. She also received a great deal of press for a swimsuit she deigned that was marketed by Catalina. The two-piece bathing suit was made of an aquarium print of gray and yellow, topped with a poncho coat made of two straight pieces of fabric, the front of which tied at the waist.

Edith kept up her hectic pace for the latter part of 1947. In June, she joined the staff of UCLA Department of Theater Arts to train advanced students in costume design for movies. She designed the costumes for Zasu Pitts' new play *The Late, Great Christopher Bean*, which opened in Chicago in October, 1947. In the same month, Edith traveled to New York for two weeks to survey fabrics and view the fashion collections. Though she was not fond of hats, it had become a tradition for her to buy a new hat each year in New York to wear to the fashion shows. Upon returning, Edith told Hedda Hopper "wait 'til you see my new hat. It makes me look like a French poodle. I never went near Central Park for fear that another poodle might recognize me."

The Supreme Court decision in *U.S. vs. Paramount Pictures* began the decline of the Hollywood studio system. The Federal Trade Commission had been investigating the way movie studios block-booked films into theatres since 1921, but also brought into question movie studios' monopolization of the business by owning their own theater chains. The process of block-booking forced independent exhibitors to buy unwanted films in a block along with the studio's prestige films. In 1928, the FTC took Famous Players-Lasky (Paramount Pictures' former name) and nine other Hollywood studios to court and won, but the result was nullified by a deal arranged with the Roosevelt administration during the Great Depression. However, in 1940 and 1945, the Justice Department brought the studios back to court.

The 1948 decision meant that movie studios would be forced to sell off their theater chains, and lose a valuable source of revenue. That same year saw the largest spurt of sales to date of television sets in the home. NBC had begun regular broadcasts in 1944, but by 1948, viewers had a choice of four networks—ABC, CBS, NBC and the BBC.

Edith had been disappointed when Mitchell Leisen requested Mary Kay Dodson to design Marlene Dietrich's wardrobe for *Golden Earrings* (1947). When Billy Wilder cast Marlene in *A Foreign Affair* (1948), Edith finally got a chance to design for the legend who had once been Travis Banton's muse. Unfortunately, Dietrich was playing a post-war nightclub entertainer and the script called for a raincoat, an old dressing gown, and a battered suit. There was one evening gown needed when Marlene sang *Illusions*, but she asked Edith to copy of one of her own gowns, originally designed by Irene, that she had worn while entertaining the troops behind the front lines. Dietrich felt that a gown that was few years out-of-style would be right for her character, who would not have been able to afford a new dress. Only one new gown was needed for a flashback sequence in an antique newsreel, and it had to be photographed crudely.

For Jean Arthur, as a Congresswoman doing battle with Marlene, Edith designed a black gown with glittering rhinestones across the bust and covering straps which circled behind Arthur's neck. It was attractive and understated, and most importantly, did not pull focus from Dietrich. Dietrich was hesitant to play a German of the Nazi era, particularly in a comedy with bombed-out Berlin as its backdrop. But Jean Arthur's fragile ego wasn't so easy for director Wilder to handle either. "I have one dame who's afraid to look at herself in a mirror and another who won't stop looking!" he famously quipped.

Sorry Wrong Number (1948) was originally a radio play starring Agnes Moorehead, and written by Lucille Fletcher, who adapted it for the screen. Barbara Stanwyck was cast in the film as Leona Stevenson, a bedridden heiress to a drug fortune. When Stevenson accidentally overhears a phone conversation between two men planning to murder her, she becomes more and more frantic as her attempts to get help fail.

The screen version was opened up considerably from the radio version, which had been essentially a one-woman show. Scenes were added showing Leona as a young woman, allowing Edith to design an expanded wardrobe for Stanwyck. The film's flashbacks went back to 1938, but since styles were similar, Edith was able to use current fashions on the extras. For other scenes, Edith compromised Stanwyck's look between 1938 and 1948 styles because Stanwyck was not yet ready to adopt the New Look, as her husband Robert Taylor didn't like it.

The wedding gown worn by Leona for her wedding to Henry Stevenson (Burt Lancaster) was shimmering silver brocade with a veil of expensive material and a six-foot train. Five yards of material were used to create the gown and the cost ran into the thousands of dollars. Stanwyck felt that as an heiress, her character should be covered in diamonds. Edith obliged to the tune of $200-250,000. The gown was accessorized with a diamond necklace and earrings that Robert Taylor had given to Stanwyck for Christmas. Edith also added a forty-karat wedding ring and a bracelet of diamonds and emeralds that were rented from a jewelry store in Beverly Hills. Diamonds were put in Stanwyck's hair, causing her to exclaim "gosh, I simply reek with rocks!" All the jewelry had to be screen-tested before it was OK'd for the wedding sequence. "Even with a 250-grand price tag, they had to have that photogenic sparkle," Stanwyck said.

More than half of Stanwyck's scenes were played in bed, which she had to perform alone (save for the crew) on a soundstage for twelve days. Edith designed five different nightgowns for the course of the film, but only one could be used for the most dramatic sequence. Edith did ten sketches of different styles until director Anatole Litvak was convinced they had the one which gave Barbara the "dressed up" look. He settled for a tailored pink Chantilly lace nightgown and bed jacket that Edith dubbed the "New Look nightie." She also accented the nightgown with thousands of dollars of rented jewelry, requiring an armed guard who had to accompany Stanwyck on the set at all times. Stanwyck was nominated for an Oscar, but lost to Jane Wyman. Critics felt this was one of Stanwyck's most Oscar-worthy performances.

Oleg Cassini once said that Edith never did anything that she didn't receive credit on, but *Winter Meeting* (1948), a Warner Brothers film starring Bette Davis, was one film on which that happened. With Bette's longtime designer Orry-Kelly gone from Warner Brothers, the actress needed someone to help her shop for her wardrobe for the film. Edith told David Chierichetti that she couldn't remember how the connection had come about. Since Edith hadn't officially been borrowed for the film, and apparently had only shopped for clothes, no one was credited as a designer on the film. The most important aspect of a costume for Bette was that it gave her the freedom to move in the way she wanted to act out a scene. "I liked Edith Head from the moment she said to me 'nobody should ever put a tight skirt on you. That isn't the way you move,'" Bette said.

Davis did officially request Edith for the film *June Bride* (1948), which was based on the unproduced play *Feature for June* by Eileen Tighe and Graeme Lorimer. The play had been nominated for the Writer's Guild of America Award for Best Written American Comedy. However, Edith found the resulting script somewhat lackluster. Bette Davis played Linda Gilman, Editor of *Home Life*, a women's magazine whose new employee is her old flame, played by Robert Montgomery.

Davis' temperament where her costumes were concerned was well-known. She was very insecure about her looks and Orry-Kelly often had trouble finding ways to hide her figure problems, and still please her. Edith made up her mind early in her relationship with Davis that

Edith designed this lounging outfit for Rhonda Fleming for her role as a French countess in *The Great Lover*.

Edith stands in front of sketches for *Sunset Blvd.*, which marked the beginning of a period of flourishing creativity at Paramount and great professional rewards in Edith's career.

the two of them would never argue. Whatever Bette wanted, Edith would give to her. Edith embraced the New Look for Bette Davis, because she found the lines of the clothes suited Bette's rounded figure more than straight skirts.

Edith designed a coat dress with pockets in which Davis' career-woman character could carry pencils and memo pads. Davis liked this idea so much, she asked Edith to make some for her personal wardrobe. Edith had several more orders of smock designs that season from actresses for their wardrobes. Maureen O'Hara had one made in white linen with a small design embroidered in black, with a yoke and collar and a flared back, worn atop a slender black linen skirt. Veronica Lake ordered an evening smock of black lace with flared back and belted with the ends in front, which she wore with a long slender dinner skirt.

To accessorize another outfit, Edith loaned Bette four small gold ornamental hands from her personal jewelry collection, which had originally been used in France as hooks for children's bibs. But for Bette, it was the performance that mattered. "Years of experience have taught me that all the flounces and ruffles in the world won't cover up a bad performance," she said. "And likewise, bare midriffs and dimpled knees won't divert attention from a dull scene, although I'll admit they help."

When Ingrid Bergman was cast in *Arch of Triumph* (1948) for the independent production company Enterprise Productions, she requested that Edith design her costumes. The film was set in 1938, against the backdrop of refugees fleeing to Paris prior to the outbreak of the war. Ingrid played Joan Madou, a woman saved from a suicide attempt by Dr. Ravic (Charles Boyer), who is planning to murder a Nazi officer (Charles Laughton).

Even though the film was set ten years earlier, Edith chose to make Ingrid's wardrobe contemporary. Her designs for Ingrid included a gown of forest green rough textured crepe with a simple drape effect at bodice and hip; a long, straight jacket treated with simulated frogs embroidered in silver thread, accented with matching green gems; and an ice blue crepe evening gown with a square-cut low neckline, and a gathered fitted bodice that worked into a draped hip detail, accessorized by a stole and green evening gloves. Edith used Lily Dache hats to top off Ingrid's wardrobe.

For a pivotal scene involving Ingrid's character, Edith designed a beautiful gold lamé dress. After the war, lamé was manufactured differently, and the pre-war material was almost unobtainable. But the studio managed to locate a precious twenty yards in Paris, which had been stored in a vault when the Nazis overran the city.

Edith didn't stick to her usual safe design motifs, and earned some criticism for it in the press. Hollywood Reporter reviewer Cecelia Ager said "Miss Bergman's costuming is particularly unfortunate. Edith Head has designed for her Hollywood glamour numbers with bizarre and asymmetrical decollatages and slinkiness elsewhere that overpower Miss Bergman's healthy beauty and make her look like a dairy maid come upon a trunk full of Theda Bara's clothes."

By the time she made the *The Sainted Sisters* (1948), Veronica Lake only had one year left at Paramount. Lake and Joan Caufield played two con artist sisters, who are taken in by Robbie Mcreary (Barry Fitzgerald) in a small Maine town, and decide to try the straight life. Veronica felt that one of the suits created for her, looked like it had just come straight out of the sewing room, and in fact it had. She asked Edith if they could distress the suit, and she and Edith cut moth holes in it. But that still didn't satisfy Lake, who took it home and slept in it over night. When her husband, director Andre De Toth, came home late, he saw Veronica asleep in bed. Not recognizing her in an old suit, he thought that one of her aunts had come to visit and she forgot to tell him. He spent the night on the sofa.

FOR THE LOVE OF OSCAR

When Billy Wilder undertook the directorial job of *The Emperor Waltz*

EDITH MADE UP HER MIND EARLY IN HER RELATIONSHIP WITH DAVIS THAT THE TWO OF THEM WOULD NEVER ARGUE. WHATEVER BETTE WANTED, EDITH WOULD GIVE TO HER.

(1948), he wanted to make a satirical look at the court of Franz Joseph of Austria. There was even a scene written about the killing of puppies as allegory for genocide. But star Bing Crosby knew what his fans wanted, and the movie was reworked as a light, frothy musical with only a bit of the Wilder cynicism remaining. Bing Crosby played a phonograph salesman romancing Joan Fontaine, as the niece of Emperor Franz Joseph (Richard Haydn). There was also a canine romance in the plot, with Fontaine's poodle falling in love with Crosby's dog.

Filmed in Technicolor, with music by Johann Strauss and Victor Young, the film was a hit. Working with Gile Steele, who costumed the male cast members, Edith felt she did some of her finest work of her career. For a number called *I Kiss Your Hand, Madame*, one can fully understand what Edith's collaborations with film personnel could bring about. Edith dressed Fontaine in a white day suit with a scalloped collar, and white hat with tulle tie. The hat becomes an integral part of the scene as Crosby tries to maneuver around it to kiss Fontaine. Finally, when he has persuaded her to let him kiss her, she pulls back the tulle tie to allow him.

Fontaine recalls an earlier visit to the studio when she met Madame Barbara Karinska, who was making the costumes for Mitchell Leisen's *Frenchman's Creek* (1944). "I was a nurse's aide during the war, Fontaine says. "I wore white stockings, and had the heaviest white shoes, and my uniform with my nurses' cap. I was called by the studio to see Karinska, and she said to them 'you promise me I do the best star you have, and what you got, you have a mouse!' That was me! So later Edith Head had to transform me from a mouse into glamour."

"We always considered what was happening in the scene," Fontaine says. "It wasn't just to put a dress on someone. Edith had to know what the movements were going to be and whether the clothes were restrictive. She was interested in your best qualities and in your acting scope. She'd ask 'what color should this be?' And you'd pick one, and she'd change it right away. There was nothing she wouldn't do to make you feel at home in your clothes. That was the most important part. Before, I had almost always supplied my own clothes for movies. For instance, in *Rebecca* (1940), almost all those clothes were mine. That's why David O'Selznick was such a great producer. He understood that shabby little girl, whose wardrobe I would have. And Hitchcock, of course, he also knew what kind of a wardrobe this girl would have."

Edith spent months in pre-production on research and costume construction and then traveled with the production to Jasper National Park in Canada, where the exteriors were filmed. Working on location was a new experience for Edith, and she found it very easy to focus on the tasks at hand, without the normal studio distractions. "The only problem we ever had were the necklines because they always tried to make it as low as possible," says Fontaine. "Then the Hays Office would send somebody when you were dressed and on the set and ready to be

Edith would often have dolls with small versions of an actress' costume made, which she would give as gifts or use for publicity purposes. Here, Joan Fontaine holds a doll wearing a tiny version of her gown from *September Affair.*

The dark glasses Edith wore were originally to help her see how a costume would look in black-and-white, but as color films became the norm, Edith still retained her trademark look

shot. They would look at your dress and say 'too much bosom' and they would have somebody there with a little piece of lace or whatever to fill in the division between the breasts, so it would be legal. But then later, I think it would slip out just a little bit."

When the company returned to Hollywood to shoot interiors, Edith began her usual media blitz to get fashion editors interested in covering the film. Stories ran on Edith and Joan having lunch to work on their French together and Edith designing outfits for the poodles. "I thought I'd been asked to do about everything, but I guess I haven't begun to live yet," Edith said of designing for the dogs.

On July 21, 1947, Louella Parsons reported that Charles LeMaire, then a costume designer at Twentieth Century Fox, had succeeded in convincing The Academy of Motion Pictures Arts and Sciences to create an award for best costume design. In fact, they created two, one for color films and one for black-and-white. The first nominees were chosen by a panel of art directors, many of whom liked Edith and had collaborated well with her. Edith and Gile Steele were nominated for *The Emperor Waltz* for color, alongside Dorothy Jeakins and Barbara Karinska for *Joan of Arc* starring Ingrid Bergman.

Edith was absolutely convinced she would win the Oscar that night. She had worked with LeMaire to have the award instituted, and had now been working in the industry for twenty-five years, and she felt her clothes for *The Emperor Waltz* were so lavish and detailed that there was no way the Academy could pass them over.

But the costumes for *Joan of Arc* had signaled a change in Hollywood costume design, and other designers had taken note. As a gritty, new realism was taking place in the stories being proposed, so it also was with the design and look of films. Jeakins and Karinska had painstakingly researched and copied fifteenth-century costumes for *Joan of Arc*, even going so far as to find similar looms to the day on which to weave the fabric.

When Jeakins' and Karinska's names were called as winners by Elizabeth Taylor at the award ceremony, Edith was devastated. In her typical fashion, she tried to hide it, and no one but her husband probably understood her true feelings. Edith remained somewhat sullen for a few days, but eventually returned to her "business as usual" attitude. But, even for a woman who tended to gloss over much in press interviews, she spoke quite openly years later about her disappointment on that night.

Edith was still busier than ever. Her radio appearances on Art Linkletter's House Party were causing her to receive a great deal of fan mail and her requests for lectures were on the rise. Only now, it wasn't just from ladies' club luncheons, but prestigious universities including the University of Southern California. At the studio, Edith estimated she was designing at least two new dresses every day. By October 1st, 1948 she figured she had designed 608 dresses, coats and gowns.

If you asked Edith what was her least favorite experience working on a film, you might be surprised to hear *Samson and Delilah* (1949) tripping off her lips. The film had everything that made a DeMille epic exciting: a biblical story, beautiful stars, revealing clothing, and an exciting climatic finish. What it lacked for Edith was any form of authenticity and any appreciation for her contributions from DeMille

THE RACE FOR OSCARS

Director William Wyler placed a great deal of importance on authenticity for the costumes of Olivia de Havilland and Montgomery Clift in *The Heiress*

WHEN SHE LOST THE OSCAR FOR THE *EMPEROR WALTZ,* Edith thought she would never understand what the Academy was looking for in good costume design. She would only have to wait a year, and to work under director William Wyler on *The Heiress* (1949) to learn what it would take.

In *The Heiress*, Olivia de Havilland played Catherine, an awkward young woman, who lives with her doctor father and is courted by the gold-digging Morris Townsend, played by Montgomery Clift. The designer Valles was brought on to design the wardrobe for Clift, as well as for Ralph Richardson, who was playing Catherine's father. Wyler was a stickler for accuracy, and Edith traveled to New York to do research for the film at the Brooklyn Museum. Every detail, whether viewed on screen, or made on an undergarment and seen only to the actors and wardrobe personnel, had to be correct down to the smallest detail.

For another designer, it might have been a daunting task to be so historically accurate, but not for Edith. Not only did her instincts as a school teacher kick in, she was also relieved that many of the details weren't up for discussion. If a costume was Edwardian, it had to have a bustle and so on. The research Edith did gave her a blueprint for the kinds of buttons, buttonholes, fabrics and other details that she would use, and she felt very comfortable working that way.

Catherine was shy and backwards from years of being made to feel inferior by her father. However, Edith could not make Catherine's clothes look inexpensive or ugly because Catherine's father was a wealthy man. Instead Edith made the clothes fit awkwardly with gaps and wrinkles in places, or by adding too many ruffles or ribbons.

Edith couldn't help but appreciate the importance Wyler placed on the costumes and the way they helped advance the story. They met to discuss how the changes in Catherine's personality throughout the film would be reflected in her clothes. In the beginning of the film, Catherine is resolved to never having attention from men and her clothing is simple. After she meets Morris, she makes overzealous choices in clothing, and her

"The Heiress"
Olivia de Havilland
Edith Head

This page and opposite page: **Two sketches, done later by Richard Hopper, for Olivia de Havilland in *The Heiress*.**

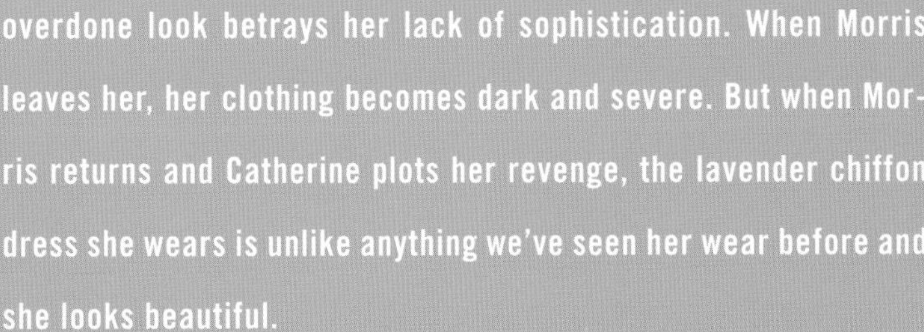

overdone look betrays her lack of sophistication. When Morris leaves her, her clothing becomes dark and severe. But when Morris returns and Catherine plots her revenge, the lavender chiffon dress she wears is unlike anything we've seen her wear before and she looks beautiful.

Edith and Olivia collaborated on the research for the gowns. They both read Henry James' *Washington Square*, the novel on which the film was based and they visited museums together, examining original clothing of the mid-nineteenth century. Olivia practiced how to move in the cumbersome costumes. All activities including walking, sitting and dancing had to be considered because the authentic undergarments were very restricting.

Edith did not have as much success with Miriam Hopkins on the authenticity angle. Miriam played the poor widower aunt to Olivia's heiress. Miriam convinced Edith that her character, no matter how poor, would most likely have embellished her gowns to make herself more attractive. This was one instance where Edith collaborating with an actress on character motivation failed. Director William Wyler overruled the embellishments and the costumes were re-worked to make Miriam look exactly as a poor aunt would have appeared in that period.

The Heiress brought Edith her first Oscar for Costume Design. And with the award also came the lesson for Edith that just simply having beautiful costumes in a film was not what made good costume design. The advancement of the character and the script in harmony with the costumes was what won over the Academy voters that year, as it had the year before with *Joan of Arc*. As confident as she had been the year prior, Edith was totally unprepared to win the Oscar for *The Heiress* and was completely speechless when the award was presented to her by actress Peggy Dow. When master of ceremonies Bob Hope realized this, he took the microphone and ad-libbed "Edith says thank you." The following day, Edith was on the phone with fashion editors all over the country offering little morsels of copy to maximize the publicity the award offered. Florabel Muir reported in *The L.A. Daily Mirror* that "Edith Head, who won the costume designing Oscar, said she didn't like the naked look and was already planning a costume in which to drape it."

"THEY WOULD LOOK AT YOUR DRESS AND SAY 'TOO MUCH BOSOM' AND THEY WOULD HAVE SOMEBODY THERE WITH A LITTLE PIECE OF LACE OR WHATEVER TO FILL IN THE DIVISION BETWEEN THE BREASTS SO IT WOULD BE LEGAL. BUT THEN LATER, I THINK IT WOULD SLIP OUT JUST A LITTLE BIT."

–Joan Fontaine

Edith has a costume consultation with Barbara Stanwyck in 1951.

ANY
CTS AND FIGURES

A wardrobe department test photo of Hedy Lamarr for *My Favorite Spy.*

DeMille had considered filming the story of *Samson and Delilah* as far back as 1935, when he embarked on a publicity campaign to find the perfect Delilah. In 1946, DeMille renewed his interest in the project, and pre-production began in the spring of 1948. Betty Hutton and Yvonne de Carlo were originally considered for the role of Delilah, but eventually DeMille cast Hedy Lamarr in the role.

Victor Mature was cast as Samson, the strongest man of the tribe of Dan, who falls in love with Semadar (Angela Lansbury). After Samson wins Semadar in a battle with Prince Ahtur (Henry Wilcoxon), her true love, she is killed accidentally when he tries to reclaim her. Delilah, who has been in love with Samson, vows revenge on him for her sister's death.

DeMille very rarely used only one designer on an epic film. For *Samson and Delilah*, the costume assignments were broken up among five designers, with Edith dressing Hedy Lamarr and Angela Lansbury, Gwen Wakeling and Elois Jenssen doing the remaining women's costumes and Gile Steele and Dorothy Jeakins doing the men's costumes. It bothered Edith that DeMille would divide up the power on various aspects of production, so that he was the only one with complete autonomy over everything.

Since there was very little reference to research the costumes, Edith's designs were based on a passage from the book of Judges in the Bible, which implied that an Assyrian atmosphere surrounded Delilah, while Samson's dress was of simpler Israelite design. "DeMille liked a great deal of glamour and sumptuousness, and we were working in a period we could not reproduce," Edith said. "We were working in a period where the censorship would not allow us to do accurate clothes. I think a lot people possibly blamed DeMille. But we couldn't show a navel. We couldn't show cleavage or any bosom. And a lot of these pictures should have been bare-bosomed."

The censors rarely complained about any of the men's costumes, but seemed preoccupied with every inch of what showed on the women's figures. It didn't help that Edith had a very unenthusiastic star on her hands either. Hedy Lamarr would constantly need to lie down during her fittings, and lack of professionalism was one thing for which Edith had little tolerance. Hedy would complain of her back hurting, but Edith thought it was just laziness. Lamarr once said that she picked her acting projects based on whatever had the shortest shooting schedule, and fittings were one more example of Lamarr not being as interested in her career as most actresses.

The costumes Edith sketched for Hedy would have been better suited to an actress with a larger bust line. But Hedy didn't want her costumes to be padded, telling Edith "I won't be able to act. I'll feel as if I'm carting balloons." Whether Hedy could really act at all was a topic Edith could debate. To keep star and director happy, Edith filled out Hedy's slim figure with careful draping of the costumes. When DeMille saw Hedy in the costumes, he smiled, an accolade Edith rarely received from the director. Edith's relationship with DeMille had always been an

"EDITH SENSED THAT YOU HAD TO BE COMFORTABLE IN YOUR CLOTHES, THE CLOTHES HAD TO BE COMFORTABLE FOR THE CHARACTER."

–Joan Fontaine

#8
CHANGE
SONG

This page and opposite: **For *Samson and Delilah*, Edith's need for authenticity was overruled by Cecil B. DeMille and the Hollywood censors, who would not allow Edith to show Hedy Lamarr's navel.**

exasperating one for her. DeMille made Edith work up many more versions of each costume than were asked for by any other director. And even when he did finally make a selection, Edith felt it was often the costume with the least amount of taste.

For the final scene of the destruction of the temple, DeMille asked Edith to create a less revealing costume for Hedy, one that would demonstrate the power that Delilah had obtained. DeMille seemed hell bent that the costume should have feathers, and Edith contacted the research department to find out what kind of feathers would have been available during Minoan times. Edith was told that perhaps there may have been peacocks, but there was no certainty of that.

Edith worked up a sketch for DeMille referencing a costume that had been created for Theda Bara in the 1917 film version of *Cleopatra*, in which Cleopatra attended a banquet for Marc Antony in an ensemble appliqued with peacock feathers. DeMille loved the idea, but it totally went against Edith's school teacher sense of authenticity. But with a story set in Minoa with a very American Samson and a Delilah with a heavy Viennese accent, the film may have already been in trouble by Edith's standards. Due to the scarcity of peacock feathers, Edith was forced to use feathers from DeMille's own peacocks, which he kept on his ranch in Tujunga. She dispatched her staff during moulting season, and they returned with nearly two thousand feathers, which were sorted and applied to the costume.

An intense marketing campaign, including lectures and tours of the costumes, helped the film to gross millions and it is still one of the most successful films produced by Paramount in its Golden Age. The "Delilah" look was copied by many manufacturers that year in their clothing lines. Russell's Department Store in New York commissioned the company Cabana to design *Samson and Delilah*-inspired clothing, including a goddess dress with a single strap, which was available for $19.95.

Shortly after the movie's release, archaeologists discovered the city of Phillistia, and proved that DeMille had indeed gotten it wrong. Though Edith had already known that creating tailored bodices on dresses was inaccurate, historians could now also see that the Philistines shaved their facial hair and wore their head hair long.

Taking a much needed break from the studio over the holidays, Edith traveled with Wiard to Guatemala for two weeks. As the 1940's drew to a close, Edith was entering the decade that would be her most prolific, and in which she would do her most memorable and critically-acclaimed work.

CHAPTER FOUR

THE STYLE ICONS

Grace Kelly and Edith review sketches for ***To Catch a Thief.***

One of the most well-known portraits taken of Edith, it properly conveys Edith's stature as one of the most important female executives in the film industry at that time

A*ll About Eve* (1950) BEGAN ITS LIFE AS AN ORIGINAL STORY BY MARY ORR BASED ON THE TRUE EXPERIENCE OF AUSTRIAN ACTRESS ELISABETH BERGNER DURING HER RUN IN THE STAGE PLAY *The Two Mrs. Carrolls* IN THE 1940S. TWENTIETH CENTURY-FOX BOUGHT THE RIGHTS TO THE STORY AND DIRECTOR/WRITER JOSEPH L. MANKIEWICZ ADAPTED IT INTO A SCRIPT CALLED *Best Performance.* MARLENE DIETRICH, GERTRUDE LAWRENCE AND TALLULAH BANKHEAD WERE ALL CONSIDERED FOR THE PART OF FIERY BROADWAY STAR MARGO CHANNING, AN AGING ACTRESS WHO BELIEVES SHE IS BEING BETRAYED BY HER ASSISTANT EVE (ANNE BAXTER).

Fox studio Chief Darryl F. Zanuck changed the name to *All About Eve* after one of character Addison DeWitt's lines in the film. The movie was all set to go into production with Claudette Colbert as Margo, when the actress suffered a ruptured disc while making *Three Came Home* (1950). Bette Davis was rushed into the production, with a stipulation that Edith be loaned to create her costumes.

Charles LeMaire was the head of the Twentieth Century-Fox wardrobe department, and had already begun designing the costumes for the cast, which also included Celeste Holm and an up-and-coming Marilyn Monroe. LeMaire was not happy with the prospect of turning the biggest star in the film over to a designer from a rival studio, but everyone in Hollywood knew what happened if you made Bette Davis mad. To keep the film on schedule, he relented.

Edith had no consultations with Mankiewicz over the clothes, and only spoke with him over the phone. "Just do what you think is right. I love your work," he told her. It was only Davis who had to be pleased, and Edith had already gained her trust. "Bette walks in here like a small, disciplined cyclone," Edith said. "You don't discuss details with Bette. She shows you how she is going to do the part—how she is going to throw herself on the bed, sit on the desk or whirl around and walk out in

One of the happiest accidents in Hollywood history was the off-the-shoulder hostess gown Bette Davis wore in *All About Eve*

a huff. 'That," says Bette, 'is the way I want the clothes to act.'"

LeMaire and Edith had worked closely to make sure that their designs for Davis and Baxter in the cockatil party scene had similarities in the neckline, the fitted waistline, fullness in the skirt, and coloring. The day of filming, Edith arrived at the studio for the final dress fitting. Everything had been rushed very quickly, but this dress was to be the centerpiece of the film, in which Margo Channing, at her most histrionic, would deliver her soon-to-be famous line "fasten your seat belts, it's going to be a bumpy night." Edith had designed a brown silk dress trimmed in brown sable with a squared neckline. The dress had a foundation built in that would support Bette's breasts without her wearing a bra. When Bette tried the dress on, it slipped down off of her shoulders.

Edith realized the measurements must have been taken incorrectly, and was just getting ready to go down the set to tell them production would need to be held up, when Davis stopped her. Looking at her reflection in the mirror, Bette asked Edith if perhaps it wasn't better with the shoulders exposed. Edith was completely relieved, and had the dress stitched up to keep it from falling further. And one of Edith's happiest accidents became one of her most legendary designs.

"I am big. It's the pictures that got small," is also one of the most famous lines in film history. Uttered by the character Norma Desmond in Billy Wilder's *Sunset Blvd.* (1950) it set the stage for a Hollywood story of megalomania and murder. In the film, Norma Desmond (Gloria Swanson) tries to recapture her youth and lost career in the arms of down-on-his-luck screenwriter Joe Gillis (William Holden). Just as Norma's life continually blurred between the past and present in her own world, Wilder used casting, to give the audience a sense of déjà vu. After offering the part to Mae West and Mary Pickford among others, director Billy Wilder finally settled on Swanson, who had been one of Paramount's biggest silent screen stars in the 1920s. Erich Von Stroheim, who was one of Swanson's directors in her heyday, was cast as Max, Norma's former director and former husband, now acting as her butler and companion. When Norma screens one of her old films for Gillis, it is *Queen Kelly* they watch, which starred Swanson and had been directed by Von Stroheim.

The present-day Paramount studio and Cecil B. DeMille also make appearances, as Norma tries to reclaim her fame. Silent stars H.B. Warner, Anna Q. Nilsson and Buster Keaton appear as "the wax works," former silent stars who now visit Norma for oddly silent get-togethers. If the audience needed a program to keep track of what was real and what wasn't, it is no wonder that film fans since have had a hard time separating the real Gloria Swanson from the character of Norma Desmond.

In truth, they couldn't have been more different. Swanson was a woman who never looked back. Though she had been absent from the screen for eight years before making *Sunset Blvd.*, she had stayed very busy with theatre work and her constant travels. The character of Norma Desmond was an egomaniacal shut-in with delusions that one day she would recapture the bloom of her successful silent career with an overlong movie script she has written about Salome, in which she also plans to star.

"THAT IS THE WAY, I WANT THE CLOTHES TO ACT."

–Bette Davis

Edith had never worked with Swanson before. Edith's tenure at Paramount began just as Swanson was marrying Henri de la Falaise in 1925, and making more films in New York. The first time Edith saw Gloria was when the actress returned from her honeymoon to the Paramount studio, and all the employees were assembled and given roses to throw at Gloria's feet as she stepped out of her car.

It was the perfect background moment for Edith to have stored away, to help her understand what kind of accolades a former silent screen star would expect as they emerged from their exile. Director Billy Wilder didn't want Norma to dress as a woman who only lived in the past. In her heyday, Norma would have always been up-to-date on the very latest Paris fashions, and Wilder saw no reason for her not to have adapted to the New Look these many years later. Edith's challenge was that Wilder also wanted just small touches in the designs to

The All About Eve dress that Edith used in her fashion shows. Above: Edith confers with blonde bombshell Marilyn Maxwell during production of *The Lemon Drop Kid.*

Gloria Swanson felt that uneven lines on her clothes made her appear taller on screen. Opposite: The finale of *Sunset Blvd.* when Swanson appears in her Salome dress and the audience realizes she has descended into madness.

show that Norma hadn't quite moved on. She accomplished this through details that harkened back to the over-the-top silent days, such as a headdress that spoke of a Mack Sennett bathing beauty, oversized accessories or having Norma sunbathing on her patio in a silk robe printed in leopard skin.

Swanson was happy to collaborate with Edith on the costumes, and she taught Edith the tricks she had learned over the years to make herself appear taller on screen, including lengthening her skirts in the back and dropping the waistline in the back. She felt uneven lines gave her height, so Gloria asked for one cuff of a jacket trimmed in fur. To minimize Gloria's broad shoulders, Edith had some of the costumes cut on the bias. Swanson's feet were so small (size 2?) that Edith had trouble finding shoes. When she asked the wardrobe department to pull what they had in stock in that size, she found that some of the shoes had been worn by Swanson some thirty years before and still had her name written in them.

The house used as Norma Desmond's decaying mansion was then owned by the ex-wife of J. Paul Getty, whose rental fee to Paramount was the cost of building the pool on the property, which figures so prominently in the film. For the famous scene in which Norma returns to Paramount, Edith dressed Gloria in a black Kasha peg top dress with a short waist-length cape lined in ermine accessorized with an ermine cuff muff and hat. Norma arrives at the gates of Paramount in an Isotta-Fraschini limousine that had been a gift from Walter Chrysler to socialite Peggy Hopkins Joyce. When she greets her old director Cecil B. DeMille on the set of *Samson and Delilah*, DeMille was, in actuality, shooting on the film at the time.

Edith relied on rich fabrics and fur pieces to convey Norma's wealth, including a pale grey woven Kasha dress with mink-lined cape and a spiral mink hat; a brocade gown topped with chinchilla fur; and black velvet hostess pajamas with a printed silk trim. In the final scene, Edith returned to the unstructured lines of a 1920s dress to show that, in her mind, Norma has completely regressed to the past as she performs the scene from Salome. To avoid tripping on the stairs, Gloria decided to play the scene barefoot.

During the filming, the buzz around the studio was that an instant classic was being made. Executives jockeyed for seats in the screening room to watch the rushes. But Wilder knew not everyone in Hollywood would be pleased with his depiction of the film industry, and while in production, he code-named the film "*A Can of Beans.*" At the premiere, Louis B. Mayer upbraided Wilder for destroying the image of his profession. But there was no doubt that *Sunset Blvd.* would catch on with moviegoers, and is almost always near the top of every best film list.

At the twenty third Academy Awards for the best films of 1950, *All About Eve* was nominated for fourteen Oscars, beating the previous record held by *Gone With the Wind* (1939). Anne Baxter and Bette Davis were both nominated in the Best Actress category, along with Judy Holliday in *Born Yesterday*, Eleanor Parker in *Caged* and Gloria Swanson in *Sunset Blvd.* Many film historians believe that Davis and Baxter being

DURING THE FILMING, THE BUZZ AROUND THE STUDIO WAS THAT AN INSTANT CLASSIC WAS BEING MADE. EXECUTIVES JOCKEYED FOR SEATS IN THE SCREENING ROOM TO WATCH THE RUSHES. BUT WILDER KNEW NOT EVERYONE IN HOLLYWOOD WOULD BE PLEASED WITH HIS DEPICTION OF THE FILM INDUSTRY, AND WHILE IN PRODUCTION, HE CODE-NAMED THE FILM "A CAN OF BEANS."

This page and opposite page: **For *Sunset Blvd.*, Edith used subtle touches to show that while Norma Desmond would be up-to-date fashion-wise for the time, she still hadn't quite moved on from her Hollywood heyday of the 1920's.**

nominated in the same category split votes for *All About Eve* and the award went to Judy Holliday.

Edith was nominated along with Dorothy Jeakins, Elois Jenssen, Gile Steele, and Gwen Wakeling for *Samson and Delilah* in the color category for costume design, and for *All About Eve* with Charles LeMaire in the black-and-white category. Edith had a theory that the popularity of a film always helped sway Academy voters, and this year she absolutely had popularity on her side. Edith wore a gown of oyster white Faille to the ceremony. To the wraparound skirt, she added an apron-like overskirt that had been lavishly jet embroidered. She wore her hair in her trademark chignon, covering by jet-embroidered net.

Actress Jan Sterling presented both costume design Oscars that evening wearing a pale yellow gown with a jeweled topaz corselet, which Edith had designed for her. In a stunning night of surprises, Edith won in both categories, taking home two Oscars that night. *All About Eve* dominated the evening, taking the Best Picture, Best Supporting Actor (for George Sanders) and Best Director (for Joseph L. Mankiewicz) categories, among others.

September Affair (1950) cast Joan Fontaine as a pianist and Joseph Cotten as an industrialist who fall in love on a trip, and after missing a plane, are reported dead when it crashes. Edith's designs for Fontaine were some of the most crisp, cleanest day clothes that she ever

A sketch by Grace Sprague for Elizabeth Taylor in A Place in the Sun, done after production for publicity purposes

designed, including a white blouse that was split in front, and lined with a dickey of striped fabric. For a scene in which Fontaine plays at a concert, Edith designed a gown of stiff white satin with a strapless neckline that resembled an open fan. The gown was embroidered lavishly in brilliants and gold thread, and the bodice fit snugly at the waistline, then fell into generous folds. Fontaine wore it with a three-strand pearl necklace and small pearl earrings. "Edith sensed that you had to be comfortable in your clothes, and the clothes had to be comfortable for the character," Fonatine says. "I never had a fraction of a dispute with her. I don't know anyone who did. Everybody loved her—amiable, charming, helpful, with a degree of friendship."

In April, 1950, *Photoplay Magazine* selected another of Edith's designs to feature as its Pattern of the Month. A shirtwaist dress that Edith designed for Barbara Stanwyck in *The File on Thelma Jordon* (1950) proved to be another popular design. Edith also accepted a commission from the Andrews Sisters for $15,000 worth of clothes to wear when they toured their nightclub act.

AH, YOUTH!

Edith missed out on designing the wedding gown of the year when actress Elizabeth Taylor married hotel heir Conrad "Nick" Hilton on May 6, 1950. The assignment went to Helen Rose, head designer at MGM, the studio to which Elizabeth was under contract. Edith had been working with Taylor in the pre-production stages of George Stevens' *A Place in the Sun* (1951), and had to settle for designing Elizabeth's trousseau. Edith devised a varied wardrobe that would allow for a minimum of suitcase space. She created a black skirt with four different types of colored blouses: a black net camisole; a light ground blouse with name embroidered at spaced intervals; a jonquil yellow corset blouse with matching gloves; and a white cotton lace scoop neck blouse with pink linen ribbon running through the neckline and tied with matching carnations. To coordinate the skirt with the blouses, Edith made a matching handkerchief for each blouse to be worn in the skirt pocket.

There had already been a film made of Theodore Dreiser's novel *An American Tragedy.*, on which *A Place in the Sun* is based. The book was based on the true story of Chester Gillette, who was convicted of murdering his pregnant girlfriend in 1906, and was executed in 1908. Since the original film had not been a hit, director George Stevens was looking for a new title for his remake of 1951. He held a contest at the studio and offered $100 for the best title. Though he never collected his prize, producer Ivan Moffat came up with the title *A Place in the Sun.*

Elizabeth Taylor had been a star for six of her seventeen years when she began work on *A Place in the Sun* (1951) in 1949. She was already an exquisite little girl when she was first brought to the attention to MGM head Louis B. Mayer, who put her under contract, and she was now on the threshold of becoming one of the most celebrated beauties in the world. Director George Stevens had borrowed Taylor from MGM and cast her in the much-coveted role of Angela Vickers, a debutante who falls for Montgomery Clift, and appeals to his desire for a life of privilege.

The challenge of costuming *A Place in the Sun* was

Left: **Richard Hopper's sketch for the black *A Place in the Sun* gown, done later for publicity.**
Opposite: **Edith fitting the gown on Elizabeth Taylor.**

Left: **Richard Hopper's sketch for the dress that launched thousands of prom dreams from *A Place in the Sun*.** Right: **Elizabeth Taylor wears the gown during production.**

EDITH DESCRIBED ELIZABETH AS "ONE OF THE PRETTIEST HUMAN BEINGS I'VE EVER SEEN."

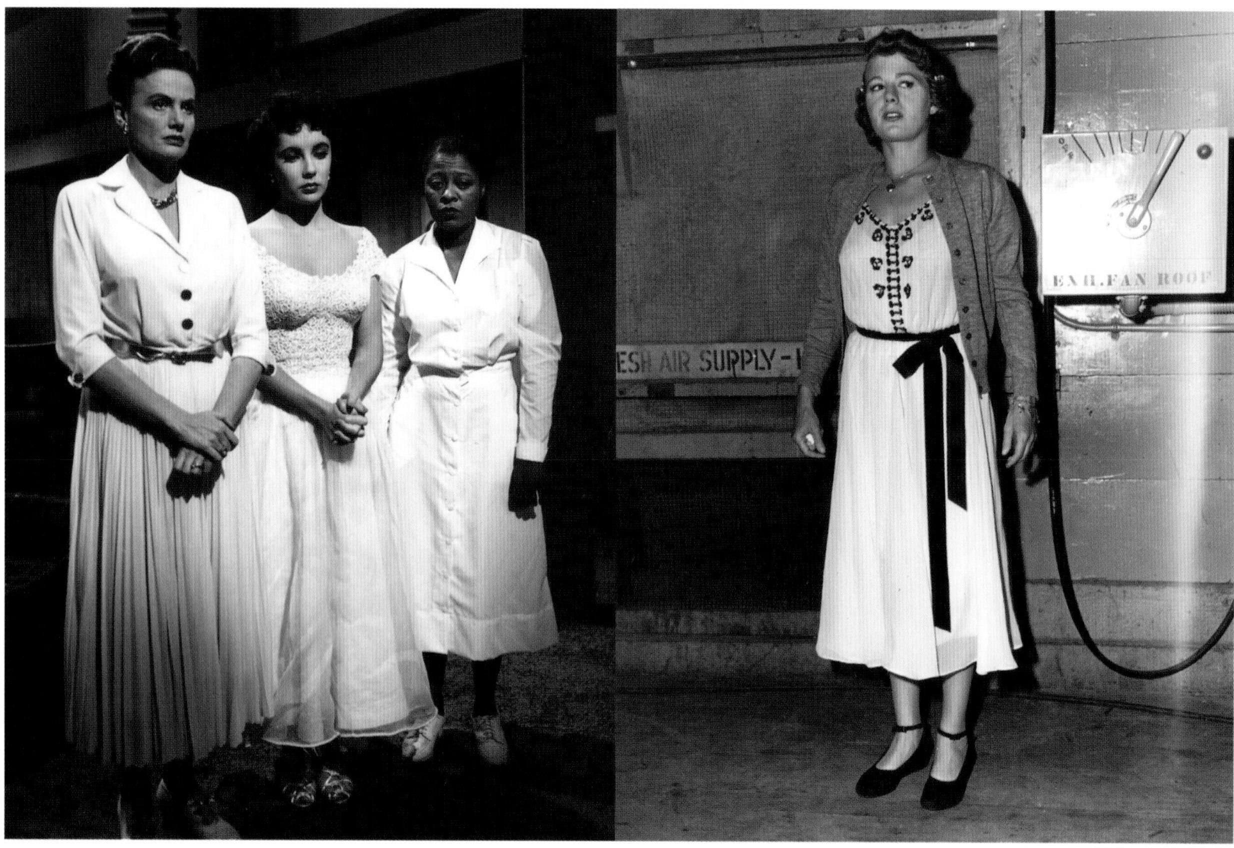

Left: Wardrobe tests from *A Place in the Sun* highlight the difference between the social standing of Elizabeth Taylor's character (far left) and that of the character played by Shelley Winters.

that it was not going to be released for more than a year from the time Edith's designs would be completed. Edith believed that the New Look would survive as a style trend during that time, so she felt comfortable giving Taylor gowns with full skirts. She kept details on all of the clothing including accessories, collars, and sleeves to a minimum because those were the trends that she felt she couldn't predict.

Edith credited Elizabeth with helping her understand the teenage point of view to fashion. There had now been two generations since Edith had come of age in the flapper years. The Depression and then a World War had made previous generations of young people have to be constantly aware of conserving. Now with the advent of blue jeans for day wear and Dior's New Look for evening, the rules had changed for young people. Edith noted that the casual look was very casual and the dressed up look was probably far beyond what a teenager should be wearing, and there was no in-between.

The fittings for Taylor proved lively and enjoyable for Edith. Taylor would often bring her mother, her tutor from MGM, and a myriad of pets with her. Edith found Elizabeth to be very well-mannered and totally in sync with the proposed designs. It must have also helped that Elizabeth had a beautiful hourglass figure and she kept trying to cajole Edith into making the waistline of the dresses as tiny as possible. Edith described Elizabeth as "one of the prettiest human beings I've ever seen."

When the audience first sees Elizabeth in the film, she is in a dance dress of white satin with Boas bands across the bodice and hip, and a petticoat of tulle underneath. As the story unfolds, Elizabeth's wardrobe is designed to keep reminding the viewer that she is a woman of privilege, in direct contrast to the blue collar wardrobes of George Eastman (Clift) and Alice Tripp (Shelley Winters). Designs for Taylor included a terry cloth "sunner" with knit waist and bra bands accompanied by a matching fringed stole; a knitted Boucle sweater, whose hood formed a collar when worn down, which Edith accessorized with matching knit gloves; and a sweater and stole of heavy white lace with double circular skirt of sheer white organdy.

EDITH NEEDN'T HAVE WORRIED TOO MUCH ABOUT PREDICTING THE FASHION TRENDS TO ENSURE THAT *A PLACE IN THE SUN* WOULDN'T LOOK DATED UPON ITS RELEASE. IN 1951, IT WAS ELIZABETH TAYLOR'S APPEARANCE IN THAT FILM THAT ACTUALLY SET THE TRENDS.

"DON'T LET HER KID YOU. SHE OWNS A 50-ACRE ESTATE SURROUNDED BY A PICKET FENCE MADE OF NOTHING BUT OSCARS!"

–Walter Plunkett

On Oscar night 1955, Edith is flanked by actresses Marla English (left, wearing Audrey Hepburn's gown from *Roman Holiday*) and Gene Tierney.

Edith and actress Helen Hayes look over sketches for the film *My Son John*.

Edith needn't have worried too much about predicting the fashion trends to ensure that *A Place in the Sun* wouldn't look dated upon its release. In 1951, it was Elizabeth Taylor's appearance in that film that actually set the trends. Manufacturers recognized that young girls would want to emulate Taylor's style, and manufactured copies of the two important gowns and had them ready in stores upon the film's release. One gown was a black velvet formal with a heavy lace that had been encrusted with pearl beads that were laced into ribbon bands cross the bust. But it was Edith's gown for Taylor, employing six layers of white net over pale mint green taffeta, studded with single velvet violets, and a bodice covered in white velvet violets with green centers, that would cause a sensation among prom-going young ladies that year. It is still considered one of the most iconic dresses designed for the Golden Age of Hollywood.

At the twenty-fourth annual Academy Awards, Edith was nominated for an Oscar for in the black-and-white category for *A Place in the Sun*, against Lucinda Ballard for *A Streetcar Named Desire* (1951), Edward Stevenson and Margaret Furse for *The Mudlark* (1950), Charles LeMaire and Renie Conley for *The Model and the Marriage Broker* (1951), and Walter Plunkett and Gile Steele for *Kind Lady* (1951). Steele, who had worked in the men's wardrobe department at Paramount, was a frequent collaborator on films with Edith and had recently passed away.

Edith wore a short evening gown of black linen net, which had been embroidered in black velvet chenille, to the ceremony at the RKO Pantages Theater in Hollywood. Zsa Zsa Gabor presented the costume awards in both the black-and-white and color categories. When Gabor opened the envelope for black-and-white costume design, the audience roared with laughter when she announced with her thick Hungarian accent, "the award goes to Edie's Head." When Edith told the reporters backstage that this was her fourth Oscar win, Walter Plunkett, who had won for *An American in Paris*, told the press reps "Don't let her kid you. She owns a fifty-acre estate surrounded by a picket fence made of nothing but Oscars!" It was a generous statement, as some resentment was growing towards Edith from other designers about her Oscars. Some felt that in the few years since the award was created, Edith so dominated the awards that it left little opportunity for anyone else to win one.

To capitalize on Edith's celebrity, Paramount created a featurette to be shown in theaters called *The Costume Designer* (1951). The film centered on Edith's creative process, as she explained how she used details in the script such as time of year and financial status of the character to come up with a picture of what the clothes should look like. Showing the same scene in a film using different gowns, Edith demonstrated how a dramatic scene with an eye-catching gown can pull the focus from the story.

Here Comes the Groom (1951) cast Bing Crosby as Pete Garvey, a singing journalist who must marry quickly so that he can bring two war orphans to the United States. For Jane Wyman, as Pete's ex-fiancee, Edith made a strapless dress of pink satin and tulle. The bodice was embroidered in pink sequins and fit Jane's form like a second skin from the bust line to the waistline, then flared out over a full tulle skirt made from three layers of delicate shades of pale pink tulle. Edith accessorized the outfit with long pink satin gloves that had been embroidered in pink sequins.

Of course, a film called *Here Comes the Groom* would have to have a wedding gown, and Edith made a beautiful one for Wyman, using thirty-nine yards of rose point lace imported from a French convent. The dress took a month to make at a cost of $5,000. To promote the film, *Photoplay Magazine* held a contest in their October 1951 issue to win a custom Edith Head-designed wedding gown or dress.

The proportions of the New Look had brought feminine curves into vogue. Across town, Marilyn Monroe was causing a sensation at Twentieth Century-Fox with her full figure in films like *Love Nest* (1951)

and *Let' s Make it Legal* (1951). Paramount's answer to Monroe was the curvy platinum-haired Marilyn Maxwell, who had toured with Bob Hope in his USO shows. Maxwell was co-starring with Hope in *The Lemon Drop Kid* (1951) when censors began complaining about the wardrobe for the actress. Edith had been asked by the producers to have Marilyn's clothing reflect the fact that her character made only $75.00 a week. Edith designed 12 changes for Marilyn in that price range, using sweaters a part of the solution. And Marilyn knew how to fill out a sweater. "Can't you do something about it?" the censors asked Edith. "You can't do a thing about it unless you cast a boy in the part," she reportedly told them. For one low-cut dress, Edith had to caution Marilyn, saying "never sit down in it, honey. If you do, there will be too much Marilyn showing. It's an eye level dress."

When the sexy French actress Corinne Calvet was making *Peking Express* (1951) opposite Joseph Cotten, she asked producer Hal Wallis for less revealing clothes. The film was the second remake of Josef von Strernberg's *Shanghai Express* (1932) and Calvet was cast in the role of the glamorous prostitute, which Marlene Dietrich had played in the original. "I don't like to show ze bare fleash. Eet takes away all ze glamour. Curves fine . . . I like to show ze curves. Zey weel all be cleenging gowns, but zey will covair me up. Ze mens will know I am underneath zem — but zey will have to imagine ze rest," Calvet said at the time.

FACING THE CAMERAS

A mild calamity struck when Art Linkletter decided to simulcast his radio show *House Party* on television in 1952. Edith had become very comfortable on the radio, dispensing fashion advice to women and discussing upcoming trends. She had spent over a decade doing all kinds of publicity to promote the films on which she worked, she spoke to ladies' groups at luncheons, held fashion shows and talked to a constant stream of fashion columnists from all around the country who reported her one-liners about bra padding and hemlines. But television put Edith more on a playing field with the actresses for whom she designed, and she knew better than just about anybody what kind of scrutiny those women were put under.

In the early televised shows, Edith was terribly self-conscious and did all she could to try to hide from the camera. She had continued to wear her dark blue glasses, even though fewer and fewer pictures were made in black-and-white, and viewers found her look affected. Edith turned to Art Linkletter for help, as she had in the early days of the radio show. Linkletter watched the kinescope playbacks with her and critiqued her performances. He encouraged her to be more accessible and use her sense of humor. Things didn't change overnight for Edith's performances, but she became more comfortable with each show.

Edith followed the advice Linkletter had given when they started the original radio show: " you can be critical, but you must be kind as well." The home audience could now actually see the transformations of the audience members, and how dramatic the results could be, sometimes with just a few accessory changes. It is impossible to measure the influence Edith had over women's fashion purchases, but you can be sure there were more women wearing solid colors, less jewelry and fewer silly hats after seeing Edith on *House Party*.

"Inside Edith Head was an independent cuss and she had her own ideas," Linkletter said. "But she got more independent outside as time went on because she became more famous and in-demand and more competitive. Because as movies got bigger and bigger, other designers were trying to use the stars that Edith might have gotten the jobs for. And she had to do politics. And she had to do little inside wiggles, so that she'd be picked."

The exposure of television gave Edith a platform like no designer had ever had, whether a Hollywood studio designer or couture designer. The average American woman might not realize that she owed the cinched waist on her dress to Christian Dior, but she could probably tell you what Edith Head was thinking about hemlines that

“SHE GOT MORE INDEPENDENT OUTSIDE AS TIME WENT ON BECAUSE SHE BECAME MORE FAMOUS AND IN-DEMAND AND MORE COMPETITIVE.”

–Art Linkletter

CASA LADERA

IN 1951, EDITH AND WIARD PURCHASED A RAMBLING ESTATE in Beverly Hills called Casa Ladera (House on the Side of the Hill). The property's main building had originally been a sheepherding ranch. Film star Robert Armstrong purchased the property and molded it into a traditional California ranch house in the Mexican hacienda style. Guests would enter through a courtyard, and wind their way up the shaded banks of ivy past the guest house with its balconied bedrooms, to the large house. The one-story house faced inward and surrounded a large terra cotta-tiled patio on three sides. The fourth side looked toward the wall of the canyon. All of the rooms spilled out onto the patio, and there were also an outdoor kitchen, dining room and bar. Edith and Wiard filled the house with the treasures they collected on trips together. Paintings by Mexican masters hung on the walls, Mexican dolls, hats and pottery were placed about and glass cases were filled with snuff boxes, jade ornaments, and perfume bottles. Edith and Wiard chose Spanish colonial furniture made of heavy woods, and cushioned them with colorful Mexican weavings.

Edith's schedule left her little time to look after the house. Wiard had been working less and less as an art director, and created a studio space in the house where he could do his fine art painting. "Aside from being her loving husband, Wiard was like a therapist," says David Chierichetti. "He would listen to all her troubles at the studio and give her advice. He was a nice man, very devoted to her. And he was willing to put up with her demanding lifestyle. He retired a lot sooner than he needed to. He was just the opposite of Edith. He worked in the movie business to make money. He wasn't interested in being famous, and once he got enough money to quit, he quit."

Wiard happily took on the chore of running the house, and the couple employed a maid and gardener. "I see nothing noble in washing dishes or pulling weeds. I just don't do it," Edith said. But when Edith got home from the studio, they enjoyed having friends over and entertaining. As she had in their previous home, Edith showed her domestic side in the kitchen.

CHICKEN AND POTATOES CASA LADERA

1 chicken fryer (about 3½ lbs.), cut up

1½ tsp. salt

1 tsp. paprika

¼ tsp. pepper

6 tbsp. butter or margarine

½ cup chicken broth or bouillon

½ cup dry white wine

3 tbsp. flour

Rice Potatoes (recipe follows) or mashed potatoes

½ lb. chicken livers

½ lb. small mushrooms

Cherry tomatoes

Watercress sprigs

Sprinkle chicken pieces with salt, paprika and pepper. Heat 2 tbsp. butter in large skillet. Add chicken pieces; sauté over medium-high heat to brown, turning once. Transfer chicken to large shallow baking dish. Add broth and wine to skillet. Stir over medium heat to loosen brown particles and bring to boil. Mix brandy with flour until smooth. Stir into broth mixture. Cook about 5 minutes until smooth and thickened. Pour over chicken. Cover and bake in 350-degree oven 30 minutes. Meanwhile, cook potatoes. While chicken and potatoes cook, heat 2 more tbls. butter in large skillet. Add chicken livers. Toss gently over medium-high heat about 5 minutes until the livers lose pink color and brown slightly. Remove livers and set aside. Add remaining 2 tbsp. butter to skillet. Add mushrooms. Saute, tossing until lightly browned, about 10 minutes. When chicken has cooked 30 minutes, add livers and mushrooms. Cover and continue to cook 15 minutes. Mound rice potatoes on center of serving platter. Surround with chicken, chicken livers and mushrooms. Garnish with tomatoes and watercress. Serve with sauce. Makes 4 to 6 servings.

RICE POTATOES

1½ lbs. potatoes, peeled

1 tsp. salt

1 tbsp. butter or margarine

Cut potatoes into large chunks of uniform size. Combine in 3-quart saucepan with salt and 1-inch boiling water. Bring to boil, cover and cook until fork-tender over medium heat, about 20 minutes. Drain; shake over medium heat to dry completely. Toss with butter. Force through ricer onto serving platter.

(Edith would serve Chicken and Potatoes Casa Ladera with a salad of finely chopped hearts of lettuce, tomatoes, celery, cucumbers, and onions, dressed with vinegar and oil. For dessert, she would serve a fresh fruit compote).

Bob Hope puts his life on the line in *Here Come the Girls*, opposite (left to right) Arlene Dahl and Rosemary Clooney

week. Eventually, the quirks that had made Edith unpopular in the early shows, became her trademarks — the dark glasses, the beige suits — and television audiences embraced her. Today we would call it "branding an image." Edith, who had realized the value of publicity early on, was becoming as famous as the stars for who she designed. With her new-found celebrity status, Edith found herself more in demand for lectures and fashion shows. Edith and her friend June Van Dyke began acquiring well-known pieces Edith had designed from Paramount and touring fashion shows as a side business, which Edith would moderate in person.

Carrie (1952) cast Jennifer Jones as the title character, whose lover (Laurence Olivier) embezzles a fortune to build a life with her in New York. Edith designed some lovely period clothing for the story, which was set in 1900, including a bare-shouldered French court dress of shimmering satin with a tiny waist and billowing shirts, topped with a white powdered wig of sculptured curls. The designs earned Edith an Oscar nomination that year. Miriam Hopkins was cast only the night before she started filming as Olivier's cruel, mercenary wife. "Willie Wyler called me one night around 11:30 to say he was having trouble with the wife part and would I take it," Hopkins said. "So I washed my hair at 2:30 a.m., got into my car at 5:45 a.m. for the studio and was ready at 7:00 to dress for the fisrt scene. Edith Head had ordered the costume department to work all night on my wardrobe. She and I were both so sleepy we had to take Benzedrene tablets to keep going. And the tablets made us so voluble, we talked like mad all day."

Jones' next project was *Ruby Gentry* (1952) at another studio. When filming a scene in which Jones has to come to fisticuffs with co-star Charlton Heston, the actress broke a small bone in her right hand. David O'Selznick called Edith and asked if she could devise a solution for Jennifer, so that production would not need to be held up any longer than needed. Jones' wardrobe for the film was designed by the couturier Valentina, and was shipped to the set, leaving only the wardrobe supervisor to deal with the problem. Edith devised a brace hidden by a ring and two bracelets, and filming continued.

Edith was also nominated for an Oscar for color costume design for Cecil B. DeMille's *The Greatest Show on Earth* (1952) starring Betty Hutton, Cornel Wilde, Charlton Heston and Dorothy Lamour. Edith told Hedda Hopper "I thought I knew quite a bit about clothes, but I find I know nothing about designing for the circus — for girls flying through the air, hanging to a strap by their teeth, or crawling all over elephants." The film was popular with audiences, and did win the Oscar for Best Picture, though film critics believe it was because Academy members resisted voting for *High Noon* (1952) because they viewed it as a parable for communism.

In 1924, Jesse Lasky had purchased the rights to *War of the Worlds* (1953) from H.G. Wells to film a silent screen version of the book. With the Cold War in full swing and Americans terrified of the idea of an invasion, the 1950s seemed a good time for an allegorical film about Martians coming to Earth. Producer Cecil B. DeMille brought director Gorge Pal on board, who was well known for his Puppetoon films, and could handle the special effects. The Martian military hardware and spaceship launch systems all had to be envisioned by the art department, and Edith had to figure out what the well-dressed Martian would be wearing that year. Since real-life space travel was still a few years off, audiences would still accept that people could travel through space not only without a space suit, but often wearing very little. Edith worked with make-up artist Wally Westmore who used greenish-gold paint to cover the Martian women. Edith's design began with a very simple leotard that formed the base of the costume. The Martian's headgear was based on the television antennas, and Edith added bracelets, anklets and a wide belt, all spray painted for a metallic look.

In July, 1952, Edith and Wiard were able to travel for a month to London, Paris and Madrid. Edith had just finished designing a slate of commissions from Paramount stars for their nightclub engagements, including Betty Hutton's gowns for her appearance at the RKO Palace Theatre in New York. Rosemary Clooney opened in Reno in August in $75,000 worth of Edith's designs. When the Andrews Sisters approached Edith about designing for their nightclub tour, they told Edith she could design anything for them "as long as it had a Peter Pan collar." Edith talked the ladies instead into glamorous black sequined gowns by the time they opened at the Coconut Grove in Los Angeles in October. Their opening night party also celebrated Edith's birthday, and they brought Edith onto the main floor to present a cake to her. A nervous Edith knew that it was always best to go for a laugh, and she pretended to adjust Patty's dress as the audience roared.

In February, 1953, Joan Crawford moved on to the Paramount lot and spent a month in pre-production for the Irving Asher production of *Lisbon*, an international spy tale. Joan's character was a very wealthy woman with great taste, and Edith and Joan pored over sketches and fabrics in Crawford's dressing room. But late in February, the film was scrapped, and though Edith did design outfits for Joan's personal wardrobe and did one uncredited film design, they never worked on a full film together.

In March, 1953, the Oscars were televised for the first time. Two years prior, the Academy had asked Edith to serve as a fashion consultant for actresses that were at a loss for what to wear to the ceremony. But television provided some new challenges. White of any kind, including gloves, just appeared as a big white blob on crude TV sets. Plunging necklines also became a worry in case cameras were placed on high. For Loretta Young, Edith designed a gown of Duchess Lace appliquéd on matching pearl tulle with a bustle and train, embroidered with mother of pearl pailettes, and worn with an ermine stole. Her jewelry was a pearl necklace featuring a 278-gram baroque pearl shaped like a swan gliding on a bed of diamond white water lilies. Terry Moore wore an Edith Head gown of pale pink French satin with full wrap-around skirt, which created a one-sided pocket that Edith filled with pink satin poppies.

Rosemary Clooney preferred white for her costumes in *The Stars Are Singing*.

Up until 1949, audiences had only seen auburn-haired actress Rhonda Fleming on screen in character parts. Producer David O. Selznick, to whom Fleming was under contract, cast the actress in moody black-and-white films such as *Spellbound* (1945) and the *Spiral Staircase* (1945). In 1949, Selznick loaned Fleming to Paramount to star opposite Bing Crosby in *A Connecticut Yankee in King Arthur' s Court*, and Frank Richardson assigned Mary Kay Dodson to do the designing duties on the color film. Technicolor seemed to be made for Fleming, but it took some getting used to for the actress. "Technicolor was far too unnatural," she says. "If your eyes were green, they were really green, and your skin was so pinky white. Suddenly they just started calling me a 'Technicolor Queen,' which I hated. I just wanted to prove I was a good actress."

Edith was assigned to dress Fleming in *The Great Lover* (1949), starring Bob Hope. "I was so relatively new when I started out, I just didn't know anything," says Fleming. "Edith was an unusual lady. She was just on business completely. She wasn't terribly friendly, but I probably didn't know how to make friends with someone like Edith, who was so self-assured. But you trusted what she came up with." *The Great Lover* was shot in black-and-white, and Rhonda's image was given an overhaul with gowns of French lace, for her role as a sophisticated French Duchess. "*The Great Lover* just wasn't me," says Fleming. "It was a French look and they cut my beautiful long hair. I didn't like it, but it was appropriate for the role."

By the time Fleming starred in *Crosswinds* (1951), the actress was comfortable working in Technicolor, and more comfortable working with Edith. "She'd give me a choice of color," Fleming says. "I don't know if I always made the right decision, but Edith knew what she was doing and I knew I was in good hands. The clothes fit so beautifully, like a glove. I just knew when I walked out of the dressing room, people would go 'wow that's a beautiful outfit.' " In *Hong Kong* (1952), Fleming was cast opposite future President Ronald Reagan. For her role as a missionary, Rhonda asked Edith to keep her as unglamorous as possible. "My hair was straight, and I didn't wear any make-up," she says. "I would have been happy staying in character parts for the rest of my career. When I did those, I never had to care where the camera was. I just concentrated on my lines and my work."

But it was back to glamour for *Tropic Zone* (1953), which cast Reagan as Dan McCloud, a freedom fighter trying to save a banana plantation owned by Flanders White (Fleming). Edith opted to do all of Fleming's fourteen changes in jungle tones. These included a dress of suntan linen with a flared skirt worn over a white starched petticoat, and a separate wraparound blouse top. To emulate water and leaves, Edith put Rhonda in a dress of navy blue silk linen with a halter bodice. The stole and skirt were in a cool print of white, blue and shades of green.

The Buster Keaton Story (1957) was a highly fictionalized account of the great silent comedian's life, starring Donald O'Connor as Keaton and Ann Blyth as a composite character of Keaton's three wives. Fleming played Peggy Courtney, a fictional film star, with whom Keaton falls in love. When Rhonda came on the set wearing a platinum wig and a black velvet negligee slit to the thigh, accompanied by two Russian wolfhounds, Edith told reporter Harrison Carroll "Isn't that negligee something! You know, if I were designing a lounging robe for a star to wear on a set today, it probably would be made of terry cloth." When Carroll asked Edith about other costumes Edith had dreamed up for Fleming, she answered, "I didn't dream them up. Nearly all of Rhonda's costumes are copied from clothes I designed for Clara Bow and Carole Lombard." Edith may have been stretching the truth a bit. The silhouettes of Fleming's clothes were more form fitting than the prevailing styles of the 1920s. "Edith kept the glamorous look of that era," says Fleming. "You could get away with it in comedy, and it certainly looked good."

Gunfight at the O.K. Corral (1957) was a retelling of the confrontation in 1881 between Wyatt Earp (Burt Lancaster) and 'Doc' Holliday (Kirk Douglas) with the Clanton-McLaury gang. With great star power on its side and the climactic five-minute shootout scene, it is one of the most enduring and entertaining films of the Western genre. Fleming played Laura Denbow, a lady gambler and love interest for Wyatt Earp. For Denbow's confrontation with Earp in the saloon, Edith designed a low-cut yellow dress with a black net accent across the bust, edged in black jet beads. But another ensemble didn't fare as well in its on-screen time. No matter how much the actress and Edith slaved over a costume, ultimately it was up to the director as to what the audience saw. "When I was getting out of the wagon, it was all done in long shot," says Fleming. "They never did come in close to show the outfit."

Alias Jesse James (1959) cast Bob Hope as an inept insurance salesman trying to buy back a life insurance policy that he had sold to the outlaw Jesse James. Fleming played Cora Lee Collins, Jesse James' girlfriend and beneficiary. Once again, the dresses of the Old West demanded Edith put Rhonda Fleming in corsets. "The dresses had no boning," Fleming says. "We wore corsets, which made me laugh because as I wore them throughout a film, my waist got tinier and tinier. You had to get used to them, and I was comfortable in them as long as I could breathe well. But in warm weather, you could roast in the heat. It seemed like every time we did a western outside, it was hot."

The Stars Are Singing (1953) starred newcomer Anna Marie Alberghetti as Katri Walenska, an illegal immigrant who wins a televised amateur contest. Rosemary Clooney played Terry Brennan, a Broadway hopeful, who secures the television appearance for Katri. "Rosemary Clooney asked for as much white as possible," Edith said. "Rosemary says she feels wonderful when she wears white. It is probably a throw back to the days when she sang with dance bands. She wore white or pastel bouffant gowns then, and with the spotlight shining on her, she feels like a princess." Edith designed a white linen dress with soft shoulders and a full skirt, rolled collar and cuffs, both of which were opened at the ends. For Alberghetti, Edith chose a dress of pale pink crossbar organdie over pink taffeta.

If Clooney felt comfortable in white for stage and screen, gray was the color she chose for her wedding to José Ferrer in July, 1953. Ferrer had brought Clooney some light gray herring bone tweed fabric from London the year before. Edith fashioned a wedding suit out of it for Clooney, who took it with her for her appearance in Dallas in *Kiss Me Kate*. "I just kind of felt that this was to be it," Clooney said. "But I honestly didn't know for sure." But when then decision was made for the couple to wed, they didn't waste any time. They traveled to Oklahoma because of the lack of pre-marital waiting time.

Glamorous Arlene Dahl first met Edith, not as an actress, but as a journalist. The red-headed beauty had begun her acting career at Warner Brothers, and then moved to MGM. In addition to her acting, Dahl had an entrepreneurial spirit and turned her interest in beauty and fashion into second and third careers as a writer and designer. In the early 1950s, Arlene interviewed Edith for her beauty, fashion and health

"WHEN I INTERVIEWED EDITH FOR MY COLUMN, I ASKED HER ABOUT FASHION AND SHE SAID 'WELL, WHEN A WOMAN REACHES 40 AND OVER, SHE SHOULD NEVER REVEAL WHAT SHE SHOULD CONCEAL.'" –Arlene Dahl

column, which was carried by the *Chicago Trubune/New York News* Syndicate. The column ran in about 100 newspapers including *The London Evening News*. "I went into her office on the second floor at Paramount and I saw this very striking, not very tall, woman dressed in black," Dahl says. "She was wearing what we called a model's coat, with a very nice patent leather black belt, and black-rimmed glasses. She'd be perfect in today's fashion climate, but that is what she always wore. She was absolutely disarming and charming and wonderful. When I interviewed Edith for my column, I asked her about fashion and she said 'well, when a woman reaches 40 and over, she should never reveal what she should conceal.' That includes the upper arms of course. She had many bon mots she would use. That was one that I particularly remembered."

When Dahl came to Paramount in 1952 to make *Caribbean* with John Payne, she was able to see Edith's formula first-hand for simplifying an actress' look on screen. "I went up to her studio and she remembered me and she said 'now let's talk about what colors you like and what your character is, and we'll go from there,' " Dahl says. "Character was very important to her, and colors that flattered the actor or actress that she was working with. Edith told me 'you're a redhead, and nobody can have more than three poster colors. Red is one of yours, so you can only have two more poster colors. It could be green or blue or whatever, and a neutral color.' "

She was easy to love. Especially for someone who won more Academy Awards than any other designer. You find that sometimes designers are very autonomous and set in their ways. They don't open up to other people and their ideas, especially the actors. She came to meet the actor or actress first because they had to be comfortable in their clothes. I had to sit in some of my costumes to make sure they sat well and that I was comfortable. Caribbean was a period piece. I had to wear these corsets, and she got me down to eighteen-inches in my waistline. She impressed me with that."

Edith knew how rough the film business could be, and watched out for young actresses in the early stages of their careers, such as Patricia Crowley.

"You couldn't have too low of a neckline because if it showed a shadow or a crease, you'd have to stick a lace handkerchief in there. You could see the outline of the breasts, but you couldn't see the shadow between the two 'positions.' Whether they were apricots or grapefruit, you had to be very circumspect! I did three costume films that Edith designed, and one modern, which was *Jamaica Run* (1953) with Ray Milland. It was a modern film where I could wear dresses without wearing waist cinchers. I had more of a natural figure."

"When Arlene began *Sangaree* (1953), her co-star was Fernando Lamas, with whom she was having an off-screen romance. Though it was technically a 'B' film that was being produced by the Pine-Thomas unit at Paramount, the producers invested a little more money in the film because of the headlines the couple were generating. "The low-budgets didn't show," Dahl says of her eighteenth-century costumes. "Edith would pick materials that were showy and colorful, but maybe the costumes wouldn't have as much French lace on them." Edith designed Dahl's wardrobe when the actress traveled on a press tour to New York and Chicago to promote the 3-D film, accompanied by Lamas. "We made headlines wherever we went," Dahl says. "*Sangaree* was the first film to be shot in 3-D, but unfortunately, *House of Wax* (1953) was released before our film. We felt that we were robbed because it was sold as the first 3-D film."

Here Come the Girls (1953) cast Bob Hope as Stanley Snodgrass, an inept chorus boy who is ordered to go on stage in place of the leading man, whose life has been threatened. Dahl played Irene Bailey, Snodgrass' girlfriend, and the film co-starred Rosemary Clooney and Tony Martin. Though the movie contained splashy 1950s musical numbers, the story was set circa 1913. "Edith did costumes as well as she did modern clothes, especially on the Bob Hope film because she had a lot more to spend," Dahl says. "She could use better fabrics that really brought out the textures and colors. There was an emerald green gown that I wore with a big picture hat, with one with a long jeweled hat pin

"THE SLIMMEST WAIST SINCE THE CIVIL WAR!" –Edith Head

which I was going to use on a thief in the film. I said 'well, he'd better not come near me,' and I showed this big pin. Edith thought of all the details to the character, to the scene, down to the last thing.

"I interviewed Edith three or four times for my column, so we became friendly. We weren't only business acquaintances, I got to know her socially. I went to her house several times for cocktails. She would have some of her favorite people over that she'd worked with, and mix with some of her other friends. She was a very good hostess. I think that's the only time I saw her wear color. She wore a hostess skirt that would match a fabric on her pillows. She was very coordinated that way. It was the same with the house. The house was a character too."

When Arlene made *Slightly Scarlet* (1956) at another studio, she was the first actress to get a designer credit for the sleepwear used in the film, that she designed and manufactured. "I talked about design with Edith, and she inspired me to go into the field," says Dahl. "I adapted one of her designs from *Caribbean*. I had it made up by my dressmaker and then it was copied by my manufacturer in Puerto Rico and put on sale. The first designs I did were covered by *Life* magazine. A store on Fifth Avenue had my designs in the window, and I remember Edith wrote me a note when she went to New York and saw them. The note said, 'well, I fully expect you to be a rival any day now.' I told her she was my inspiration to continue my designs."

Far left: **Edith designed Audrey Hepburn's dress for her Oscar win for *Roman Holiday.*** Left: **The formal ball gown for *Roman Holiday.*** This page: **Hepburn and Gregory Peck in a scene from the film.**

EDITH WAS QUITE TAKEN WITH HEPBURN AND RECOGNIZED INSTANTLY THAT HEPBURN HAD A FIGURE THAT WOULD WEAR CLOTHES MORE LIKE A FASHION MODEL THAN THE ACTRESSES EDITH WAS USED TO WORKING WITH IN HOLLYWOOD.

ENTER MISS HEPBURN

Roman Holiday (1953) was originally conceived in the 1940s as a vehicle for Elizabeth Taylor and Cary Grant, to be directed by Frank Capra. When budget restrictions kept the film from being produced, Capra sold the script to Paramount when his production company met with financial difficulties. The studio turned the script over to William Wyler, who was unable to get RKO to lend Jean Simmons for the role. Needing to save on budget to compensate for the expensive Rome location shoot, Wyler finally settled on an unknown Belgian actress named Audrey Hepburn. Hepburn had screen-tested for the role in London, and won the part when the cinematographer left the camera running after her audition, allowing her charm to come through in the unguarded moments that he captured. Audrey was cast in the role of Princess Ann, who escapes her royal restraints to walk among the normal folk in the streets of Rome, and meets reporter Joe Bradley (Gregory Peck).

In April 1952, Hepburn was appearing on Broadway in *Gigi*, and Edith and Wyler traveled to New York to meet her and to test wardrobe. Audrey accompanied Edith to Lilly Daché to select hats that would be right for the test. Among others, they chose a simple black sailor hat in Milan straw, a soft white horsehair hat with white chiffon draped around the crown and a gray bonnet made of a new material called "Plastic-Sheer."

Edith was quite taken with Hepburn and recognized instantly that Hepburn had a figure that would wear clothes more like a fashion model than the actresses Edith was used to working with in Hollywood. But Edith felt there were some figure problems. Hepburn had suffered from malnutrition during World War II and had prominent collarbones and not much of a bust. Alternately, her legs were more developed from her training as a ballet dancer. Edith used a diamond necklace to hide Hepburn's collarbones and also created dresses with full skirts to camouflage her legs.

Edith brought two gowns for the test. One was a black velvet gown, which was seen briefly in the final film. The other gown was a long torso brocade ball gown with wide off-shoulder collar, and a smooth hipline that rose into a low-cut "V" at front over a softly gathered skirt. Edith had added Jewels to the dress to help pick up the pattern, and with a sash and full royal regalia, the dress became the centerpiece of the film. Some of Audrey's original screen test was later included in a theatrical trailer for the film, along with the wardrobe test footage that Edith oversaw.

The first time we see Audrey in the brocade gown in the film, she looks beautiful, but we understand from her manner and from the design that this is a woman who feels restricted. The Embassy Ball was filmed inside the famous Palazzo Brancaccio, the first time a movie studio had been permitted to film inside the eighteenth-century palace. William Wyler contacted Princess Virginia Ruspoli, the Queen of Italian society, and suggested that she and her friends appear as nobility in the scene. They wore their own clothes and jewelry, and donated their pay to charity.

When Princess Ann makes her escape in the film, Edith put

(left to right): Cynthia Bell, Rhonda Fleming and Theresa Brewer in *Those Redheads from Seattle.*

Edith and actress Jane Wyman confer over sketches for the film *Here Comes the Groom.*

Audrey in ill-fitting clothes because she thought it was essential to the story that Ann not stand out on the streets of Rome. Edith thought Hepburn's arms were too thin, so she dressed Audrey in a plain blouse with the sleeves rolled up, and a gathered cotton skirt and flat shoes. The light costume proved to be a bit of a relief for Audrey, as the summer was particularly hot in Rome, with the temperatures reaching the high 90s. For the press interview at the end of the film, Edith put Audrey in a short lace coat dress, wrapped to one side, with full sleeves and a wide-standing collar. Edith chose a hat that was a close-fitting swirl of antique silk, to show off the Italian haircut that comes earlier in the film. Paramount presented Audrey with her entire wardrobe from the film, including hats, shoes, handbags, and jewelry as an engagement gift for her impending wedding to James Hanson. However, Hepburn ended the engagement before the marriage took place.

Initially, Gregory Peck was hesitant to take on the role of Joe because it was obviously secondary to Ann. Before shooting began, the studio offered him billing above the title, with Hepburn's name going below. But after the film wrapped, it was Peck who realized most that it was going to be Hepburn's performance that would make the film a success, and that she would most likely win an Oscar. He convinced the studio to put her name above the title, alongside his.

The film catapulted Audrey Hepburn to stardom. Instantly, everyone wanted to know about the young, stylish star. Edith talked her up in the press, saying she had a "lovely, audible face, an expressive body—and the slimmest waist since the Civil War—nineteen and a half -inches. You could get a dog collar around it!" Hepburn returned the favor, telling Patty Calvin of *The Washington D.C. Times Herald*, "I'm too long for a nine and too slim for a twelve, so eleven is my regular size, but nothing in ready-made fits me, unless I belt it in. This usually gives the dress a bad line. Edith Head solved my problems with what she calls the "dropped waistline." The dresses she designed for *Roman Holiday* all have fitted bodices which are longer in back due to an inset band."

Edith designed a gown of bouffant blue silk tulle, which Hepburn wore to the film's premiere in Los Angeles. When Hepburn won the Best Actress Oscar for the film, she accepted the award in New York wearing an ivory-colored French lace gown that Edith had created for her. That same night Edith was in Los Angeles at the RKO Pantages Theater for the bi-coastal ceremony, nominated for black-and-white costume design for *Roman Holiday*. Edith won the award over Helen Rose and Herschel McCoy for *Dream Wife* (1953), Jean Louis for *From Here to Eternity* (1953), Walter Plunkett for *The Actress* (1953), and Charles LeMaire and Renie Conley for *The President' s Lady* (1953). *Roman Holiday* also won Best Screenplay for the film's credited writer Ian McLellan Hunter, who had fronted for the real writer Dalton Trumbo. Trumbo had been blacklisted as one of the Hollywood Ten, and could not receive screen credit. In 1993, the Academy presented Trumbo's widow with an Oscar for his screenplay.

MIXING IT UP

In late 1953, designer Sheila O'Brien and a group of studio costume designers formed a union to ensure proper working conditions and fair wages for designers. Edith had resisted the idea at first, but when it was inevitable that a union was going to happen, she went along with the idea. Serving as the first President was Leah Rhodes, head of the costume department at Universal. Other members included Michael Woulfe of RKO, Milo Anderson of Warner Brothers, and Edith from Paramount. Edith would sit on the board at interval periods during the remainder of her life.

When people wonder how Edith Head accomplished as much as she did in her career, the truth was that she had help. Just as Edith had come up with ideas in sketches for Howard Greer, she relied on a team of sketch artists for their input and creativity in her design process. The various levels of contribution can never be fully documented. Ideas could change as the costume went through the approval process, and

Top right: **A sketch from Edith's studio of a dress lent by Hubert de Givenchy for Audrey Hepburn in *Sabrina*.** Above: **Edith's design for a coat for Hepburn in *Sabrina*.** Opposite: **A later sketch done by Richard Hopper in Edith's studio, of a design that was originally Givenchy's concept for *Sabrina*.**

Audrey Hepburn in *Sabrina*. Hepburn is wearing a gown by Hubert de Givenchy, which was credited to Edith in the film.

could still change more as it was built in the workroom. In the 1940s, sketch artists like Rudi Gernreich and Waldo Angelo were two of the creative forces on whom she would rely when her creative well was dry.

"Edith was criticized by other designers for copying things rather than coming up with ideas of her own" says David Chierichetti. "She had a lot of ideas of her own, but because of the volume of work that she had, she relied a lot on her sketch artists. She would say to her sketch artists 'give me some collars for a woman's blouse.' And the sketch artist would make up a whole bunch of sketches and Edith would look at them and maybe find one or two that were interesting and incorporate them into the next sketch that was done for the whole outfit. Some designers like Walter Plunkett would not work this way. Plunkett wouldn't let his sketch artists give him any input at all. He could do beautiful sketches himself. But just because he was too busy, he had to delegate the work to a sketch artist. But he would not allow them to give him any ideas."

In the early 1950s, Pat Barto moved from being a sketch artist to being Edith's full-time assistant. "Pat Barto was the shadow Edith Head," says Shirley MacLaine. "Pat was the person who would make it happen, or not make it happen. She was the one who was stashed in the back in a little cubicle. I don't know how Edith could have done it all without Pat. Pat was an excellent designer. I would go after I finished my talks with Edith and I'd go in the back and see what Pat was doing. And it was Pat's dress that would show up in the design that Edith thought I should wear." Grace Sprague was brought on as a sketch artist in 1954. Because of her quick sketching style, she could come up with dozens of variations for just one dress. In the 1960s, Edith employed Bob Mackie and Richard Hopper as sketch artists, also relying on their input into the design process. Hopper worked for Edith up until her death.

By most accounts, Edith was a fair boss. Of course, things didn't always run smoothly. Often people were asked to work all through the night to have clothes ready for a shoot in the morning. "Nothing's fair in a studio," says David Chierichetti. "Everybody puts up with a lot of stuff. That's why they had the union and all those union rules. Frank Richardson's sister-in-law worked with Edith in the late 1930s and she thought Edith was really nice. There was an article published about Edith in *Vanity Fair* in 1998 that was very negative and she told me 'that wasn't the Edith I knew. She was very nice to us, as much as she could be with having no time and having a million things on her mind.' "

Just after Audrey Hepburn completed *Roman Holiday*, Billy Wilder cast her in *Sabrina* (1954), based on the play *Sabrina Fair* by Samuel Taylor. Hepburn played Sabrina, a chauffer's daughter, who causes an uproar in the wealthy household of her father's employer when his two sons, played by Humphrey Bogart and William Holden, fall for her. In the film, Sabrina must transform from a young duckling into a beautiful swan after a trip to Paris.

As Audrey Hepburn's tour for *Gigi* wrapped up in San Francisco, Edith traveled to the city to consult with her about her costumes for *Sabrina*. Knowing how much fashion meant to Audrey, Edith had sheets of drawings of Audrey's figure made up, on which they could collaborate drawing the dresses. After Edith returned to Los Angeles, Billy Wilder told Edith that Audrey had asked if she could wear a real Paris dress in the film. Edith was shocked, but after all, there had been Paris fashions blended into films since the days of Travis Banton. Edith approved the idea, but not without some reluctance, as the film would give her some great opportunities for designs for the young star.

Billy Wilder's wife sent Audrey to Cristobal Balenciaga in Paris for the dress, but Balenciaga was too busy to see her. He sent Hepburn to his friend Hubert de Givenchy, who was then a fledgling designer in the city. "When the door of my studio opened," Givenchy said, "there stood a young woman, very slim, very tall, with doe eyes and short hair and wearing a pair of narrow pants, a little t-shirt, slippers and a gondolier's hat with red ribbon that read 'Venezia.' I told her, 'Mademoiselle, I would love to help you, but I have very few sewers, I am in the middle

of doing a collection, I can't make you clothes.' So she said, 'Show me what you have already made for the collection.' She tried on the dresses. 'It's exactly what I need!' And they fit her too. Later I tried to adapt my designs to her desires. She wanted a bare-shouldered evening dress modified to hide the hollows behind her collarbone. What I invented for her eventually became a style so popular that I named it 'décolleté Sabrina.'"

Hepburn borrowed enough clothes from Givenchy for the entire post-Paris wardrobe. All that was left for Edith to design were the unglamorous outfits that Sabrina would wear early in the film. Edith's department also was to create a dress from a sketch by Givenchy, a black cocktail dress with small bows on the shoulder and a boat neckline. They also had to manufacture duplicates that would be needed in case a dress was soiled during production. Confusion about the designs in the film began as sketches were done in the wardrobe department to execute all the clothing needed. Edith began sending the sketches out to publicize the film, leading to the assumption that all the clothes were her designs.

Since no contract existed between Paramount and Givenchy, there was no legal obligation for the studio to credit his designs. However, Paramount did have a contract with Edith that did require she receive credit on any films on which she worked, including films in which she may have only supervised clothing pulled from stock. It had never occurred to Hepburn or Givenchy to secure a screen credit for him, and both were flummoxed when Edith's singular credit appeared on the film. Once again, Edith's detractors were fueled by the notion that she was taking credit for designs that weren't hers, and indeed she was. It is impossible to say how much of this may have been influenced by sheer studio politics and her desire to maintain her position. But more than likely, Edith saw the brilliance in Givenchy's designs, and could not bear the idea that when people praised the clothes in the film, she would only be able to take credit for the lesser designs. When Edith won another Oscar for *Sabrina*, many found it hard to for-

Wardrobe department stills of Shirley Booth in *About Mrs. Leslie*. In a rare instance at that time, Edith actually shopped for some of the clothes, carefully considering the character's budget for clothing

give her not acknowledging or thanking Givenchy from the podium during her acceptance speech.

Clothing manufacturers reproduced the black cocktail dress by the thousands that year. It became known as The Sabrina dress, and the boat neckline became known as The Sabrina neckline. Over the years, Edith had her sketch artists make up dozens of sketches of that dress and other Givenchy designs for books and appearances, and signed them with her name. She also marched the original black cocktail dress down the runways of her fashion shows. Only after Edith's death did Givenchy confirm that the black cocktail dress was his original design, and had been made under Edith's supervision at Paramount. It is unfortunate that her omission in properly crediting Givenchy has tarnished her legacy and that she never fully corrected the record, even years later.

THE ROSTER OF TALENT GROWS

About Mrs. Leslie (1954) was based on the novel by Vina Delmar, about a woman who goes from being a singer in a cheap nightclub to the stylish girlfriend of a government executive. Shirley Booth was cast as Mrs. Leslie, and asked Edith to give her wardrobe the same realism that she had in *Come Back, Little Sheba* (1952). Edith estimated that she couldn't have spent more than $15.98 on the simple clothes for Sheba, but in this film, Booth would need thirty-three ensembles costing $17,0000 including suits, evening gowns and negligees. "Both Shirley and I agreed not to cheat or try to make her a hot glamour doll in the picture," Edith said. "She wanted to be true and real in her character. So we deliberately underplayed things and whenever possible, we actually bought her clothes in the stores in the price ranges that matched Mrs. Leslie's circumstances in the picture."

Paramount tried to recreate the success of *All About Eve*, by dusting off a forty-year-old play by Sir James Barrie called *Rosalind*. Screenwriters Philip and Julius Epstein added a comedic twist, and the project became *Forever Female* (1954). Ginger Rogers was cast as

FORM 750—G-46

PROD. No. 10205 DIRECTOR Daniel Mann ASSISTANT Dick McWhorter

ARTIST Shirley Booth CHARACTER Vivian Leslie

No.	DESCRIPTION		ACCESSORIES
	#16 Tan + wht ch wool skirt		HAT
	Tan cable knit sweater		BAG
	Wht Blouse - silk - high roll collar		GLOVES
		sht sleeves	JEWELRY
	Above in cab		HOSE
		(out)	FURS
	Int Florida patio - Sc		
	#17 Red plaid cotton shirt		
	Blue Jeans		
	Ext Sea - Sc 101 (Falls in)		
	#17 A Blue linen skirt - self belt		HAT
	Blue striped Blouse		BAG
			GLOVES
	Wht Blouse (silk)		JEWELRY
	Bl linen Skt		HOSE
	Tennis shoes		FURS
			SHOES
	Tennis Sc 102		TIES
			SCARFS
			SHIRTS
			SUITS

"I WAS VERY INTIMIDATED, BUT NEVER BY HER. SHE WAS TOTALLY PROFESSIONAL IN THAT YOU WERE THERE TO GET A JOB DONE, BUT THERE WAS STILL A FEELING THAT SHE WAS IN YOUR CORNER."

–Pat Crowley

Opposite: **A wardrobe department continuity log for Shirley Booth in *About Mrs. Leslie.***
Right: **Grace Kelly in *The Bridges of Toko-Ri.***

Beatrice Page, an actress vying for an ingénue role against younger actress Sally Carver (Pat Crowley).

Edith decided to create about seventy-five-percent of Rogers' wardrobe in wool because she felt the clothes would hold their shape for a tailored, crisp look that an actress of Beatrice's stature required. Ginger's wool wardrobe included a salt-and-pepper Donegal tweed suit with slim skirt topped by a sleeveless jacket, lined in a black wool jersey, worn with a sweater of black wool jersey with a shallow rollover collar; a coat of black-and-white Harlequin tweed with a crushed collar and a companion suit is of charcoal gray flannel bound in charcoal grosgrain ribbon; a wool trouser skirt made of flannel in a milk-chocolate color and blouse and cardigan in white flannel with cocoa used in edges and lining. For a formal dress, Edith chose red slipper satin with a rolled collar that plunged deeply at the sides of the bust and a full-skirt with a gently puffed harem-type hemline.

As this was her first film for the studio, Pat Crowley got the Paramount publicity treatment. She was photographed with a million-dollar wardrobe that had been designed for her including gowns and jewelry, in which she would make a string of personal appearances all over the country to promote the film. In the photo, she wore one of Edith's dresses and the photos were published alongside photos of her in blue jeans with a quote, suspiciously sounding like it could have been written by a man: "I don't think any girl can look attractive in blue jeans or sloppy shirts or sweaters. I think this type of clothes makes girls look like slobs. And that's not good for romance or morale."

Crowley has fond memories of working with Edith, and of the watchful eye that the designer kept on her. "She was wonderful to me,"

A wardrobe continuity log for actress Freida Inescort in *Casanova's Big Night.*

Crowley says. "Of course, I knew who she was from childhood. That was a name that everybody knew connected to costuming in Hollywood. And then to meet her, and then to have her doing sketches, which just made the character come alive for me, was just unbelievable. I was a kid. I was green behind the ears. I'd done a lot of stuff in New York on Broadway and live television, but this was completely different. She knew this was a big thing that I wasn't really taught to handle, and thank God, that I ran into people like her. I was very intimidated, but never by her. She was totally professional in that you were there to get a job done, but there was still a feeling that she was in your corner."

Vivien Leigh was in England during pre-production of *Elephant Walk* (1954). She had been cast as Ruth Wiley, a British beauty who is romanced by a tea plantation owner (Peter Finch) and brought to a doomed plantation house in Ceylon. Edith made fifty sketches for the thirty-two changes of wardrobe and sent them to England for Vivien to approve. The clothes that Vivien was to wear for the location shooting in Ceylon were made in England. The remaining wardrobe (about half) was made in Hollywood and was to be ready when the company came to the Paramount Studio to film the interiors.

Vivien, who had been having an affair with Finch, arrived in Hollywood at the end of February, 1953, and suffered a nervous breakdown. Producer Irving Asher had already spent $1,000,000 on the production, including the location trip to Ceylon where 10,000 feet of film had been shot. The plantation set at the studio was already constructed at a cost of $125,000. An offer was made to Elizabeth Taylor to replace Leigh. Taylor had been Asher's first choice for the role, but the actress had declined because she was pregnant when filming began.

Elizabeth accepted the role on March 15th and spent the entire weekend at Paramount having the dresses refitted. Edith had to alter twenty costumes and build six from scratch. Both Vivien Leigh and Elizabeth Taylor were size ten, but different in strategic points. "It's not as hard as it may seem. It's mostly a matter of taking a little material out of the waists and adding it to the bosoms," Edith said of making the changes.

Filming resumed at Paramount on March 23rd. Taylor hadn't read the full script, since it was still being written during production. On replacing Vivien Leigh, Elizabeth said "I'm just not worrying about it. I haven't seen the film she made and I don't plan to play the same part. I can't." Only ten-percent of the shoot in Ceylon had to be scrapped, and Vivien Leigh is still visible in the long shots done on location in the final cut of the film.

The incredible wardrobe worn by the character of Ruth throughout the film is explained in the script by a reference that the newlywed couple stopped off in Paris to buy a trousseau on the way back to Ceylon. The standout design was a gown of draped white chiffon with a gold corselet, which was very similar to a gown Edith had designed for Patricia Morison in *The Magnificent Fraud.* Edith also incorporated Indian design in a dress of silk linen with a molded halter neckline with a full skirt that resembled an East Indian sari, that was accessorized with a narrow belt embroidered with gold and pink pearls and a pink East Indian sari stole.

THE MAGIC OF THE MUSICAL

Television was beginning to present itself as a real threat to movie-going as it had been known, as more people began staying at home for their entertainment. Instead of producing entertainment for the new medium, Paramount chose to fight it with huge spectacles in a big screen processes they called VistaVision.

White Christmas (1954) offered Edith the unusual opportunity to supervise the men's costumes of a film, as much as she did for the women. Generally, men's costumes were either pulled from stock or purchased at men's clothing stores by the actors themselves, and reimbursed by the studio. Most of the designs for the men in movies for which Edith was credited were not done by her. They were done by a

FORM 750—8-46

PROD. No. 11503 | DIRECTOR Norman McCleod | ASSISTANT Mickey Moore

ARTIST Fredia Inescourt | CHARACTER Signora Castelbello Digambetta

No.	DESCRIPTION
	#1 Dress
	Tan Brocade
	wht pett and side h[illegible]
	Tan pett Taffeta
	Int Elena Rm.
	Sc 39
	Int Digambetta Hall
	#2 Dress
	Blk Vel
	wht pett - side hoop
	elaborate jewelry -
	E[illegible] s G[illegible]
	72
	#3 Wedding Party
	Int Ballroom
	Sc 150 thru 162

Clothing designed for Vivien Leigh, the original star of *Elephant Walk*, had to be re-worked when Elizabeth Taylor (pictured) took over her role.

"MEN ARE TEN TIMES EASIER
TO WORK WITH.
THEY HAVE NO TEMPERAMENT ABOUT IT."

–Edith Head

Opposite page: **Rosemary Clooney and Bing Crosby on the set of *White Christmas.***

Above left: **Edith confers with Danny Kaye and director Michael Curtiz on *White Christmas.***

Above right: **Rosemary Clooney and Vera-Ellen perform the song *Sisters.***

left?
no jacket

This page and opposite page: **Grace Sprague's sketches for three designs for Rosemary Clooney in *White Christmas.***

series of designers employed in the men's wardrobe department over time including Gile Steele, Valles, and Yvonne Wood.

Even though women's costumes gave her more opportunity for creativity, Edith liked working with men more than with women. "It's easier to do men, but not as creative—unless you're doing Casanova," Edith told an interviewer. "Men are ten times easier to work with. They have no temperament about it. With women there's a basic female instinct of caring deeply about the way they look; women stars have a narcissist complex."

Though she may not have had a hand in the original sketching or construction of the costumes, director Michael Curtiz had some very specific requests for Edith to oversee in the design of the costumes. Bing Crosby and Danny Kaye played famous song-and-dance men Bob Wallace and Phil Davis, respectively. For Kaye's dance numbers, Curtiz asked Edith to keep the color extension of Kaye's costumes going all the way down to his feet. For the number *The Best Things Happen While You' re Dancing*, Kaye is in a gray suit, gray socks and gray shoes dancing on a bridge with Vera-Ellen in a pink chiffon dress with a full skirt. In another number, Kaye wears a Dubonnet jacket worn over gray pants, with a Dubonnet tie and gray shoes, topped with a Dubonnet band around his straw hat.

One of the most memorable scenes has Crosby and Kaye, pant legs rolled up, appropriating the bright blue fans, sashes and hair ornaments worn by Vera-Ellen and Rosemary Clooney to sing the song *Sisters. White Christmas* was the first film made in VistaVision and was also shot in Technicolor. "Technicolor gives us an entirely new field which can be applied to men's clothes," Edith said. "Fabrics become so much more important."

This page and opposite page: **A costume sketch and wardrobe department log for Rosemary Clooney's costumes in *Red Garters*.**

FORM 750—G-46

PROD. No. 11499 DIRECTOR M. Leisen ASSISTANT J. Coonan

ARTIST Rosemary Cloon CHARACTER Calaveras Kate

No.	DESCRIPTION		ACCESSORIES
#4			HAT
			BAG
			GLOVES
			JEWELRY
			HOSE
			FURS
			SHOES
			TIES
sc. 93	Int. Dressing Room. Kate comes from behind scene fully dressed.		SCARFS
			SHIRTS
			SUITS
#5			HAT
			BAG
			GLOVES
			JEWELRY
			HOSE
			FURS
			SHOES
			TIES
			SCARFS
sc. 105 thru 111	Ext. Temperance House & Street. Rocking on Porch - Hear of July 11th celebration that afternoon - Bob & Rafael return from quest of killer.		SHIRTS
			SUITS
#5			HAT
sc 112 thru 132A	July 11th celebration - Rafael and Shelia do Vaquero - Kate stops duel.	That afternoon	BAG
			GLOVES
			JEWELRY
			HOSE
sc.			FURS
			SHOES
			TIES
			SCARFS
			SHIRTS
			SUITS

Because her costumes covered Vera-Ellen's neck throughout the film, including her sleepwear, rumors persisted through the years that the pencil thin Vera-Ellen's neck had been damaged by anorexia. This was not true, but most likely Edith did this to not draw attention to the actress' collar bones.

Red Garters (1954) was a stylized musical Western, originally to be directed by Mitchell Leisen as a vehicle to showcase Rosemary Clooney. The creative intent was that the project would be filmed like a stage show, with color used for emotional effects. No scenic backdrops were used, only suggested outlines of sets and solid-color backgrounds. Art directors Roland Anderson and Hal Pereira based their sets on a photograph in *Life* magazine that showed the cast of the film *Yellow Sky* (1948) standing in front of the false front sets of the film.

Before filming began Paramount replaced Leisen with director George Marshall. Though Leisen and Edith had their differences over the years, it was Leisen who had a vision for much of the project. David Chierichetti learned that even though the studio told her not to, Edith would still sneak her sketches over to Leisen for his input after he was off the project. The costumes were a creation of fancy, done mostly in pinks, reds and blues, often employing swirling stripes and plaids that resembled candy confections. Everything about the film had a fanciful, surreal quality. Yvonne Wood, who did the men's costumes, dressed Guy Mitchell in skin-hugging beige glove leather.

The film's plot centered around Reb Randall (Mitchell), who rides into town seeking to avenge his brother's death. "I was a last minute replacement and probably didn't have the amount of time that I would have, had I been cast sooner," says Pat Crowley, who played Susan Martinez De La Cruz. "But it all worked out, and the clothes are darling in that. It was a very stylized experimental film poking fun at Westerns." To create the unusual lines of some of women's clothing, Crowley remembers that Edith's attention to detail was essential. "Everything would fit you like a glove," she says. "Little pins would come out and they'd go back in. And that's when I learned that we all had one leg that's shorter than the other, and the same with the arms. They measured, and measured and measured. And Edith cared about everything. She concentrated on whatever was going on there."

The film was originally released in 3-D to help give the audience the sense that they were watching a live stage production. "We will have to design costumes more carefully for 3-D," Edith said at the time of the film's release. "Something that looks all right in a 'flat' picture can look pretty frightening when it comes and sits in your lap." The film's box office receipts were disappointing however, given the enormous success of another musical set in the West, *Seven Brides for Seven Brothers* (1954), released by rival studio MGM.

A TOUCH OF GRACE

Filming began on *The Bridges at Toko-Ri* (1954) in January of 1954. Grace Kelly played the role of Nancy Brubaker, visiting her husband, Lt. Harry Brubaker (William Holden), while he is on leave before he begins a dangerous mission during the Korean War. Kelly was becoming as well-known for her fashion sense as Audrey Hepburn. Whatever disappointment Edith had experienced with Hepburn was more than made up for in the joy she had working with Grace Kelly. Grace's role was a small but pivotal one, with the real stars of the film being Holden and the climactic tense bombing sequence. Edith dressed Grace appropriately for her role as a middle-class American wife, but Edith must have hoped for a more fashionable collaboration in the future with the young star.

Grace was under contract to MGM, and the studio couldn't quite figure out what to do with their patrician leading lady. Grace fought hard to be loaned out again to Paramount for *The Country Girl* (1954) when Jennifer Jones bowed out of the production. Based on the play by Clifford Odets, the film didn't allow for a lot of great design opportunities, but it was a great critical success. Grace played Georgie Elgin, a woman who feels crushed under the burden of caring for her alcoholic husband (Bing

Edith looks over some hats in the workroom at Paramount in 1955

Seaton
George Seaton

Opposite: **Wardobe department test photos for the dowdy clothes worn by Grace Kelly in *The Country Girl.*** Right: **The black dress worn by Kelly at the end of the film.**

Crosby) after their son is killed. Grace was more concerned than Edith that the dowdy wardrobe did not show her off well, but Edith was able to convince Grace that the clothes were right for the character. "No one has looked at me as a woman for years and years," Georgie tells Bernie Dodd (William Holden) in the film and Edith dressed Grace for the part in plain brown wool clothes, cardigan sweaters and low-heeled Capezio shoes.

A flashback scene allowed the audience to see the lovely young woman that Georgie had been. And by the end of the film, for the opening night party scene, Edith put Grace in a black dress with a low "V" neckline and a jeweled accent at the waist and a single strand of pearls around her neck. It was just a hint of the stylish collaborations that were to come between designer and actress.

Edith designed an ice blue satin gown and matching coat for Grace to wear to the premiere of *The Country Girl*, and Grace chose to wear the same ensemble to the Oscars when she was nominated for the film. Kelly won the award against heavyweight contender Judy Garland in *A Star is Born* (1954) and in the following week she was photographed by Phillipe Halsman for the cover of *Life* in the gown Edith had designed.

Women began emulating the classic style of Kelly's clothes: her understated gowns, pillbox hats, tweed suits and the white gloves with which she became synonymous. The French haute couture house Hermes created a handbag known as The Kelly Bag, similar in style to a handbag with which Grace was often photographed.

Grace and Edith were working together so much that they struck up a close friendship. During lunch hour, Grace would often visit Edith in her salon and discuss the interests they shared in all things cultural. The relationship grew even closer when Alfred Hitchcock chose them both to work on *Rear Window* (1954). Finally Edith was able to design the wardrobe she'd dreamed of for Grace, who was playing Lisa Freemont, a well-to-do New York fashion model, opposite James Stewart as a wheelchair-bound magazine photographer.

While Edith had found Hitchcock somewhat difficult to work with on *Notorious*, their relationship fared much better this time. Edith appreciated that Hitchcock had a very clear idea of how he wanted the clothes to advance the story of the film. Hitchcock's instruction to Edith was that Grace was to look like a piece of Dresden china, nearly untouchable. The script called for Jeff (Stewart) to be wary of Lisa's advances toward him due to his insecurity about the differences in their lifestyles.

In what may be one of the most famous close-ups in film history, we are introduced to Lisa in the film in a scene where the dozing Stewart awakes to a full close-up of Lisa coming toward him for a kiss.

This page and opposite: **The famous eau de nil suit worn by Grace Kelly in *Rear Window*.**

pearl top – sk. tone
pearl top
ok?
add fabric

Edith's wardrobe for Grace Kelly in *Rear Window* highlighted the differences in lifestyles between the character of Lisa and that of photojournalist L.B. Jeffries, played by Jimmy Stewart

EDITH TOLD GRACE, "MR. HITCHCOCK IS WORRIED BECAUSE THERE'S A FALSE PLEAT HERE. HE WANTS ME TO PUT IN FALSIES."

Edith made sure that the neckline was kept very simple so that Grace's face was framed by it for the close-up. When the camera pulled back, Hitchcock wanted the audience to know immediately that Lisa was a woman who came from wealth. A dress "fresh from the Paris plane" was how Lisa described her dress, with a fitted black bodice and a deep off-the-shoulder "V" neckline atop a full skirt to mid-calf, gathered and layered in chiffon tulle, with a spray bunch pattern on the hip. Grace wore the dress with a narrow black patent leather belt, white chiffon shoulder wrap, white elbow-length silk gloves, and a single strand of pearls.

When Lisa arrives to spend the night at Jeff's apartment, she is wearing an eau de nil midi-length jacket with stand-up collar, with rounded shoulders in a nod to the designs of Cristobal Balenciaga. Underneath she wears a white silk halterneck, gathered at the waist with a wrapover front that sits atop an eau de nil pencil skirt. Edith accessorized the ensemble with a white pillbox hat with half veil, a single strand of pearls, stud earrings with glass cameo, and a gold and silver pearl bracelet with lockets.

Inside her Mark Cross overnight case, Lisa produces a nightgown which she calls "a preview of coming attractions." When Grace put the sheer nightgown on, Hitchcock took Edith aside and told her that he felt that the bust area needed some padding. Edith told Grace, "Mr. Hitchcock is worried because there's a false pleat here. He wants me to put in falsies." Grace didn't want to wear them, and felt that they would show through the material. Edith's solution was to make some quick adjustments to the pleat, and Grace went back out on set, standing as straight as she possibly could. Edith looked at Hitchcock and, not letting on that the pads had not been added, said, "see what a difference they make?"

"Edith was more liberal in her designs in the 1930s," says David Chierichetti. "As time went by, she became more conservative. In the 1950s and 1960s, she just didn't use prints, which was a big limitation. She was worried with prints that the picture would be delayed and they would look funny. In *Rear Window* there is a print at the end of the picture because it serves a certain dramatic purpose. Grace Kelly is trying to sneak into Raymond Burr's apartment and she wears a print dress. It's a fluffy dress with lots of petticoats underneath it, and she has high heels on. All of this make her more vulnerable, more feminine, and it makes her going into the apartment more foolhearty."

At the end of the film, Hitchcock wanted Lisa in a casual outfit to show Lisa is trying to prove to Jeff that she is the sporty type. Edith dressed Grace in slim indigo denim jeans and a pink casual men's shirt with button-down collar and pushed up sleeves, and accessorized the outfit with a scarf ring that forms the shirt tails into a side sash, and dark brown loafers.

Lisa Freemont's wealth was nothing compared to the wealth of Francie Stevens, the character Grace would play in *To Catch a Thief* (1955). The film was the next collaboration between Grace and Hitchcock, for

GRACE WENT BACK OUT ON SET, STANDING AS STRAIGHT AS SHE POSSIBLY COULD. EDITH LOOKED AT HITCHCOCK AND, NOT LETTING ON THAT THE PADS HAD NOT BEEN ADDED, SAID "SEE WHAT A DIFFERENCE THEY MAKE?"

Edith and Grace Kelly work on fabric selection during the making of *To Catch a Thief*.

Opposite: Grace Kelly and Cary Grant in *To Catch a Thief.* Right: Grace in the layered blue chiffon gown in *To Catch a Thief,* flanked by Jessie Royce Landis and John Williams.

which Edith would design the clothes. Cary Grant played opposite Kelly as John Robie, a reformed cat burglar who is being accused in a new string of robberies. Hitchcock stressed to Edith that since the film was set in France, the fashion capital of the world, and the plot involved jewel robberies among the very wealthy, high style was of the utmost importance.

Grace had become Edith's perfect muse. She was an actress who was interested in clothes, but who relied on Edith's judgment. She also had no figure problems that Edith would need to cover, and she had a beautiful face that could be filmed from any angle. On this production, Hitchcock gave Grace more reign with clothing than he usually gave to his actresses. This allowed Edith more latitude to work out the costumes first with Kelly and then to bring the ideas to Hitchcock. When making a Hitchcock film, the director always requested that Edith be on set as much as possible. Since *To Catch a Thief* was to be made partly on the French Riviera, Edith traveled with the crew to France in June of 1954.

When Robie first meets Francie and her mother Jessie (Jessie Royce Landis), Francie is in a gown of draped blue chiffon in various shades. Hitchcock wanted Edith to use cool colors to play up the idea of Francie as an ice princess. Jessie comments that when she sent Francie to finishing school, she thinks "they finished her." A strapless gown of white chiffon was chosen to show off a diamond necklace that Francie wears in a scene in her hotel room. To underscore Francie's flair for the dramatic, Edith created a lounging outfit of black Capri pants with a white overskirt and an oversized round white hat. For the picnic when Grace uttered her famous line "do you want a leg or a breast?" Grace asked Edith to put her in a dress because she was "making a play" for Robie. Edith chose a feminine pink dress with a pattern of swirls of white, accessorized with a pink scarf.

Near the end of the film, a fancy masquerade ball is held at a mansion on the Cote d'Azur, and all of the extras wore costumes in the style of the court of Marie Antoinette. It was the most expensive costume scene Edith had ever done. One of the biggest challenges for Edith was designing dresses for the extras that allowed for the cameramen to shoot close-ups of the glittering necklaces the actresses were wearing. The necklines had to allow a clear view of the jewelry, but if a dress was strapless and the camera shot too tight, the actress could appear as if she were wearing nothing at all. Edith was able to design gowns with simple lines that still gave Hitchcock the elegance he sought to show off the gems. Hitchcock instructed Edith to dress Grace as a "fairy princess" for the ball. Edith created a ball gown with a huge skirt of gold mesh adorned with fabric birds and accessorized with a golden mask, and topped Grace's head with a golden wig.

The almost always diplomatic Edith broke her rules to name Grace Kelly her favorite actress with whom she worked, and *To Catch a*

P4056 – 111

Far left, top: **Grace Kelly and Cary Grant in *To Catch a Thief.*** Far left, bottom: **Hitchcock asked Edith to make Grace look like a "fairy princess" in the fancy ball sequence.** Middle: **A dramatic sun suit for Grace to walk to the beach.** Above: **Grace Sprague's sketch for the gold ball gown.**

WHILE EDITH COULD HOLD BACK TELLING AN ACTRESS OR DIRECTOR WHAT SHE REALLY THOUGHT, SHE HAD NO TROUBLE LETTING LEMAIRE KNOW HER TRUE FEELINGS ABOUT THE LOSS.

Thief her favorite film. So it was a very difficult pill to swallow when Edith was nominated for an Oscar for *Thief*, only to lose that year to Charles LeMaire for *Love is a Many Splendored Thing* (1955). She called the loss the "single greatest disappointment" of her costume design career. She chalked it up to the fact that LeMaire's film was very popular with the movie-going public and spawned an equally popular theme song. But Edith still felt, even many years later, that her ornate gowns for *Thief* were better than the traditional Chinese cheong sams that Lemaire designed for Jennifer Jones. And while Edith could hold back telling an actress or director what she really thought, she had no trouble letting LeMaire know her true feelings about the loss.

ALL ABOUT EDITH

Lucy Gallant (1954) had all the makings of the ultimate women's picture: a New York socialite moves to a desolate Texas town and decides to open a fashion salon, while her love interest (Charlton Heston) strikes it rich in oil. The movie was produced by the B-picture unit of Paramount Pictures known as Pine-Thomas Productions. The unit was operated by William H. Pine and William C. Thomas, who were known as "The Dollar Bills" because they kept their budgets so in line that they never lost money on a film.

Jane Wyman starred as the title character and concurred with the producers' idea to have Edith moderate the film's fashion show that takes place in Lucy's salon. For the first time, Edith had to turn for someone else for advice on what she should wear, and it was Jane Wyman who suggested that she just stick with her traditional suit. But director Robert Parrish wouldn't let Edith appear with her glasses. And worse, once Edith's make-up was on the day of shooting, she couldn't even put her glasses on for off-camera script studying until Jane Wyman fashioned some cotton around the frames to protect Edith's make-up.

Edith had come a long way in battling her shyness. The girl who was once taunted by other children because of her smile, could now stand with assuredness in front of television cameras and radio microphones telling women how they could look more attractive. But in *The Dress Doctor*, Edith said that without her glasses, she was especially anxious and in rehearsal, mumbled her lines as Wyman tried to coach her. This story may have been embellished for good dramatic effect. Those on

Opposite page: **Grace arrives with Edith at the 1955 Academy Award ceremony, wearing the ice blue gown that Edith had designed for her.** This page: **A gown inspired by the flowing oil of Texas for *Lucy Gallant*.**

Below: The fashion show sequence from *Lucy Gallant.* Opposite: A dress designed by Edith for Jane Wyman in *Lucy Gallant.*

the set, including her husband Wiard, did not witness a nervous Edith. Edith's on-screen time was hardly a blip, but the fashion show allowed Edith to delve back into the kinds of fantasy fashion show sequences that were so popular in the late 1930s films, but had been relatively absent from Paramount films, except for a few like *The Stork Club*.

Governor Allan Shivers of Texas also had a cameo in *Lucy Gallant*, and asked Edith if she would copy one of the gowns in the fashion show for his wife Marialice to wear to his inauguration, should he be re-elected. The popular Governor succeeded in winning an unprecedented third term that year. In the film, the gown was a black creation strewn with mother-of-pearl to represent the flowing oil of Texas. Edith recreated the dress in a more appropriate white fabric. Wayman Adams painted Marialice's portrait in the dress and it hung in the Shivers' home for years. Edith got to see the dress and the portrait years later when she visited Texas for a fashion show, and was hosted in the Shivers' home for a cocktail reception.

In March, 1955, NBC dedicated its new studio in Burbank, called NBC Color City. The studio boasted that it was the first TV studio equipped exclusively for color broadcasting. Rosalind Russell was chosen to host the opening night TV special. Even though the studio was all about color, Edith would take no chances that untested colors may appear garish under the television lighting. Edith designed a gown of charcoal chiffon with flat sequins that photographed black, accented by a large black fox muff and a feathered hat—the very essence of a movie star.

June Allyson and James Stewart had played husband and wife twice before they made *Strategic Air Command* (1955). Edith had a little

Left: **A sketch for June Allyson in *Strategic Air Command*.** Opposite page: **Edith celebrates her 1955 Oscar victory for *Sabrina* at the Mocambo nightclub with the costume designer Renie (far left) and the ladies' husbands.**

trouble convincing June to bare her shoulders to wear a white Swiss organdy dress embroidered in cherry red, that Edith had designed for the film. Allyson felt the shape of her neck and shoulders did not lend themselves to a bare top. Edith compromised and made the dress with thin straps and promised Allyson that they would rework the top if she was unhappy with the finished product. Allyson ended up buying the dress for her own personal wardrobe.

If belts were the sticking point for Clara Bow, it would be a slip that would be the hurdle for Anna Magnani in *The Rose Tattoo* (1955). The great Italian actress and her interpreter were brought to Edith's salon by producer Hal Wallis. They began to go over each change as the character goes from a happy, normal woman to a woman lost to life, in mourning for her late husband. The one thing Magnani railed against was the idea of being turned into a Hollywood glamour girl.

When discussions turned to a scene where Magnani wears only a slip, the actress asked that the slip look disheveled and slovenly, with plenty of décolleté. Edith re-worked an old slip, so that the material would appear worn. The seamstresses reconstructed the slip so that it would have little shape, the way it might have been constructed in an old Italian town. Magnani was very pleased with the result. The development of character through costume paid off for Magnani, who won an Oscar for Best Actress that year. Edith was nominated for an Oscar for her designs, but lost to Helen Rose for *I'll Cry Tomorrow* (1955).

The Trouble with Harry (1955) was one of Alfred Hitchcock's best black comedies, and a personal favorite of the director. The plot centered around the corpse of a man that is discovered in the woods of Vermont, and a group of offbeat locals who think they had something to do with his murder.

Hitchcock was experimenting with how audiences would react to a film without a major name star. He cast Edmund Gwenn, John Forsythe and a young dancer and actress named Shirley MacLaine, who producer Hal Wallis had just brought from New York. The film would mark the beginning of one of the most successful collaborations for Edith with an actress since Dorothy Lamour. In addition to experimenting with star power, Hitchcock also decided to experiment with the concept of shopping for a wardrobe for an entire film, as opposed to having all or part of it designed. Though it has become common practice since the 1970's, it was still a radical idea in the 1950's.

Like Pat Crowley, MacLaine was another young girl from New York, who Edith was keeping an eye on, but in a different way. "Hitchcock wanted me to have breakfast with him every morning, and that

“OH, QUIT FUSSING,”
EDITH FINALLY TOLD HIM DURING A FITTING.
“WOMEN GO THROUGH THIS
ALL THE TIME.”

Danny Kaye only sought comfort in his wardrobe for *The Court Jester.* Opposite page: **Angela Lansbury as *Princess Gewndolyn.***

meant I was eating for four!" MacLaine says. "So I gained weight. I had everything. You don't even want to hear what I would have for breakfast. And I put on weight and that upset Edith. It was my first picture after I had lived for years on lemonade and peanut butter sandwiches in the chorus of many Broadway shows. She talked to Don Hartman (later a producer of *The Matchmaker*), and I got a call from Don saying 'you have to lose some weight, you're looking fat.' And I saw the dailies and he was right. Edith was a stickler for that, but we didn't have too much trouble with it because I basically had a dancer's body. After that first foray into 'oh my gosh, I can eat for free,' I didn't do that any more." Hitchcock regarded the film as the most British of his American films, which could explain why even though it was not a commercial success in the United States, it played for a year in England, Italy and France.

Artists and Models (1955) was a vehicle for the comedy team of Dean Martin and Jerry Lewis, who been making films at Paramount since 1949. They also starred in their own enormously popular radio show *The Martin and Lewis Show* which aired from 1949-1953. Dean played the handsome crooning straight man to Lewis' goofy child-like comedy style. The plot of the film had Rick Todd (Dean Martin) as a budding comic book writer, who uses the dreams of his roommate Eugene Fullstack (Lewis) for plots in his stories. Dorothy Malone played Abigail Parker, a comic book illustrator who uses her roommate Bessie Sparrowbush (Shirley MacLaine) as a model for her comic *The Bat Lady*.

Malone had a knock-out figure, MacLaine had the sinewy body and shapely legs of a dancer, and Edith's goal seemed to be finding ways to keep the ladies in the briefest swimsuits and nighties that the censors would allow. For the comical number *Innamorata*, Edith designed a bright yellow figure hugging one-piece swimsuit with a winged collar and white belt, in which MacLaine had to perform almost entirely on a staircase banister. Dance numbers always required more care in their design because they had to allow the dancer to perform the steps that had been laid out by the choreographer prior to the costume consultation. "Dancing was a whole other thing," says MacLaine. "The costume had to be able to move, and it had to be able to split correctly. "It had to not constrict and to have great lines commensurate with the body."

For MacLaine's costume as *The Bat Lady*, two versions were done, one for posing and a sequined version for the finale. Shirley spent long hours being fitted for the costumes, and said to Edith "if I'm going to be playing a bat, I should know something about bats. Am I a mammal or a reptile? And how do I have my babies?" The fitters were perplexed. "That's the first reasonable request made of me today," Edith told her, and phoned the research department to get answers.

"We wore a lot of body make-up on that film, which I hated," MacLaine remembers. "And I used to watch Anita Ekberg and think 'how do you get to look like that?' That was an interesting picture because it was nearly the last picture for Dean and Jerry together and they did not get along. And Dean was the funny one!" Jerry Lewis eventually became a director, working with Edith often. "Jerry was very involved in all the aspects of a film. He was just that kind of a person" says Pat Crowley, who worked with Martin and Lewis on *Hollywood or Bust* (1956). "Dean was more into getting out of there and playing some golf."

Edith had another chance to do men's costumes for Danny Kaye in *The Court Jester* (1955), in which the actor played a carnival performer trying dethrone the evil Sir Ravenhurst (Basil Rathbone). Kaye was never that interested in his costumes, and when he did show up for fittings, he was often anxious for them to be over. Kaye was concerned about his comfort when wearing the suit of armor required for the film. Edith devised a suit made of lightweight aluminum, which wouldn't be too warm or too heavy for Kaye to wear during long takes. "Oh, quit fussing," Edith finally told him during a fitting. "Women go through this all the time."

Edith was frequently on the set during scenes in which costumes were the critical focus

CHAPTER FIVE

EDITH HEAD SUPERSTAR

Edith at the 1960 Academy Awards ceremony with (left to right) Robert Stack, Edward Stevenson and Barbara Rush.

Anne Baxter as Nefretiri in *The Ten Commandments.*

CECIL B. DEMILLE'S *The Ten Commandments* (1956) WAS A REMAKE OF HIS 1923 SILENT VERSION AND BECAME THE LONGEST AND MOST EXPENSIVE FILM IN PARAMOUNT'S HISTORY. CHARLTON HESTON WAS CAST AS MOSES, WHO LEADS THE SLAVES OF EGYPT INTO THE DESERT, WHERE HE RECEIVES THE LAW OF GOD. ANNE BAXTER HAD ORIGINALLY BEEN CONSIDERED FOR THE ROLE OF SEPHORA, BUT DEMILLE MOVED HER INTO THE ROLE OF NEFERTIRI, MOSES' LOVE INTEREST, AFTER DECIDING THAT AUDREY HEPBURN WOULD BE WRONG FOR THE PART. BOTH EDITH AND ANNE FELT THAT BAXTER WAS A LITTLE MISCAST IN THE ROLE OF NEFERTIRI. EDITH'S RESEARCH SHOWED NEFERTIRI HAD HAWK-LIKE, BROODING FEATURES WHICH WERE NOTHING LIKE ANNE'S IRISH FEATURES

Charlton Heston was one of the few stars of *The Ten Commandments* still under contract to Paramount. Many studios were now abandoning the idea of the contract system because of the sweeping changes to the industry caused by the breaking up of the studios' theater chains and the rise of television.

Because, as Edith said, "there were no fashion hints in the bible," she worked with an expert who had done eleven years of research on biblical clothing. Records indicated that the Hebrews of Moses dressed like the more humble of the Egyptians. Some of the cues for the film's costumes were taken from the pre-production drawings made by John L. Jensen and Arnold Friberg. The costume for Moses was patterned after a painting Friberg had done for the magazine *The Children's Friend*, published by the children's organization of The Church of Jesus Christ of the Latter Day Saints. Many of the costumes that appear in The Ten Commandments were originally made for the film *The Egyptian* (1954) and were bought from Darryl F. Zanuck for use in the film. Clint Walker, as an Egyptian royal guard, uses a sword that had been used by the Hitite princes in The Egyptian.

Princess Grace sails off on her honeymoon with Prince Rainier III of Monaco, wearing the gray suit that Edith designed for her.

DEMILLE HAD FOCH GO FAR INTO THE WATER, AND THE DRESS BECAME TOTALLY TRANSPARENT. "HOW SHOULD I KNOW THAT MR. DEMILLE'S IDEA OF WADING IS WHAT I CALL DEEP SEA DIVING?" EDITH ASKED.

Friberg and Jensen had originally been brought to the project as production illustrators, and not to contribute to costume ideas necessarily. But as was typical with a DeMille epic, the costume responsibilities were still broken up among several designers including Edith (who was designing the principal female leads), Dorothy Jeakins, and Ralph Jester.

For Nina Foch, as the Pharaoh's daughter, Edith put the actress in a nude-colored sheath, in which she was to wade into the water and retrieve baby Moses floating in a basket. Edith got a frantic call the day the scene was shot, and rushed down to the set. Normally, Edith would have tested water on the fabric before making the costume, but the script only called for the character to wade. But DeMille had Foch go far into the water, and the dress became totally transparent. "How should I know that Mr. DeMille's idea of wading is what I call deep sea diving?" Edith asked. Until the release of *The Passion of Christ* (2004), *The Ten Commandments* was the highest grossing religious film in history, earning $65.5 million in 1956.

While Grace Kelly had been in France making *To Catch a Thief,* she toured the Royal Palace of Monaco with Prince Rainier as her guide for a magazine layout in *Paris Match*. The Prince had been searching for a wife, and began courting Grace after she came back to the United States. When Grace announced her engagement, Edith assumed that because of their close friendship, she would be asked to design Grace's wedding dress. It wasn't a completely incorrect assumption. Up until that point, Grace's home studio of MGM had lent her to Paramount and Warner Brothers for most of her greatest commercial and critical successes. But with news of an impending royal wedding, MGM was making sure Grace completed the last two films of her contract there, and cashing in on all the publicity that went along with it.

Helen Rose, head of the costume department at MGM, was now working closely with Grace on her final two films, and was chosen to design Grace's suit for the civil wedding ceremony and her wedding gown for the religious ceremony. Edith was upset at the loss of the commission, but Grace reminded her that MGM was picking up all costs for the dresses, and that Paramount most likely would not have done that. Rose designed a gown with a high-necked bodice of antique Brussels lace with flower designs, embroidered with seed pearls, topping a bell-shaped skirt of ivory peau de soie. The gown is still considered one of the most beautiful ever designed for a high-profile wedding.

Edith settled for designing Grace's going-away suit for her honeymoon, for which Paramount did pay. Edith designed the light gray suit to be worn with white gloves, an acknowledgement of the fashion accessory she and Grace loved. Naturally, Helen Rose's wedding gown received the lion's share of publicity for months after the wedding, and very little acknowledgement was made of Edith's simple, tasteful contribution to what was then called "The Wedding of the Century."

Grace and Edith stayed great friends throughout the years,

Eva Marie Saint realized that glamour was the right choice for her character in *That Certain Feeling.*

and Edith traveled to Monaco several times to visit Grace. When Grace made her yearly trip back to Hollywood, Edith was always invited if Alfred Hitchcock threw a dinner party in Grace's honor. And years later, when Edith was at Universal, she received Grace in her bungalow at the studio, with Hitchcock and studio head Lew Wasserman as guests.

THE PSYCHOLOGY OF FASHION

Paramount purchased the rights to the hit Broadway Play *That Certain Feeling* (1956) and cast Bob Hope as a played-out cartoonist and Eva Marie Saint as his ex-wife. This was Saint's follow-up film to her Oscar-winning performance in the gritty groundbreaking drama *On the Waterfront* (1954). Trained as a method actress, Saint was one of the actresses, such as Geraldine Page or Joanne Woodward, who believed in immersing themselves totally in their character. *That Certain Feeling* had more slick production values than Saint was used to on the New York stage or live television. Edith said that the one thing Saint stressed to Edith before their initial costume consultation was that she did not want the typical Hollywood glamour look.

Edith brought no sketches when she first met with Saint, only a copy of the script. The two sat down to analyze her secretary character, and what would be best for her. Edith convinced her that the New York setting and the high-fashion world in which the character lived would require very elegant, very feminine clothing. Eva Marie told Edith that she would prefer to not wear a lot of jewelry, and since the script didn't call for it, Edith selected only pearl earrings and a strand of pearls for the actress to wear. Saint looked every inch the New York beauty she was portraying in smart outfits such as a black velvet evening gown with a velvet stole lined in ermine. The wardrobe was such a hit that a New York manufacturer marketed versions of the clothes, which Saint modeled in an advertisement in *Life Magazine*.

Carol Ohmart was a former Miss Utah, who Paramount was building up to be the next Marilyn Monroe. In *The Scarlet Hour* (1956), she played a restless young woman driving her lover to commit a crime. Since this was the first time Edith was working with her, Edith studied how the actress walked and moved and wore her clothes. "I couldn't identify her with any Hollywood type," Edith said, "so I knew I'd have to start from scratch. I noticed that Carol looks like a cat and moves like a cat — so I simply dressed her like a cat in a skintight tawny beige dress made of jersey and fur."

One of Edith's big challenges was that she was often asked to design clothes that would be photographed under numerous different lighting conditions. One dress she had to make for Ohmart would be worn for nearly half the film. The dress would have to be photographed in both day and night scenes, and be simple enough for a cocktail party and seductive enough for a love scene. Edith's solution was a dress of soft, pale smokey-blue-grey dull satin for the actress.

Alfred Hitchcock was known for his penchant for cool blondes in peril. He developed a stable of blonde actresses including Madeleine Carroll, Eva Marie Saint, Grace Kelly, Vera Miles, Kim Novak and Tippi Hedren with whom he worked on a strand of continuing themes throughout his films. Since color often played such an important part in his films, these colors were often repeated on the actresses, such as the eau de nil suits that Grace Kelly wears in Rear Window and Tippi Hedren wears in The Birds (1964).

In *The Man Who Knew Too Much* (1956), Hitchcock asked Edith to design a tailored gray suit for actress Doris Day, that would be reproduced and pored over by film historians when Kim Novak wore it in *Vertigo* (1958). Doris Day was not the typical cool Hitchcockian blonde. More of a girl-next-door type than a finishing-school-type, Day's character of Jo McKenna is resourceful and self-reliant. James Stewart played her husband Dr. Benjamin McKenna, who accidentally stumbles on to the plot of an assassination, resulting in the kidnapping of his son to keep him quiet.

Jo McKenna is an American woman, a former star of the musical stage, who is now a full-time doctor's wife and mother. "I always looked forward to fittings with Edith," Doris said. "She was witty, quick and very exciting. She dresses actors for the part, not for themselves alone. They (the clothes) weren't right for me. But they were just what a doctor's wife would wear. And that's what I was playing."

The Rainmaker (1956) offered Edith a chance to finally work with Katharine Hepburn. Loosely based on the real-life story of Charles M. Hatfield, the project had begun as television drama, and then became a successful New York play. Hepburn played Lizzie Curry, a woman who was raised in a household full of men, and is on the verge of becoming an old spinster. Because of her slim figure, Hepburn had worn clothes by Adrian and Walter Plunkett in films, like few actresses could. But Lizzie was a plain woman, wearing mostly farm clothes, who tries to transform herself with the arrival of the rainmaker (Burt Lancaster). Edith admired Hepburn's desire to transform herself based on the script. The script directions included Lizzie's father telling her to wear lots of ruffles, flowers and frills. Edith designed a yellow dress, ill-fitting and full of flounces, that demonstrated perfectly the awkwardness of Lizzie's plight.

Edith referred to the film *The Proud and the Profane* (1956) as basically "costumeles," since Deborah Kerr spent a good deal of the film in an army nurse uniform. Nevertheless, Edith was nominated for an Oscar that year for the film in the black-and-white category, and for *The Ten Commandments* in the color category. She lost in both categories to Jean Louis for *The Solid Gold Cadillac* (1956) and to Irene Sharaff for *The King and I* (1956) respectively.

Witness for the Prosecution (1957) didn't give Edith many more design opportunities for Marlene Dietrich than she had with *A Foreign Affair.* The film was based on the play by mystery writer Agatha Christie, and directed by Billy Wilder. Tyrone Power played Leonard Vole, a man accused of murdering a rich widow, who is defended by Sir Wilfred Robarts (Charles Laughton). Dietrich played Christine, Vole's wife, whom he had rescued from war-torn Germany and brought back to England. Because the Voles had little money, Wilder asked Edith to put Dietrich in two slightly outdated tailored suits that a middle-class English woman would wear. Since the action was taking place in winter, Edith thought tweed would be the right choice for the suits. In a flashback sequence, audiences were at least treated to a little of Dietrich's famous legs in a breakaway sailor costume, which is ripped by a serviceman during a cabaret performance.

"I FRANKLY DO NOT KNOW MISS DIETRICH WELL, AND I'M SURE SHE WOULD NOT CHOOSE ME OF HER OWN VOLITION, IF SHE COULD PICK A DESIGNER. EVERYBODY JUST DOESN'T LIKE EVERYBODY."

–Edith Head

In *The Dress Doctor*, Edith goes into great detail about her fittings with Dietrich. She described Dietrich as indefatigable, with a large thermos of coffee to keep her going. She said Dietrich would talk about her reflection in the mirror in the third-person, as if it was a character she was playing on top of the character she was already playing in the film. "I have been reading the script," Dietrich said to Edith. "We are

STOCKMAN
PARIS

Edith with fashion photographer Richard Avedon, on whom Fred Astaire's character was based, on the set of *Funny Face*.

going to have trouble with this woman? This woman is not going to be so easy." "The producer and director are worried," Edith told Marlene, "they want you to look like a hausfrau." "Why don't they ask me?" Dietrich reportedly shot back. "I was one! I was not dowdy." Most likely, Edith didn't design the tweed suits at all, instead possibly purchasing them from a store, and then supervising their refitting.

There was also the matter of the pivotal gaudy costume of the cockney streetwalker, in which Dietrich must be unrecognizable. Edith said Dietrich decided she should wear red platform shoes with ankle straps. To find them, Marlene thought they should visit the weekend vendors markets in downtown Los Angeles to find just the right kind of "hussy" accessories Dietrich wanted. Edith continually contradicted herself about her working relationship with Dietrich. Years later, she said "I frankly do not know Miss Dietrich well, and I'm sure she would not choose me of her own volition, if she could pick a designer. Everybody just doesn't like everybody." While it is possible that Billy Wilder requested Edith's services on the independent production, it still is probable that Dietrich would have been allowed to weigh in on the choice for designer. But whatever the real story is, Dietrich did not get her red "hussy" platforms. She wears black flats in the film.

Melissa Galt, the daughter of actress Anne Baxter, and Edith's goddaughter, says that Edith's storytelling was due to Edith fabricating her persona. "It gets tricky," she says. "Edith had some similar personality traits with my great-grandfather, Frank Lloyd Wright. They were both mavericks at self-promotion. Part of the way you do that is making yourself larger than life, despite your detractors. So there are times when you'll say something you won't remember, and it will come out differently later on when you retell it. I don't think it was a deliberate decision to mislead. I think it was simply a desire to embellish and augment. And even my mother would do a bit of that. She was a brilliant storyteller. And 'Aunt Edie' was every bit the story teller my mother was. So when you become a story teller like that, every time you tell a story, it grows a little bit, and eventually the true part and the not so true part become completely blurred."

By the time *Funny Face* (1957) was made, Audrey Hepburn was a bona fide fashion icon. Even though Hubert de Givenchy had not received a screen credit on *Sabrina*, his business had flourished, due in part to Hepburn choosing to wear his clothing in her personal wardrobe. Because he was designing all of the clothes for this picture specifically tailored to the script, Givenchy was given screen credit. "His design, his thought centered and focused on her physical being. It's like a great composer when he writes for a great artist. She was the physical expression of what Givenchy did," director Stanley Donen said of the collaboration of Heburn and Givenchy.

In the film Fred Astaire played Dick Avery, a fashion photographer in search of "The Quality Woman" for magazine editor Maggie Prescott (Kay Thompson). He finds her in the form of Jo Stockton (Hepburn), a bookish young woman who accepts the title and a trip to Paris to meet a philosopher in the city.

Edith was assigned to create the wardrobe for Thompson's no-nonsense editor clothes. Edith only had to look in the mirror for the inspiration. As a fashion editor who "wouldn't be caught dead" in the clothes she promoted, Edith gave Thompson a uniform — a two-piece suit with a short skirt and a long jacket with a sailor collar, made of different fabrics for different scenes. Her wardrobe seemed to be modeled on the streamlined suits Edith had become famous for wearing.

For the *Think Pink* number, Edith was able to indulge in fantasy. Though, even with no limitations, the gowns were not the serious fashion-forward haute couture provided by Givenchy. Edith still kept her philosophy of playing the safe design game, so that the clothes would not look dated by the time of the film's release. Givenchy, on the other hand, who would have been looking toward the fashion season ahead, having

Audrey Hepburn (in a gown by Givenchy) enters the editor's office in *Funny Face.*

Ruta Lee and Kay Thompson (far right) were costumed by Edith

1520-153

CASSIE #1 SC 84-89
DOOR JOE'S DR. RM.
(N.Y 1937)

Opposite page: **Edith based Kay Thompson's no-nonsense wardrobe in *Funny Face* on the suits that Edith wore herself.** This page: **A concept sketch for Beverly Garland in *The Joker is Wild.***

Left: Anna Magnani's dress for *Wild is the Wind* was based on a dress of Magnani's own design. Opposite page: Mamie Van Doren compares the concept sketch to her costume for *Teacher's Pet.*

the confidence that whatever fashion he created in the film would set the trend, rather than follow it.

Wild is the Wind (1957) was one of the last films that Anna Magnani would make in the United States. Magnani played Gioia, an Italian woman who comes to America to marry her late sister's husband (Anthony Quinn). The film was set in Nevada on a sheep ranch. Magnani showed up at the costume consultation with photos of cowgirls and Western wear, but Edith explained that since these were sheepherders, the dress would be considerably different, utilizing a lot of fleece and flannel.

In *The Dress Doctor*, Edith cited the qualities that made up Magnani, describing her as "a human Vesuvius; nothing is tranquil, nothing sloughed off, and being around her is exciting." In one instance, when Magnani felt a scene did not go well, Edith saw her leave the set, tear off the coat she was wearing, and weep on the floor.

In the film, Magnani's husband gives her money to buy a dress. Edith chose a typical party dress for the actress to wear, but it just did not work on Magnani - it was simply not her style at all. Instead, Maganani brought to Edith, a sleeveless dress with a high neck that the actress had designed herself. The wardrobe department copied the dress in black linen and had it embroidered with pink carnations, and it fit Magnani's style and the scene perfectly.

Sophia Loren and Cary Grant were having a love affair when they were signed to make *Houseboat* (1958). Complicating the matter was Loren's marriage to Carlo Ponti, which happened right in the middle of filming. Grant played Tom Winters, a widowed father of three, who enlists Cinzia (Loren), a runaway socialite, to be the family's maid on a houseboat.

In *The Dress Doctor*, Edith tells of a flamboyant gold dress that Sophia wears in the film. The dress was made of jersey impregnated with 14-karat gold, which Edith had never used before. While filming the scene where Sophia is dancing with Cary Grant, the gold on the dress rubbed off on Grant's dinner clothes making him look "a little like Sir Galahad in shining armor" according to Edith. She said she had to

call the studio paint shop, and the solution came in a spray gun with fast-drying lacquer that was blasted on to Sophia while still wearing the dress. When Sophia's husband Carlo Ponti came onto the set later that day Sophia told him "You think this is a dress? It is not. I am like an Oscar, sprayed on."

The story could be another one of Edith's embellishments. Director Melville Shavelson remembers that it was actually co-star Martha Hyer's body make-up that ended up all over Cary Grant's clothing. Still, Edith's outfits proved Sophia Loren's philosophy that "a woman's dress should be like a barbed wire fence: serving its purpose without obstructing the view."

BRUSHES WITH GREATNESS

"To be a good designer in Hollywood, one has to be a combination of psychiatrist, artist, fashion designer, dress-maker, pin cushion, historian, nurse maid and purchasing agent too," Edith mused. "I don't usually get into battles, but dressing Kim Novak for her role in Alfred Hitccock's *Vertigo* (1958) put to the test all my training in psychology." Based on the French novel *D' Entre les Morts* by Pierre Boileau and Thomas Narcejac, *Vertigo* was written specifically for Alfred Hitchcock after his unsuccessful attempt to secure the rights to one of the pair's James Stewart was cast as John "Scottie" Ferguson, a San Francisco detective who suffers from acrophobia, and is hired to follow Madeleine (Kim Novak), the wife of a former college acquaintance. Scottie falls in love with Madeleine as he trails her, and because of his fear of heights, is unable to save her when she commits suicide.

Hitchcock originally cast Vera Miles as Madeleine, but the actress had to bow out of the production when she became pregnant. In the same way that Scottie tries to form a woman into something she does not want to be, Hitchcock tried to mold a reticent Novak into the character. Hitchcock's script specifically called for Madeleine to wear a gray tailored suit. He explained to Edith that he wanted the character to

For Kim Novak in *Vertigo*, Edith had to design a dress that would be practical when Novak's character tried to drown herself

Opposite and below: **Edith only had to follow Hitchcock's costume directions in the script for *Vertigo*, but came upon a challenge with actress Kim Novak over the famous gray suit (far right).**

"TO BE A GOOD DESIGNER IN HOLLYWOOD, ONE HAS TO BE A COMBINATION OF PSYCHIATRIST, ARTIST, FASHION DESIGNER, DRESS-MAKER, PIN CUSHION, HISTORIAN, NURSE MAID AND PURCHASING AGENT TOO," EDITH MUSED.

Costuming for *Vertigo* was of the utmost importance to separate the personas of the characters Madeleine and Judy

"Vertigo" 1958
Candy
Enjoy

appear mysterious, as if she had just come out of the San Francisco fog, and that gray was absolutely essential.

Edith maintained that it was the color gray that Kim resisted so fervently, and that she tried showing various shades of gray with different color hues to try to come to terms. Edith said she even designed a black satin gown with a black satin coat lined with emerald green for a restaurant scene, that was so beautiful, Edith felt it might sway Kim to compromise on the suit.

But it wasn't the color gray so much that put Novak off, as much as the manufactured stylization of Madeleine. In 2003, Novak reflected on her *Vertigo* ensembles with author Stephen Rebello, and cleared up some of the mystery that has long surrounded her costumes: "Once we were making *Vertigo*, Hitchcock never questioned anything about what I was doing character-wise. Before shooting started, he sent me over to Edith Head, who showed me a set of drawings. When I saw them, the very first thing I said was, 'I'm sorry. I don't wear black shoes.' When she said, 'Alfred Hitchcock wants you to wear these shoes,' I said, 'I'm sure he doesn't mind.' I didn't think it would matter to him what kind of shoes I wore. I had never had a director who was particular about the costumes, the way they were designed, the specific colors. The two things he wanted the most were those shoes and that gray suit. When Edith Head showed me that gray suit, I said, "Oh, my God, that looks like it would be very hard to act in. It's very confining.' Then, when we had the first fitting of the dress, it was even worse and I said, 'This is so restrictive.' She said, 'Well, maybe you'd better talk to Alfred Hitchcock about this.'

I went in and he said, 'I understand you don't like these black shoes.' He asked me why and I said, 'I tell you, black shoes always sort of make me feel I'm pulled down. I've always felt that your feet should be the same as the top of your head, so that you're connected. Wearing the black shoes would make me feel as if I were disconnected.' He heard me out. And then he said, 'Fine. When you play the role of Judy, you will not have to wear black shoes. When you are playing Madeleine, you will wear them.' When he put it like that—after all, he's the director—I said, 'OK.'

I really wanted the chance to express myself and he allowed me that chance. It felt OK because he had heard me out. He felt my reasons weren't good enough, they weren't right. I just wanted to be heard as far as what I felt. So, I thought, 'I'll live with the grey suit.' I also thought, 'I'm going to use this. I can make this work for me. Because it bothers me, I'll use it and it can help me feel like I'm having to be Madeleine, that I'm being forced to be her. I'll have it as my energy to play against.' It worked. That suit and those shoes were a blessing. I was constantly reminded that I was not being myself, which made it right for Madeleine. When I went out of Alfred Hitchcock's office, I remember his wonderful smile when he said, 'I'm so glad we had this talk.' I think he saw that this was going to be good. He didn't say to me, 'Now use that,' he allowed me to arrive at that myself.

"When I played Judy, I never wore a bra. It killed me having to wear a bra as Madeleine but you had to because they had built the suit so that you had to stand very erect or you suddenly were not 'in position.' They made that suit very stiff. You constantly had to hold your shoulders back and stand erect. But, oh that was so perfect. That suit helped me find the tools for playing the role. It was wonderful for Judy because then I got to be without a bra and felt so good again. I just felt natural. I had on my own beige shoes and that felt good. Hitchcock said, 'Does that feel better?' I said, 'Oh, yes, thank you so much.' But then, I had to play 'Madeleine' again when Judy had to be made over again by Scottie into what she didn't want to be. I could use that, again, totally for me, not just being made over into Madeleine but into Madeleine who wore that ghastly gray suit. The clothes alone were so perfect, they were everything I could want as an actress."

When the film opened, it was not the critical or financial success for which Hitchcock had hoped. In later interviews, he questioned the casting of the much older Stewart opposite Novak. But over the

"WHEN I PLAYED JUDY, I NEVER WORE A BRA. IT KILLED ME HAVING TO WEAR A BRA AS MADELEINE."

–Kim Novak

Though not overwhelming well-received at the time of its release, *Vertigo* is now considered Alfred Hitchcock's masterpiece

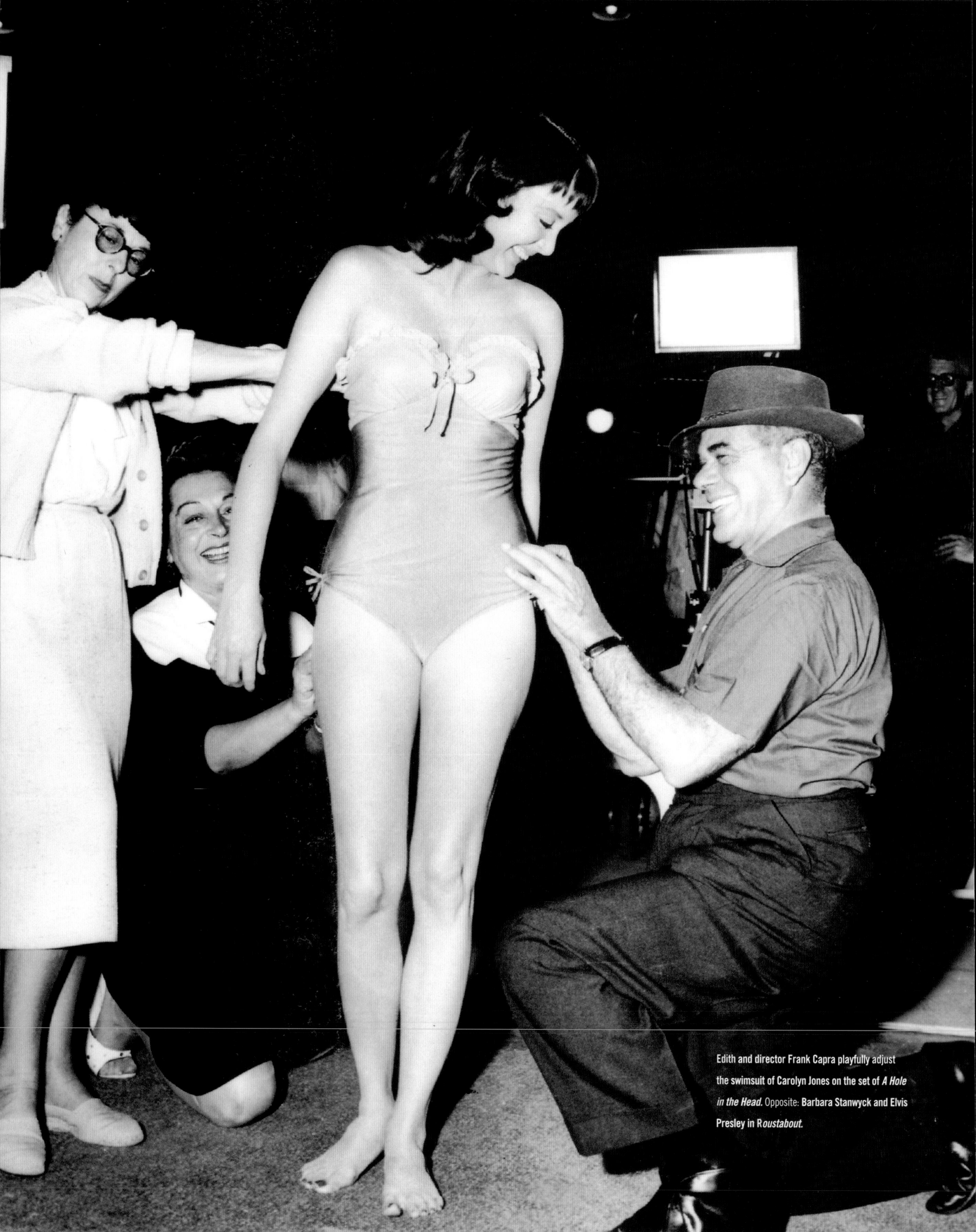

Edith and director Frank Capra playfully adjust the swimsuit of Carolyn Jones on the set of *A Hole in the Head.* Opposite: Barbara Stanwyck and Elvis Presley in R*oustabout.*

years, the film achieved a cult status among serious film students and scholars, even with it being pulled from circulation for a time, and it is now considered Hitchcock's great masterpiece.

In 1956, producer Hal Wallis had a young man screen tested for the role in *The Rainmaker* that eventually was given to Burt Lancaster. Wallis still signed the man to a non-exclusive seven-year-contract and, realizing that heavily dramatic parts were not necessarily his best fit, began to develop light frothy musicals to showcase him. Elvis Presley had gyrated his way to fame on the Milton Berle, Steve Allen and Ed Sullivan shows the year before and his public eagerly awaited his first feature film.

Elvis' first film for Paramount was *Loving You* (1958). Originally titled *Lonesome Cowboy*, the name was changed to help promote the song *Loving You* in the film. The script was based on a story by Margaret Agnes Thompson about a young singer called Lonesome Harris and his path to stardom. Hal Wallis asked Edith to oversee the image of his young new star. As a delivery man who gets his big break when he is discovered by a publicist (Lizabeth Scott), Elvis' stage wardrobe had a decidedly rockabilly flair, including a red and white cowboy suit worn when Elvis sings *Teddy Bear*.

Elvis Presley films were the only sure moneymaker in Hollywood. Even though they were generally not critically well received, Elvis' films generated so much revenue for the studio that they were able to put into production more prestigious films that made less profit. The unfortunate part was that Elvis kept hoping as the years went on that he would be able to take on more serious roles, but it happened only a few times.

Before Elvis came to the studio he had already developed his persona. It was really up to Edith and the men's wardrobe department to make sure that his clothes conveyed the Elvis style. Occasionally things went wrong—Elvis preferred not to wear an untucked short sleeved shirt to sing Marguerita in *Fun in Acapulco* (1963), but scenes had already been shot of his double wearing the shirt and it was too late to change. But he liked the black silk shirts made for the flamenco number so much that he asked Wallis if he could keep them.

Elvis understood he was playing a character and it wasn't often that he refused to wear something that had been designed for him. A formula was developed, usually dark pants, a sport coat and two-tone loafers. Frequently, the scripts found a way to get him out of his shirt by having him play a boxer or cavort on a beach in Hawaii. Elvis was not a big fan of blue jeans or overalls, which he associated with his working class upbringing.

When Edith traveled to Hawaii for the location shooting of *Blue Hawaii* (1961), she got a first-hand account of the power of Elvis. Thousands of screaming fans nearly broke through barricades at the airport and constantly surrounded the hotel, which housed the crew. Elvis' contract stipulated that he would be paid extra if he was asked to provide any part of his wardrobe for production. On a cloudy day of shooting, just as the sun was breaking through and shooting was resuming, Elvis' manager Colonel Parker yelled "cut!" as the cameras rolled. Exasperated director Norman Taurog asked Parker what was so important that he had to halt production. Parker pointed out that Elvis was wearing his own watch in the scene, and if it was used, Parker would charge the production an additional $25,000.

THE CLINIC OPENS

The Matchmaker (1958) was Shirley Booth's only comedic film role. Based on Thornton Wilder's stage play, Booth played Dolly Levi, a matchmaker from Yonkers, New York. She falls in love with Horace Vandergelder (Paul Ford), as she's trying to find a suitable mate for him in a another woman. Shirley told Edith that she felt that her character would be the kind of woman who might run up her own dresses at home. After looking at Edith's sketches, Shirley asked her to switch around various pieces of her 1890s costumes to make them appear more homemade and patchwork. *The Matchmaker* was later turned into the musical *Hello, Dolly!* by composer Jerry Herman.

Laurence Olivier was originally set to direct *Separate Tables* (1958) with his wife Vivien Leigh in the role of Ann Shankland, as a woman trying to reclaim an old lover. When Olivier dropped out of the production, so did Vivien. James Hill, who was presenting the film with Burt Lancaster, was married to Rita Hayworth and she was cast in Vivien's place. Mary Grant had already been acting as costume supervisor throughout the pre-production process, but with the addition of Hayworth, Edith was asked to design Rita's costumes. Edith said she was expecting the "movie star" treatment from Hayworth, which could sometimes mean intimidating remarks about their preferences for couture designers.

Edith said she was happy to find Rita very relaxed with no hint of movie star persona and the only suggestions Hayworth made were about preferring warm colors. Edith decided to do most of the wardrobe in colors such as topaz, sherry, and caramel, that would match Rita's eyes and hair. For the big love scene, Edith designed a dress of black wool embroidered with small black jewels that Edith felt would highlight the motion of Rita's figure. Rita was so focused and quiet during her fittings that Edith wasn't even sure that she liked the clothes. However, when Edith saw a photo in the newspaper of Rita and her husband, and she was wearing the caramel-colored suit Edith had designed, she knew she'd hit a home run.

Cecil B. DeMille had intended *The Buccaneer* (1958) to be a musical version of his swashbuckler epic of the same name from 1938. Set against the war of 1812, the film detailed the alliance between General Andrew Jackson (Charlton Heston) and Jean Lafitte (Yul Brynner). DeMille's health faltered during pre-production, and he turned the film over to his son-in-law Anthony Quinn to direct. Edith did the costumes for female leads Claire Bloom and Inger Stevens, sharing screen credit with John Jensen and Ralph Jester. The trio was nominated for an Oscar for costume design for the film, losing to Cecil Beaton for Gigi (1958). DeMille died a month after its premiere.

Producer Hal Wallis was known to like very simple clothes. He'd always liked the tailored look of the clothes Edith designed for his contract star Lizabeth Scott. The actress, on the other hand, was not always so fond of them. But when the actress recorded an album of standards in her trademark smoky voice simply titled *Lizabeth*, she wore a high-necked dress of blue jersey, designed by Edith. Opera singer Dorothy Kirsten, on the other hand, loved Edith's work and had been using her designing services for her many concert and television appearances since Edith designed for her in *Mr. Music* (1950). For Kirsten's appearance in Tosca in Miami in 1958, Edith designed a second-act gown of royal garnet velvet trimmed in diamonds with a full-length cape of the same material trimmed in gold lamé.

With her continuing TV appearances on *Art Linkletter's House Party* and other shows such as 1959's *This is Your Life: Frank Capra*, Edith was easily the most well-known costume designer in Hollywood and someone that women had come to trust for fashion advice. A book seemed like the logical next step when she was approached by writer Jane Kesner Ardmore to collaborate on a project. Since Edith was reluctant to divulge any important details of her personal life, it was Jane who came up with the concept of Edith presiding over a fashion clinic and calling the book *The Dress Doctor.*

Edith's penchant for self-promotion helped the book reach the

Edith confers with actor Jeff Chandler and director Melvin Frank on the set of *The Jayhawkers*.

PRINCESS
LOGGIA - POOL
Sprague

Grace Sprague's sketch for Anna Maria Alberghetti as the princess in *Cinderfella*.

"TO LOOK LOVELY, A WOMAN WILL SUFFER. SHE'LL WEAR A WAIST CINCHER THAT SQUEEZES HER, BONED BRAS THAT DIG HER, HEELS THAT TILT HER TO THE SENSITIVE BALLS OF HER FEET."

–Edith Head

best-seller list in a few months. Edith did an exhaustive tour of interviews for print and radio, as well as a tour of her fashion show, which she combined with book signings. The book was a breezy tome of behind-the-scenes stories of Hollywood. Edith did not often betray stars in print, stating "I may have to work with them again," but a few stars such as Hedy Lamarr did not fare all that well. Edith donated the proceeds from the sale of her books to charities for American Indian children, a subject near to heart because of her love for the Southwest. The book has been translated into over eleven languages.

A *Time* magazine review of *The Dress Doctor* titled *How Not to Wear a Tub*, quoted Edith as saying: "To look lovely, a woman will suffer. She'll wear a waist cincher that squeezes her, boned bras that dig her, heels that tilt her to the sensitive balls of her feet. Clothes have to do with happiness, and can actually give a woman personality. A woman in a bathtub has little personality; she's just a woman without clothes."

Career (1959) finally gave Edith a chance to dress Shirley MacLaine in a contemporary fashion picture. Her relationship with MacLaine was one she guarded and treasured, and the feeling was mutual. "She was one of the joys of my contract with Hal Wallis," MacLaine says. "And there weren't that many." Anthony Franciosa played Sam Lawson, an actor on the brink of success and MacLaine played Sharon Kensington, his alcoholic wife. Edith had worked with director Joseph Anthony on *The Rainmaker* and *The Matchmaker* prior to *Career*. "Directors were always a little intimidated by Edith because she was such an intellectual and she really knew what she was doing," says MacLaine. "They usually deferred to her, unless she was way off track, and that was rare."

Edith was nominated for an Oscar for best black-and-white costume design for *Career* and for best color costume design for her 1920s jazz-age costumes for Barbara Bel Geddes in *The Five Pennies* (1959). She lost the awards to Orry-Kelly for *Some Like it Hot* (1959) and Elizabeth Haffenden for *Ben-Hur* (1959) respectively.

"She was a good designer," says David Chierichetti "People liked her stuff. I don't think she was the best designer, personally. For instance, Walter Plunkett was more schooled in the period clothes. She would do research, and she would turn out a product that was quite acceptable. But she didn't just intrinsically know it the way Plunkett did. And Orry-Kelly was frequently very funny. The clothes he came up with for Marilyn Monroe in *Some Like it Hot*, Edith would not have come up with those ideas. She would have made nice looking things, but they wouldn't have had the humor that Orry-Kelly's dresses had. But then none of those people ever turned out the volume of work that Edith did. Sometimes she did forty films in one year. She obviously had help on them, but she was the main person doing it. And it was ultimately her responsibility whether it worked or didn't work, and whether people were happy or not happy."

CHAPTER SIX

THE STUDIO SYSTEM IN DECLINE

Edith with Debbie Reynolds and George Seaton on the set of ***The Pleasure of His Company***

EXIT
214
BNC 238

Edith discusses sketches with actress Stella Stevens for the film *Girls! Girls! Girls!*.

NOW THAT TELEVISION WAS A STAPLE OF NEARLY EVERY HOME IN THE UNITED STATES, PRODUCERS BEGAN TO LOOK FOR WAYS TO TRIM FILM BUDGETS. THE NEW REALISM IN STORIES BEING DEVELOPED ALSO OPENED THE DOOR FOR CLOTHING TO BE BOUGHT FROM STORES, RATHER THAN DESIGNED SPECIFICALLY FOR FILMS. THE CHANGE HAPPENED SLOWLY THROUGHOUT THE BEGINNING OF THE 1960S, STARTING WITH 'B' PICTURES. IT WAS UNFORTUNATE THAT CLOTHES IN FILMS WERE BEGINNING TO BE TAKEN FOR GRANTED, FOR FASHION WAS VERY MUCH ON THE MINDS OF EVERYONE IN THE COUNTRY.

Edith's old rival Oleg Cassini had been selected by First Lady Jacqueline Kennedy as her chief designer, and her geometric dresses and pillbox hats were being copied by women everywhere. Edith called Mrs. Kennedy "the greatest single influence (on fashion) in history." Cassini designed more than 300 outfits for the First Lady, and in 1961, her clothing bill was more than John F. Kennedy's salary as President.

The Facts of Life (1960) walked the middle of the road between comedy and drama, and proved that Bob Hope was a pretty good actor when he wasn't hamming things up. Hope played Larry Gilbert, who falls in love with a friend's wife (Lucille Ball) when they are thrown together on a vacation. When Lucille Ball signed on for the project, she requested to use her own costume designer Edward Stevenson, who had worked on her television show *I Love Lucy*. Producers Hal C. Kern and Norman Panama preferred using Edith because they knew that the publicity she generated would help to sell the film to audiences. Edith found a diplomatic solution and worked out an arrangement with Stevenson to divide their duties, with Stevenson overseeing the production of costumes at Desilu, Lucille Ball's studio.

Edith and Stevenson won Oscars for their work on the film, up against Marik Vos-Lundh for *The Virgin Spring* (1960), Theoni V. Aldredge for *Never On Sunday* (1960), Bill Thomas for *Seven Thieves* (1960), and *The Rise and Fall of Legs Diamond*. Not that the costumes for *The Facts of Life* were all that noteworthy, but the better costumes in films were now being done in color films, such as *Spartacus* (1960) and *Can-Can* (1960).

The Rat Race (1960) also gave Debbie Reynolds a chance to work more in the dramatic vein, as a taxi dancer cracking under the pressures of living in New York City. Tony Curtis played a jazz musician with whom she shared an apartment. It was one of the first films in which the maturing Reynolds could really explore her sensuality. Edith put Debbie in an eye-popping blue dress with a laced-up front bodice, which was unusual, as Edith almost always eschewed low-cut designs. But it was perfect for her character. When a customer tells her "I'm ready if you are, sweetie," she answers "I was born ready."

In 1944 Edith had done the costumes for *Our Hearts Were Young and Gay,* based on a book by Emily Kimbrough and actress and author Cornelia Otis Skinner. Cornelia asked Edith to design her costumes for the Broadway production of *The Pleasure of his Company,* which Cornelia had written and in which she was starring. She wanted Edith to dress her character as a smart, modern woman, telling her "the audience must know who she is the moment she walks on. They make an instant judgment before they've even heard her speak; and they resent deeply being deceived. She can't look like one thing and be another."

William Perlberg secured the rights for the film version of The *Pleasure of his Company* (1961) and cast dapper Fred Astaire as the absentee father showing up for his daughter's (Debbie Reynolds) wedding. Edith even had a small part in the film, appearing as a bridal consultant at a department store. Lili Palmer was cast as Reynolds' mother and Astaire's ex-wife (the part that Skinner had played on Broadway). Palmer was in Europe during all of the pre-production, and was only scheduled to arrive in Hollywood just as shooting was to begin. Edith sent sketches to Palmer for approval, and they were sent on to Palmer's dressmaker for size notations. When the sketches came back, Edith's staff created the dresses and then they were shipped back to the dressmaker to make the final adjustments on Palmer in Europe.

At the time, Debbie Reynolds had her own ready-to-wear line that was marketed through department stores, with an estimated $4 million dollars worth of merchandise produced. Fans of the actress could buy Debbie Reynolds dresses, pajamas, hosiery, rain coats, lingerie and jewelry. One of the clauses in Reynolds' contract with Perlberg-Seaton Productions allowed her to keep all the modern clothes that she wore in the film. This included the $4,000 wedding gown, which Reynolds said she would keep for her daughter Carrie. When MGM sold off the contents of its wardrobe and prop departments, Reynolds began a quest to preserve the history of Hollywood. She amassed a collection of 3,000 costumes from the silent era to the 1970s including the white dress Marilyn Monroe wore over the subway grate in *The Seven Year Itch* (1955).

Stella Stevens was twenty-five when she came to Paramount to make *Li' l Abner* (1959), in which the beautiful blonde star appeared as Appassionata Von Climax. Though Edith wasn't assigned to that film, she did work with the actress on several films, including *Man-Trap* (1961), *Too Late Blues* (1961), *Girls! Girls! Girls!* (1961) and *The Nutty Professor* (1963). Stevens' first films had been at Twentieth Century-Fox, where she says she felt like designers really didn't take any interest in grooming young stars and explaining to them what worked best for

Opposite page: **A wardrobe test photo for Debbie Reynolds in *The Pleasure of His Company.*** This page: **The daring blue dress Reynolds wears in *The Rat Race.***

EDITH PUT DEBBIE IN AN EYE-POPPING BLUE DRESS WITH A LACED-UP FRONT BODICE, WHICH WAS UNUSUAL, AS EDITH ALMOST ALWAYS ESCHEWED LOW-CUT DESIGNS. BUT IT WAS PERFECT FOR HER CHARACTER. WHEN A CUSTOMER TELLS HER "I'M READY IF YOU ARE, SWEETIE," SHE ANSWERS "I WAS BORN READY."

A costume sketch and wardrobe test for Lili Palmer in *The Pleasure of His Company.* Opposite page: **One of the gowns worn by Palmer in the film.**

them on-screen and off. "Edith was a genius of a woman" says Stevens. "She taught me that simplicity is the essence of style—the more simple things are, the more striking they can be. She also taught me that wearing things like big earrings would draw attention away from a woman's face. She took me under her wing, and told me what colors worked best for my light blonde coloring. All her clothes were flattering and perfect for the pictures."

At Bette Davis' request, Edith was loaned for Frank Capra's production of *Pocketful of Miracles* (1961). Davis played Apple Annie, an alcoholic old woman, dressed in rags, who sold apples on the street to theatre-goers. But Annie has a secret—a daughter (Ann-Margret) that no one knows about, that Annie has been supporting while she grew up in a Spanish convent. The girl contacts Annie because she is planning a trip to New York with her fiancée and his father, a Count. Glenn Ford played Dave the Dude, a mobster that believes that Annie's apples bring him luck, who makes a lady out of Annie so that she can receive her daughter.

It was a total feel-good tale told by a man who was a master of the art, and it became Capra's final film. The film was a remake of his earlier film *Lady for a Day* (1933), which originally starred May Robson. Capra had tried to interest Shirley Booth in starring in the remake, but when Booth viewed the original, she declined stating that she felt she could never match Robson's performance. Davis took as much interest in Apple Annie's distressed clothing to ensure that they looked as right for her character, as she did for her more elaborate finer gowns worn later in the film. In a 1974 interview Bette Davis said of Edith, "she's a thorough professional. You get the right kind of clothes from her without the nonsense and temperament that some designers give you."

If Edith had to conserve in areas to save money on the budget, she would pull clothing from stock wardrobe and reuse it. This was a common practice at any studio, but it was mainly done for extras and more minor characters. It wasn't often that a piece of wardrobe that was used on a major star would be reused on another star. But Edith wasn't above doing it, and she put Hope Lange, who played Dave the Dude's girlfriend, in a black dress with a rhinestone décolletage that had originally been designed for Rhonda Fleming in *The Buster Keaton Story.* Edith shared the designing responsibilities with Walter Plunkett, who did the men's costumes. They were both nominated for an Oscar for best color costume design, losing to Irene Sharaff for *West Side Story* (1961).

A NEW BREED OF WOMAN

Edith's final collaboration with Audrey Hepburn and Hubert de Givenchy was on *Breakfast at Tiffany's* (1961). Based on the novella by Truman Capote, troubled call girl Holly Golightly's (Hepburn) character was softened for the screenplay. George Peppard played Paul Varjak, a writer who is being kept by a wealthy woman (Patricia Neal). Capote had sold the rights for $65,000 to Paramount, and George Axelrod was hired to adapt the book with Marilyn Monroe in mind for the role of Holly. It would have been Edith's first chance to design for Monroe. But Paula Strasberg, Monroe's acting coach felt that playing a call girl was not good for her image, and Monroe dropped out of the production. Capote was disappointed when Audrey Hepburn was cast, though today it is hard to imagine anyone else in the role.

Pauline Trigère was brought in to design the four changes for Patricia Neal. Givenchy did not design Audrey's wardrobe specifically for the script as he had done with *Funny Face*. Instead, he allowed Hepburn to borrow pieces from his latest collection. However, Audrey didn't borrow enough clothes to fill out the entire film. Edith was responsible for Holly's everyday wear, including her casual ensemble for the fire escape scene when she sings "Moon River." A scene was cut from the final film in which Holly is taking a bath and has to improvise a gown on the spur of the moment. The audience was left to wonder why she is wearing a bed sheet at her cocktail party.

When Givenchy provided Audrey Hepburn with just a partial wardrobe for *Breakfast at Tiffany's*, Edith filled out the remainder of the needed costumes, including the ensemble in which Hepburn sings *Moon River* on the fire escape.

on scene w/cat
12 - only -
more okay
Winter
make sure all parts are done
double collar
find belt

Opposite page: **A wardrobe plot by sketch artist Grace Sprague shows how Edith envisioned some of the *Breakfast at Tiffany's* costumes based on the script, prior to Givenchy's loan of wardrobe.**

This page: **A sketch from Edith's studio of the dress worn by Holly Golightly when she visits Sally Tomato in jail.**

3a at second trip – with hat as well.
3a back – full mock back no big hat – check
4 2nd party gown second dress
sc. 35–38
optional – on arms?
6 – party Int
big column skirt.
8 option fabric with the.
#9 #9a
10 party option ?

Another wardrobe plot from *Breakfast at Tiffany's* shows the famous Givenchy gown worn by Audrey Hepburn outside of Tiffany's at the beginning of the film, was not always intended for that particular scene

"VERY DEPENDABLE. BUT YOU BETTER NOT BE LATE FOR A FITTING. SHE HAS TREMENDOUS AUTHORITY. WHEN THAT LITTLE THING WALKS IN TO A ROOM, YOU KNOW SHE'S THERE."
–Joan Crawford

Screen credits were once again spelled out carefully, with Givenchy given screen credit for principally designing Audrey's wardrobe, and Edith was credited as costume supervisor. Part of Edith's duties was to create double and triples of the Givenchy originals, so that production would not be held up in case any were soiled. One of the three copies of the black Givenchy gown from the opening scene of the film was sold at Christie's in 2006 for $923,187. The dress was presumed to have been made in Edith's studio, and because of the slit up the front, was believed to be the dress Hepburn wore for photography on which to base the poster. It was just one of the many testaments to the film as an enduring influence on style and fashion. In her book *Audrey Style*, Pamela Keogh Clarke writes, "the Hepburn Givenchy partnership reached the apogee of refined elegance as Holly Golightly's hangover chic caused a run on triple strand faux pearl necklaces, sleeveless dresses and oversized dark sunglasses that continues to this day." Amazingly, the film was not even nominated for an Oscar for costume design.

When the film *Lisbon* with Joan Crawford fell through, the actress ended up purchasing the clothes that Edith had designed for her. Joan continued to make requests for Edith to design for her personal wardrobe. Edith told David Chierichetti that she felt pressured to socialize with Crawford as well, and wasn't sure what Joan's intentions were toward her. Though many people over the years came to assume that Edith was a lesbian because of her demeanor, there is no evidence to corroborate that. In 1962, Edith did do some designs for Crawford, including a coat with an ancient Peruvian design that was hand-screened in bright pink and orange. "Edith's a sturdy woman, emotionally," Joan said later. "Very dependable. But you better not be late for a fitting. She has tremendous authority. When that little thing walks into a room, you know she's there."

Many of the pretty young women on the Paramount lot were utilized in many of the Elvis Presley films. Stella Stevens didn't want to make *Girls! Girls! Girls!* (1962), and was nearly suspended by the studio because of it. She relented when the studio promised a better role in an upcoming project. Elvis Presley played Ross Carpenter, a sailor who is caught between an insensitive nightclub performer (Stevens) and an idealistic young woman (newcomer Laurel Goodwin). For Stevens, Edith designed a dress of black lace over white crepe, edged in jet bangles

STELLA STEVENS DIDN'T WANT TO MAKE *GIRLS! GIRLS! GIRLS!*,
AND WAS NEARLY SUSPENDED
BY THE STUDIO BECAUSE OF IT.

Opposite page: **A sketch by Richard Hopper for Elvis Presley in *Girls! Girls! Girls!*** This page: **Stella Stevens plays an insensitive club singer in the film alongside Elvis.**

by EDITH HEAD

I DRESS THE *Stars*

Gowns for Audrey Hepburn, armor for Danny Kaye! My job is one wonderful fashion whirl!

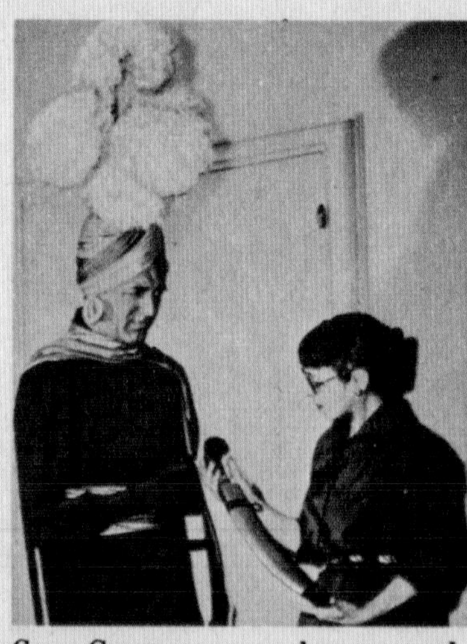

Cary Grant never makes me rush.

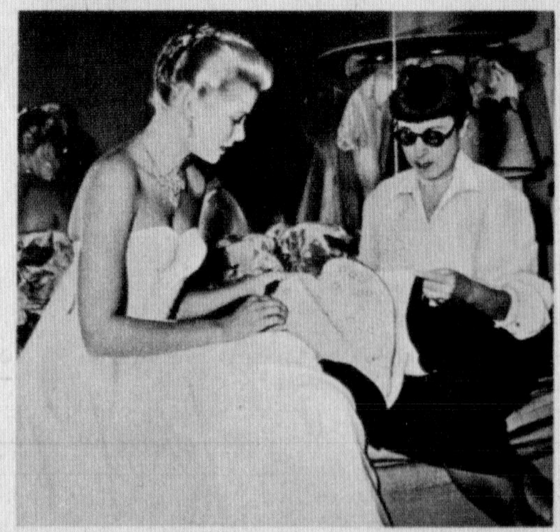

Grace Kelly's figure is a designer's dream.

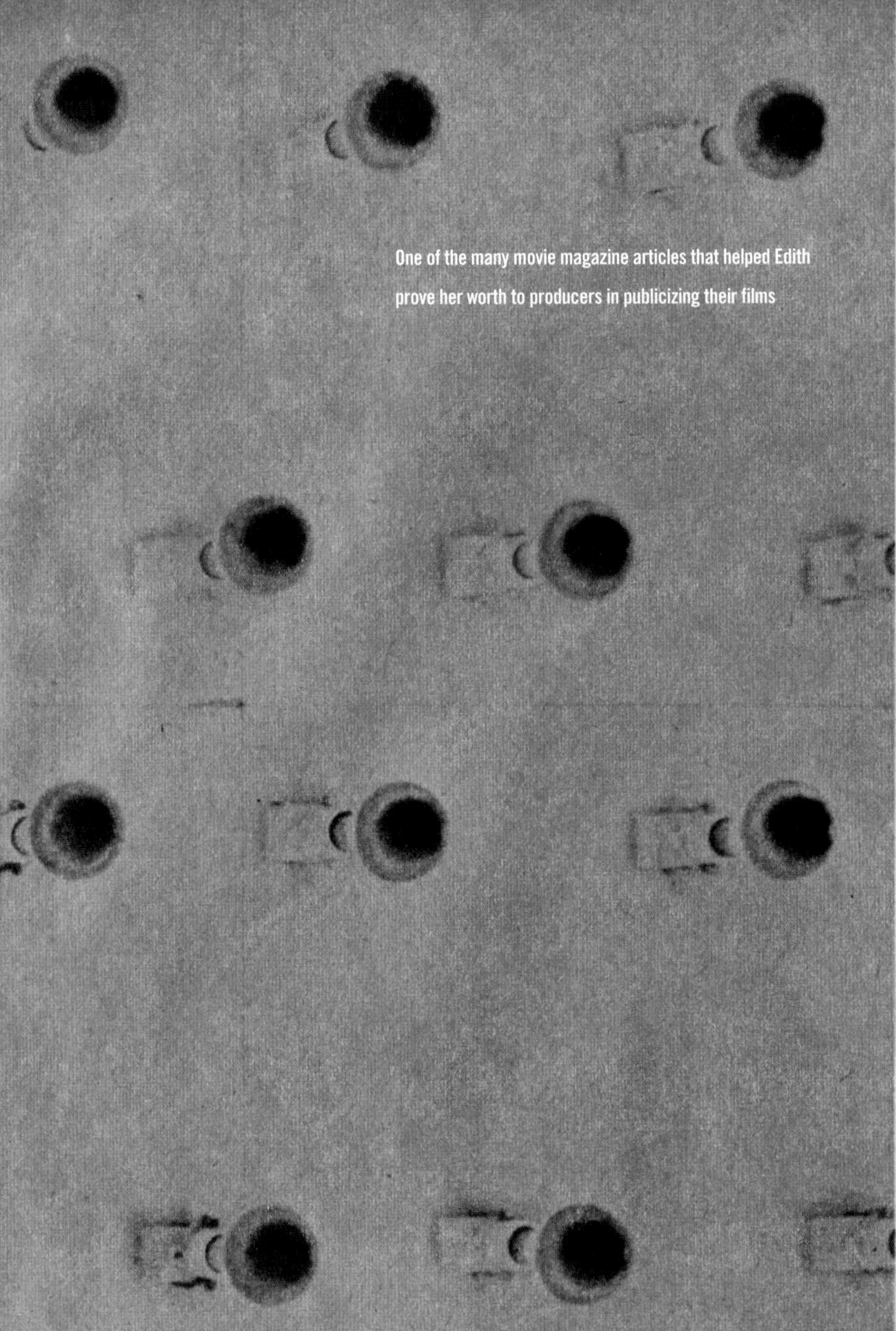

One of the many movie magazine articles that helped Edith prove her worth to producers in publicizing their films

Edith Head is fashion chief at Paramount Studios and has designed everything from a cat's collar to wardrobes for filmdom's greatest stars. Called "The Dress Doctor" of Hollywood, Miss Head is the winner of six Academy Awards and has been nominated every year since the award was established. Here is her very own story about her fabulous job.

Fitting a necktie on a cooperative snake is very difficult. Fitting a necktie on an uncooperative snake is impossible. I know because I've tried. The snake's name was Emma and she wanted to be comfortable and neckties didn't coincide with her idea of comfort. I happened to be thinking of Emma today because of a wonderfully zany man named Danny Kaye.

Danny is one of my favorite men. He's also, at the moment, my most pressing problem. For *On The Double* I have to make him look like a beautiful blonde siren. Now what makes this so difficult is that Danny, who is genuinely interested in costume, characterization and authenticity, is chiefly concerned—like most men—with comfort. Start fitting him into something uncomfortable and he's as cooperative as Emma. I know. I've already had to make him uncomfortable twice. The first time was in *The Court Jester* when the script called for him to wear a suit of armor.

"A nice comfortable suit of armor?" asked Danny.

I must have looked dubious. I know some tricks but they didn't include making a comfortable suit of armor.

"Drop the picture," said Danny—and he meant it.

I finally enticed him into flexible aluminum but he hated it and I'm not sure whether he's ever forgiven me.

In *The Five Pennies* Danny had to wear a tight costume of a Northwest Mountie complete with tight boots he couldn't get off once he had them on.

Jerry Lewis is a cut-up at fittings.

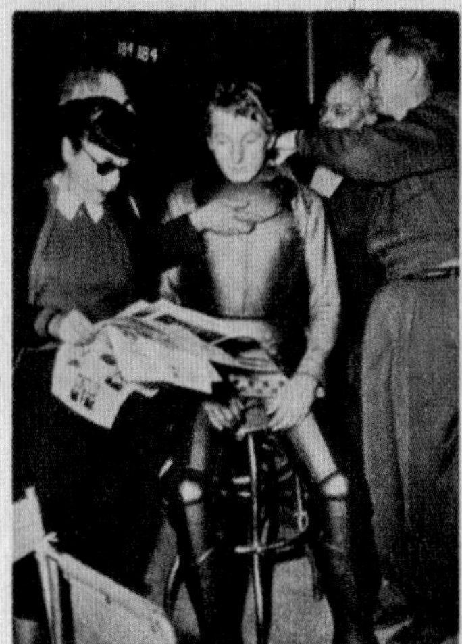

Danny Kaye longs for comfort.

over bodice and hem, for the nightclub performance. Goodwin wore a hyacinth-colored alencon lace dress with a gypsy-influence, held out by layers of matching hyacinth net.

Who's Got the Action? (1962) was Edith's first chance to work with screen legend and fashion icon Lana Turner. Lana had been under contract to MGM during the years that Adrian and Irene were designing there, and if there was one thing Lana knew how to do well, it was to wear clothes. Turner played Melanie Flood, whose husband Steve (Dean Martin) is a compulsive gambler. After loss upon loss, Melanie devises a scheme with his friend Clint (Eddie Albert), in which she will act as his bookie unbeknownst to him, so at least if he loses the bet, the money will not be lost. The trouble occurs when his horses start winning.

Lana still had a great figure, and part of the attraction of a Lana Turner film to audiences was to see what she would wear. Edith was assigned a budget of $50,000 for Lana's clothes. Two lace nightgowns had to be engineered with several layers of nude soufflé underneath to appear sheer, but to ensure that the audience didn't see too much of Lana. The cost of those alone was $750 each. Lana fashion news made great editorial copy, and Edith touted what she called the new "Action Look" to fashion writers all over the country when some of the designs were copied by manufacturers.

Escape From Zahrain (1962) was originally envisioned as a sweeping epic that would be filmed on location in Malaysia. Star Yul Brynner asked Ronald Neame to come onto project as director and producer. "Paramount changed their minds and said they thought there were plenty of Arabs here in Hollywood," says Neame. "So it became a rather second-rate Hollywood picture than what was intended." The story involved a captured leader of a rebel movement and four other prisoners who make their getaway, and must make a long trek across the desert to the border. Even Elsworth Fredericks' beautiful Technicolor cinematography of the desert, couldn't compensate for deficiencies in the script.

Edith never consulted Neame about the costumes and he believes they may have been pulled from the studio stock, with copies made to cover the long shoot. "There was no costume design really involved," he says. "The whole story took place in the desert. We shot it in Barstow on the desert there. But they all wear the same khaki outfits from the beginning of the picture to end. They were just dressed in suitable outfits to cross the desert.

"Edith was quite a modest person in a way, but she intimidated all the big stars. She received credit on most Paramount pictures, no matter who the designers were. In some cases, she had very little to do with the production. But that was the policy, and therefore she did have a lot of Oscars. When she had a meeting with any new actress, who was about to demand what she wanted, Edith would have all her Oscars out in a circle on a round table in her office. And all the people that came to see her were so intimidated, she got whatever she wanted."

Even if critics took a few knocks at *The Man Who Shot Liberty Valance* (1962), the combination of the great director John Ford teamed with James Stewart and John Wayne made for a very popular film with audiences. But that same audience had to suspend belief a little bit when the script called for the fifty-somethings John Wayne and James Stewart to play characters thirty years younger in flashback, as Stewart recounts the tale of shooting the violent villain Liberty Valance (Lee Marvin).

Leah Rhodes was brought on to the project for designing duties, and the remainder of the wardrobe was pulled from stock. Edith was receiving credit for the film, but really had very little to do but approve selections. Still, because of the film's popularity, she was nominated for an Oscar for best costume design for black-and-white, in what people thought was a very slim year in the costume design category. The award went to Norma Koch for *Whatever Happened to Baby Jane* (1962).

Bette Davis was nominated for an Oscar for Best Actress for her performance in *Whatever Happened to Baby Jane?* but Joan Crawford was not. The two actresses had been able to make it through the shoot-

Because of the studio's cuts to the original production budget, *Escape from Zahrain* starring Yul Brynner, did not live up to its potential

BETTE DAVIS WAS FURIOUS WHEN NEWSPAPERS ACROSS THE COUNTRY THE NEXT DAY, WERE FILLED WITH PHOTOS OF JOAN HOLDING THE BEST ACTRESS OSCAR, MAKING IT LOOK TO THE CASUAL OBSERVER AS IF SHE HAD WON FOR *WHATEVER HAPPENED TO BABY JANE?*

Opposite: Bette Davis as the apple-seller-turned-socialite in *A Pocketful of Miracles.* This page: A wardrobe test photo for Dorothy Lamour in *Donovan's Reef.*

ing of the film, but not without the flares of ego for which both women were famous. Joan decided to petition all the Best Actress nominees that year, except for Bette, and offered to accept the award on their behalf, if they were unable to attend the ceremony. Anne Bancroft, nominated for *The Miracle Worker* (1962), accepted Joan's offer. Bancroft did indeed win the award that night and Joan took to the stage in a gown designed by Edith. Bette Davis was furious when newspapers across the country the next day, were filled with photos of Joan holding the Best Actress Oscar, making it look to the casual observer as if she had won for *Whatever Happened to Bobay Jane?, Time* magazine called Joan's look the "triumph of the evening," saying "announcing that she would make 'my first appearance with the silvery look,' Joan washed the red out of her hair, hired Designer Edith Head to create a grey little something to match, slung a chinchilla around her shoulders, and topped the production with a ton of diamonds. Crawford's investment paid off with interest: as stand-in for Best Actress Contender Anne Bancroft (stationed cross-country in the Broadway production of *Mother Courage*), Joan emerged as the most photographed, autographed star in all that night's sky."

From 1963 to 1965, Edith hosted a series of five-minute radio segments that were produced by Paramount for CBS Radio. The shows were titled *Fashion Notes* and *Fashionscope*. Paramount paid Edith an additional $150 per week to produce between five and fifteen pre-recorded shows a week. Edith could expound for the entire five minutes or interview celebrities with whom she was working on topics like

Edith compares her sketch to the final dress for a fashion show sequence in *A New Kind of Love.*

"Men's Thoughts on Glamorous Women," "The Importance of Gloves," and "Throwing a Color-Themed Luncheon." "The handbag is one accessory that belongs to women only," Edith began one of her segments, "because men have so many pockets. But sometimes when I look at the different pocket bulges where men carry pipes, tobacco, bill folds, keys and lighters, I think I'd better invent a masculine carry-all, perhaps some version of the brief case. However, I understand it's pretty difficult to make men take up a new fashion, so perhaps I had better wait until men themselves rebel."

Edith re-teamed with director John Ford on *Donovan's Reef* (1963). The story involved a group of American ex-servicemen, played by John Wayne, Lee Marvin, Jack Warden and Mike Mazurki, living it up on a South Seas island, until the arrival of a young woman from Boston society (Elizabeth Allen, playing Warden's daughter) throws a wrench in their fun. Edith's former assistant, Pat Barto, had designed for Allen earlier that year for the film *Diamond Head* (1963). Elizabeth Allen was one of the rare stars that Edith could not find a common ground, and Edith worked hard to get Allen thrown off the film and replaced by Vera Miles.

Donovan's Reef gave Edith a chance to work with Dorothy Lamour again. By this time, the actress was forty-eight when production began and Edith and Dorothy must have been relieved that no one was screaming to put the actress in a sarong, despite the tropical location. Instead, Edith designed some kaftans in tropical patterns for the actress to wear.

Melville Shavelson actually used Edith for inspiration when he wrote *A New Kind of Love* (1963) starring real-life husband and wife Paul Newman and Joanne Woodward. Joanne played Samantha Blake, a "semi-virgin" who works as fashion consultant that knocks off high-end dresses. When Blake takes a trip to Paris to view the collections, she pays a visit to St. Catherine, patron saint of spinsters, and is advised to get a Paris makeover at Elizabeth Arden. Samantha proceeds to try to convince newspaper writer Steve Sherman (Newman), that she is Mimi, an International call-girl. She saves his career when he turns her made-up debauched adventures into newspaper columns with horrible sports metaphors.

Bob Mackie had begun working in the Paramount costume department making sketches for a designer who was doing a film in Europe, and was renting space there. "That was Edith Head's territory and she was always coming in to see what her guests were doing and I met her there then" said Mackie. When an artist in the department got sick, Edith called Mackie in to work as a sketch artist on *A New Kind of Love*. "I was the new boy," he said. "I was twenty-two years old and it was just amazing for me, all of a sudden from nowhere, to be in the middle of all that, working at the studio and having access to all the soundstages. I was soaking it up like a sponge. I was there at Paramount, and

WOODWARD WORE TAILORED SUITS OF TWEED, BUT AS MIMI, THE WIGS WERE SKY HIGH AND HER FASHIONS OUTLANDISH. "IT'S A TERRIBLE MOVIE. SHE LOOKS LIKE A DRAG QUEEN," MACKIE SAID.

WHEN CAROL BURNETT SAW ALL OF EDITH'S OSCARS LINED UP, SHE GASPED "MY GOSH, I GOT INTO WALT DISNEY'S BY MISTAKE!"

Set against the backdrop of the fashion industry, Joanne Woodward starred in *A New Kind of Love.*

I was looking at Edith Head, who was turning out all these movies and everything, and I thought 'God, she must be at least sixty-something. She's going to retire any minute. I better hang around here, maybe I can get the job. You know, when you're twenty-two, you're really stupid. And I realized, after watching her that she wasn't going to give up."

In her incarnation as Samantha, the fashion consultant, Woodward wore tailored suits of tweed, but as Mimi, the wigs were sky high and her fashions outlandish. "It's a terrible movie. She looks like a drag queen," Mackie said. But the film has achieved kind of cult status among fashion students and camp movie lovers.

A New Kind of Love was filmed on Paramount's Stage Five. A set was designed after the major Paris fashion palaces, and, duplicated authentically their couture salons and dressing rooms. When a $2,000 dress of brocade and mink comes down the runway in the film, Samantha surmises "in rayon and rabbit fur, I figure we can do it for about $89.95." The film included fashion shows by Lanvin (who got a "perfumes by" credit), Dior and Givenchy. The designers had sent sketches of their clothes, which were then built in the Paramount workroom. In May of 1963, Edith went on a tour of ladies' club luncheons around country with a fashion show of $200,000 worth of gowns from *A New Kind of Love* and other films. Dubbed the *A New Kind of Love Fashion Tour*, newspapers carried extensive coverage of the shows and interviews with Edith.

Bob Mackie left Paramount after only a few months to begin a partnership with Ray Aghayan, who was about to start work on *The Judy Garland Show*. Mackie would go on to great fame designing for Carol Burnett and Cher, among many other stars, as well as developing his own couture and ready-to-wear lines. In the late 1970s, as Edith's workload slowed down, she was often asked to speak at symposiums about fashion on the history of Hollywood. On some occasions, Mackie would also be asked to speak alongside her on the new glamour of Hollywood.

Who's Been Sleeping in my Bed (1963) gave Edith her first chance to work with Carol Burnett. Burnett co-starred along with Dean Martin, who played an actor on a medical television series. When Carol Burnett showed up for a fitting in Edith's salon and saw all of Edith's Oscars lined up, she gasped "My gosh, I got into Walt Disney's by mistake!" Later Edith interviewed Carol for her radio show, and the topic was What Do Clothes mean to you? Carol answered: "They keep me warm."

A JOB FOR THE BIRDS

ASSISTANT DIRECTOR JIM BROWN WAS SENT TO HEDREN'S DRESSING ROOM THE MORNING OF THE SHOOT TO EXPLAIN THAT MECHANICAL BIRDS WOULDN'T WORK, AND THAT SPECIALLY TRAINED RAVENS AND CROWS WOULD BE USED.

Opposite and this page: **Edith resurrected and reworked the eau de nil suit from *Rear Window* for Tippi Hedren in *The Birds*.**

ALFRED HITCHCOCK HAD MOVED HIS PRODUCTION OFFICES TO UNIVERSAL, AND WAS NOW WORKING THERE. He had made a tremendous impact in the horror genre with his film Psycho (1960). Looking for his next project, he became intrigued by news stories he had read about people being attacked by birds. Hitchcock turned to a short story written by Daphne Du Maurier, who also wrote the novels on which *Rebecca* (1940) and *Jamaica Inn* (1939) were based. In Du Maurier's story, a peasant farmer and his family are attacked by murderous birds in their small Cornish village.

When Anne Bancroft proved to be too expensive to cast in the lead of *The Birds* (1963), Hitchcock took an interest in an actress he saw in a commercial for a diet drink aired during the *Today* show. She had just the kind of cool blond good looks that Hitchcock liked. Tippi Hedren was asked to come to Universal and went through several meetings with executives before they would tell her it was Hitchcock who was interested in hiring her. She was given a three-day color screen test with actor Martin Balsam, for which Edith designed her wardrobe. Hedren was under the impression that Hitchcock only wanted her for his *Alfred Hitchcock Presents* television show, but at a dinner at Chasen's, the director presented her with a gold pin of birds flying, and told her that she had the lead in The Birds.

The screenplay's plot had socialite Melanie Daniels (Hedren) chasing after handsome Mitch Brenner (Rod Taylor) to a town where birds are mysteriously attacking people. Hitchcock originally had planned to use mechanical birds in the scenes, but soon abandoned the idea when they didn't appear realistic on screen. Production designer Robert F. Boyle and cinematographer Robert Burks investigated the sodium vapor process, in which an original negative was created as a "matte," which would allow for the special effects needed. Dummy birds could be used for background scenes, and Hitchcock hired bird trainer Ray Berwick to wrangle live birds, which would be used with the actors.

Hitchcock changed the locations in the story to San Francisco and a town 60 miles North of the city called Bodega Bay. Hitchcock had made *Shadow of a Doubt* (1943) in nearby Santa Rosa, and liked the area very much. Principal photography took six months, two months in Bodega Bay and four months on the Universal lot.

Hitchcock was planning on a lot of green being used in the production, and limited Edith to using green and blue in Hedren's wardrobe. Green to Hitchcock evoked a chaste, cool quality. Edith resurrected the idea of the eau de nil suit worn by Grace Kelly in *Rear Window*, this time with a structure more akin to a Chanel suit. Six copies were made of the suit, since Hedren would wear it for a large part of the film, and most would need to be distressed as the birds continued their attack.

Since Hedren only had three changes, her entire film wardrobe cost just $5,000. The nightgown she wears in the film was supposed to have been purchased at an inexpensive variety store, so that's just what Edith did. "There are wonderful designers who make you look good, very elegant," Hedren said. "But Edith taught me that you not only design to make a person look according to their character, you have to make sure that the person can do the action."

No. 2
"The Birds"

Opposite: The fur coat that Tippi Hedren wears as Melanie Daniels in *The Birds*. Right: A dress for Hedren's screen test.

Hitchcock personally selected Hedren's jewelry in the film: a bracelet, a ring, and a single strand of pearls. It was important that Melanie be elegant to show her privileged position and materialistic nature, so Hitchcock selected things of quality for her such as a scarf and a mink coat. Howard Smit and Bob Dawn were hired to do the make-up. Prosthetic pieces were manufactured from latex and attached to actors' faces to replicate punctures in the flesh. Smit also had his own formula for making realistic-looking screen blood.

When creating the script, Hitchcock gave the screenwriter a free hand, telling him nothing would be too difficult to shoot. For the climactic scene in the attic, Hedren assumed that most of the birds used would be mechanical or would be added optically. Assistant director Jim Brown was sent to Hedren's dressing room the morning of the shoot to explain that mechanical birds wouldn't work, and that specially trained ravens and crows would be used.

A large cage had been built with room for the camera, camera man and five or six prop men wearing gloves, who would pull large crows and sea gulls from cartons. The birds were thrown at Tippi at very close range. "The birds weren't so much angry as they were unable to direct their flight correctly when tossed so close to me," Hedren said. "The poor things were frightened and didn't know what they were doing. I was bitten on the lip and scratched directly under one eye." Costumer Rita Riggs stood by, scissors in hand, to distress the green suits as the action progressed. When it was all over, Hedren burst into tears, cried for two hours, and then went to bed for four days on doctor's orders.

Hitchcock paid to have Edith design a personal wardrobe for Tippi to wear to press conferences and various premieres of the film around the world. Tippi's "tour" wardrobe cost $18,000 and included long shifts for morning wear, daytime cocktail clothes to formal dresses. Each outfit Edith designed represented a bird, allowing for interesting conversation about the clothes with reporters. The evening clothes were all black-and-white, with many different coordinated pieces, to allow for variety when Tippi could only travel with one suitcase.

Original test audiences for *The Birds* were left grappling for answers when the film ended without explaining a reason for the bird attacks. The script's original ending was cut, which showed Bodega Bay engulfed with birds, and the Golden Gate Bridge completely covered with them. The film was met with a somewhat frosty reception by critics who used words like "plotless" and "pointless." But what were originally viewed as some of the film's shortcomings are exactly what intrigue audiences today, and it has become a favorite of film fans and college professors, who include it in courses taught to film students.

A wardrobe department continuity log for Phyllis McGuire in *Come Blow Your Horn.*

Come Blow Your Horn (1963) was based on the successful Broadway play by Neil Simon, and adapted into a screenplay by Norman Lear. Frank Sinatra starred as Alan Baker, whose swinging bachelorhood is hampered by his young brother's (Tony Bill) attempts to copy it. Edith made designs for four different types of characters in the film: a free-thinker and changes every minute (Carol Wells); a glamour girl (Jill St. John); a buyer for Neiman-Marcus (Phyllis McGuire); and the girl that Alan Baker marries (Barbara Rush). For the wedding, Rush wore a white wedding suit with yellow chiffon trim. "The perfect penthouse costume for anyone" was how Sinatra described the midnight blue jersey sheath with a floor-sweeping train and tunic of midnight blue coq feathers that was designed for Jill St. John.

On November 14, 1962, Paramount held a penthouse party on the *Come Blow Your Horn* set, complete with an Edith Head fashion show. Fashion editors from all over the country were in Los Angeles as part of the California Fashion Press Creators Week, and were invited by the studio to attend the party. Jill St. John, Barbara Rush, and other stars from the film also attended. The spectacle paid off with scores of mentions in fashion columns in every major newspaper in the country.

REALITY VS. FANTASY

In the days of stringent censorship, a film like *Love with the Proper Stranger* (1963) could have never been made without drastic alterations. But as the 1960s progressed, audiences wanted more character-driven plots with real-life dramatic situations. Natalie Wood was twenty-four when she signed on to the project. She had already been a star for sixteen years since winning audience's hearts in *Miracle on 34th Street* (1947). Performances in *Rebel Without a Cause* (1955), *Splendor in the Grass* (1961) and *West Side Story* (1961) helped establish her as a major box-office attraction and serious actress with two Academy Award nominations.

In the film, Wood played Angie Rossini, a salesgirl at Macy's who, after a one-night fling with Rocky Papasano (Steve McQueen), discovers she is pregnant. When she tells Rocky she is carrying his child, he finds a doctor who will perform an abortion (the procedure was illegal at the time the film was made). When Rocky sees the squalid conditions under which the operation will be performed, the couple flees and consider marriage.

Edith "was afraid Natalie would ask for one of the designers

FORM 750—8-46

PROD. No. 10385 DIRECTOR Bud Yorkin ASSISTANT Danny McCauley

ARTIST Phyllis McGuire CHARACTER Mrs Eckman

No.	DESCRIPTION	ACCESSORIES
(1)	Dress - Blk Velvet Sheath - Belt - Blk Cummerbund w/ Buckle Necklace 1 diamond Bracelet - gold Earrings Int Alan's Apt Living Rm Sc 42-43-44	
(2)	Blk Sheer top all over " Blk crepe skirt Stole - Blk crepe w/ Int Mrs Eckman Hotel Rm Sc 56-86-87-88	

145

162

from Warner Brothers for her clothes, because she'd been at Warner Brothers all those years," Bob Mackie said. "Because she'd started as a little kid, they kind of took her for granted, and nobody was really courting her." When Matha Hyer was scheduled to be fitted in Edith's salon at the same time Natalie was available for her first consultation, Edith had a great moment of Hollywood ingenuity. She took over designer Leah Rhodes' office down the hall and dressed it up Hollywood style to look like her own salon. "Edith pulled out all the stops," Mackie said. "They were fluffing up this back room and putting all these flowers, and bringing in hors d'oeuvres. And they were bringing the Oscars down the hall, cleaning them up, dusting them off, and, of course, it worked."

When Judy Garland was readying for *I Could Go on Singing* (1963), the producers chose Edith to do Garland's wardrobe. The film was to be shot in England, and Edith did Judy's fittings in Los Angeles. "Judy arrived in England with a wardrobe already done by Edith, director Ronald Neame says. "But the trouble was Judy put on about ten pounds during her stay in England before production began, and there was no way we could use any of Edith's lovely clothes. We had to get in a designer in England and we had to make all new clothes." The designer chosen was Beatrice Dawson, who had been nominated for an Oscar for *The Pickwick Papers* (1952).

Judy Garland played Jenny Bowman, a successful singer, who returns to London and begins a relationship with the child she's abandoned. "The performance was Judy being Judy," says Neame. "There is one scene in the hospital with Dirk and she really became herself. The lines changed and Dirk adjusted to them because he was a very professional actor. I had planned close shots and I realized when we were shooting that this was a piece of magic I would never get again. So I signaled to the dolly pusher to creep in closer because I knew I would only get this once. Dirk knew that the camera was coming in closer, and moved in closer to Judy so that I was finally able to finish on the heads. It was Judy exactly as Judy was in real life. We all loved her. She was a

Ronald Neame directs Judy Garland and Dirk Bogarde in *I Could Go on Singing*.

"THE TROUBLE WAS JUDY PUT ON ABOUT TEN POUNDS DURING HER STAY IN ENGLAND BEFORE PRODUCTION BEGAN, AND THERE WAS NO WAY WE COULD USE ANY OF EDITH'S LOVELY CLOTHES."

–Ronald Neame

pain the ass, but we all loved her."

Because Edith was contracted to have her name appear in the credits, everyone assumed Edith had done all the costumes. Dawson was only credited with "additional costumes." *Variety's* review was none too flattering saying, "Miss Garland was rather on the plumpish side when this film was shot, and neither Edith Head's costumes nor Pearl Tipaldi's hair styles are very becoming to her." Edith didn't seem to want to correct the record, as long as the reviews weren't too bad, but she took particular exception to a *Time* Magazine review that said, "Costume Designer Edith Head has not helped by giving her (Garland) a red chiffon outfit that makes Garland look like somebody had tried to stuff eight great tomatoes into a little bitty gown."

Edith fired back a letter to the editor saying "of course, since I was credited as costume designer, your critic would have no way of knowing this, but please, just for the record, I designed all of Judy's costumes for the picture with the exception of one. Uh-huh. You're right. I don't know how that red number slipped in. I plead innocent. Hollywood gremlins, I imagine. It's always a pleasure to appear in *Time*, but please, not as a tomato specialist."

By the time Judy returned to Los Angeles to begin work on her television show *The Judy Garland Show*, she was more svelte than she'd been in years. Judy asked Edith to do her wardrobe, the first time Edith was to design for an ongoing series, and Edith kept the designs to short, black dresses for the first show. "The producers don't want your listening pleasure to be spoiled by forcing you to look at elaborate gowns and production numbers," Edith told the press. Lawrence Laurent, writing in *The Washington Post*, said "Cheers too, for designer Edith Head. She gets credit for being the first person to properly costume Miss Garland for a television performance. In the past, pudgy Judy has appeared in toreador pants, ballooning skirts and frill-covered blouses."

Judy's requests for her clothes were requiring more time than Edith had allotted for the project, and she couldn't meet the demands

Opposite page: **One of Edith's unused designs for Judy Garland in *I Could Go on Singing*.**
Below: **Lucille Ball in *Critic's Choice*.**

of a weekly television show from her office at Paramount. The producers liked the work that Ray Aghayan and Bob Mackie were doing for the show's other cast members, and Edith was relieved when they were asked to take over the designing responsibilities for the remainder of the series.

Lucille Ball requested Edith for *Critic's Choice* (1963). Based on a Broadway play by Ira Levin, it was the last film pairing of Bob Hope and Lucille Ball. Hope played a New York theater critic who must somehow get out of reviewing his wife's new play. Levin had written the play in response to an essay by critic Walter Kerr, in which he surmised the worst possible scenario for a drama critic would be to have to review a play that his wife had written. Unfortunately, some of the best meat of the play was excised to tailor the material for Hope, and the film itself fell flat with critics.

But Edith's reviews for Ball's simple black dresses and unstructured suits were good. In a review for the Hollywood Reporter, critic James Powers noted: "Edward Carrerre's art direction is colorful, but not authentic. His Manhattan newspaperman inhabits a duplex of such bursting splendor that it must command a monthly rental of $2,000. Things aren't that good. Edith Head's costumes, on the other hand, are chic, but do not strain the credulity for Miss Ball's probable income bracket."

Wives and Lovers (1963) was a sex comedy with Van Johnson as Bill Austin, a stay-at-home writer, who is none too happy about his wife Bertie (Janet Leigh) leaving the house to re-join the workforce. When Bill's agent (Martha Hyer) starts making overtures at him, and an actor makes a play for Bertie, the fun begins.

Producer Hal Wallis was romancing the beautiful actress Martha Hyer, and gave Edith a little more leeway than usual. Typically, Wallis liked to keep things even more simple than Edith's simple style. Hal took a great personal interest in the costumes for Hyer, Janet Leigh and Shelley Winters. In one scene, Hyer wears the gold ball gown that

Lucille Ball – Katie

sc. 17 pg. 109
entrance w/ Hope

yellow
tent

easy release
for ball.

test.

Lucille Ball

appliqued
back?
quench jean

Edith Head

This page and opposite page: **Two designs for Lucille Ball in *The Facts of Life*.**

had originally been designed for Grace Kelly in *To Catch a Thief*. Edith removed the birds from the gown, and replaced them with roses, which is how the gown was originally designed when Edith did her first sketches for Hitchcock.

For the first time Edith received three Oscar nominations in one year. *Love With the Proper Strange*r and *Wives and Lovers* were nominated for best black-and-white costume design, losing to Piero Gherardi for *"8½"* (1963). *A New Kind of Love* was nominated for best color costume design, but lost to Irene Sharaff, Vittorio Nino Novarese and Renié for *Cleoptara* (1963).

Much like what Edith had to go through with Anna Magnani, so was it was with director Martin Ritt for *Hud* (1963). Ritt began in the business as an actor in Harold Clurman's celebrated Group Theater. He practiced Stanilslavski's acting technique in which an actor always approaches a role as directly as possible. Ritt wasn't so sure that Edith Head, responsible for so much Hollywood glamour, could pull off the costumes for his gritty tale of an amoral and destructive young rancher. Ritt was so adamant that the clothes not be a focal point, Edith had to be careful that nothing could distract on the clothes—not buttons, belts—and he wanted no flashy cowboy gear of any sort.

In typical Edith fashion, she gave Ritt almost too many choices. He settled on clothes that hugged Newman's physique and played up the idea of a sexy arrogant antihero. The posters and ads for Hud capitalized on this with full-length shots of a brooding Newman, full of swagger, looking directly at the camera. For Patricia Neal's character of Alma, the housekeeper, Edith took the actress to the wardrobe department and pulled clothes from stock so that they would have a worn look. Edith had to be careful that Alma's clothing showed that she was world-weary, but not be too ragtag, so the audience would still see her as an unconventionally beautiful woman.

Edith's services were lent out when Shirley MacLaine went to Twentieth Century-Fox to star in *What a Way to Go!* (1964), a black comedy that producer Arthur P. Jacobs had originally intended for Marilyn Monroe. MacLaine played Louisa, a poor girl who wants "only a simple life with one man to love." Her curse is that she can find plenty of love, but each of her husbands meets his untimely end in the pursuit of riches, leaving her wealthier and wealthier. As Shirley appears in each new gown, they reflect her growing financial status. Moss Mabry dressed the men playing opposite MacLaine in the film: Paul Newman, Robert Mitchum, Dean Martin, Gene Kelly, Robert Cummings and Dick Van Dyke.

For Edith, the assignment was like a return to the 1920s when budgets were limitless. She was given a half-million dollar budget for clothes, and borrowed $3.5 million worth of jewelry from Harry Winston in New York. "The whole picture was basically about the clothes and the men," MacLaine says.

MacLaine wrote that, for as happy as she was to have such a lavish wardrobe, adjusting to a different co-star and their individual idiosyncrasies every two weeks in the shooting schedule, was difficult for her. "Each actor had different ways of working," MacLaine says. 'Paul Newman liked to work like a method actor. And on a picture like *What a Way to Go!* that was really silly. I was having a love affair with Robert Mitchum, so that was easy."

For MacLaine, the film is the most memorable for her in terms of costumes because she had to endure fittings during every lunch hour. "They didn't have time to make all those clothes before the start date," she says. "I had a bungalow on the Fox lot, and all the fittings happened there. Edith and I would talk about life, love and the pursuit of happiness and my travels. I made friends with Candy, the chimp. This was in the days of smoking. And Candy the chimp would come into my dressing room and smoke and drink with me." The production kept thirty seamstresses working full-time.

The story lines called for some of the most outrageous designs of Edith's career. Newman, as a self-centered artist, paints an abstract expressionist gown for Louisa to wear to one of his openings. In a scene

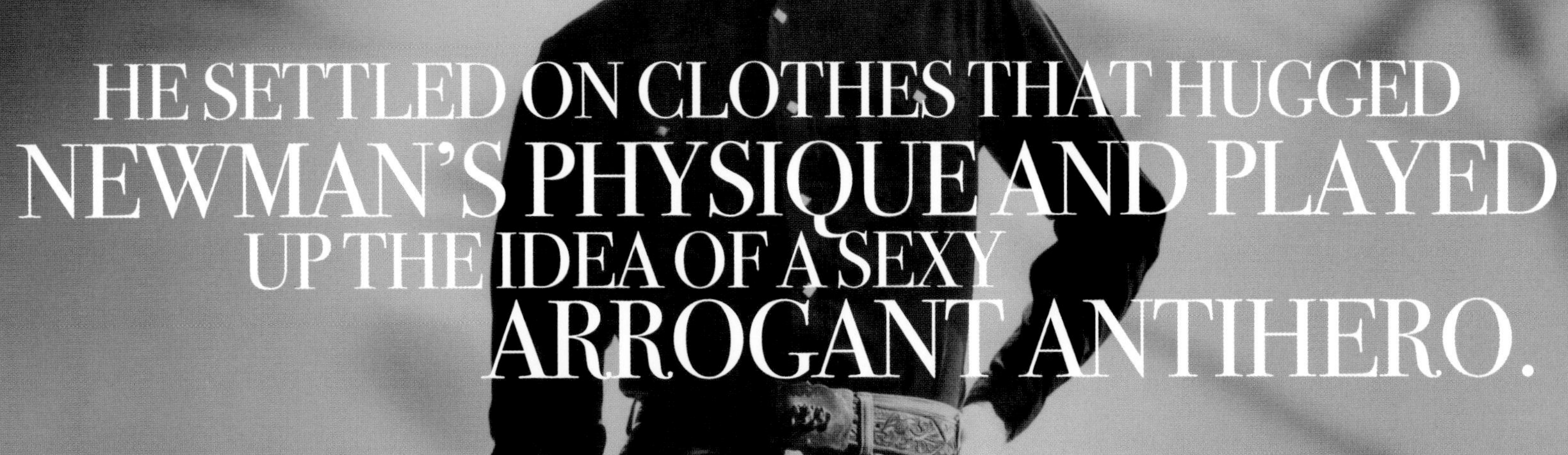

HE SETTLED ON CLOTHES THAT HUGGED NEWMAN'S PHYSIQUE AND PLAYED UP THE IDEA OF A SEXY ARROGANT ANTIHERO.

Though director Martin Ritt had his doubts about Edith at first, she understood what he needed to help Paul Newman to bring his character to life in *Hud.*

with Gene Kelly, who plays Pinky Benson, MacLaine wears an all-pink chinchilla coat and pink wig. Even the veils on Louisa's widow's weeds are longer than the hem on her skirt. But in a film of over-the-top gowns, the most remarkable was the one dubbed "the diamond dress." It was a split-up-the-side rhinestone-encrusted sheath topped by thousands of dollars in diamond jewelry. In MacLaine's wig were two large diamond pins and a diamond necklace, placed by Sidney Guilaroff, who designed the hairpieces that MacLaine wore in the film.

The reviews weren't always favorable, but no one could overlook Edith's contribution to the movie. *Time magazine* said "For all its talent and occasional forward thrust, *What a Way to Go!* never really gets anywhere. The reasons why are neatly capsuled in Shirley's cine-fantasy with Mitchum, described as "one of those Hollywood movies all about love and what'll-she-wear-next?

"This gag sequence, credited as A Lush Budget Production, offers four minutes' worth of opulent sets and a whole spring collection of Edith Head's most improbable costumes. But What a Way itself is so extravagantly overdrawn that the audience well may wonder where parody leaves off and plot begins."

Even with a costume picture as *What a Way to Go!*, Edith couldn't top the opulence of Cecil Beaton's period clothes in *My Fair Lady* (1964), and the Oscar for best color costume design went to him that year. Edith was also nominated for *A House is Not a Home* (1964), but lost to Dorothy Jeakins' designs for *The Night of the Iguana* (1964).

When Grace Kelly married Prince Rainier of Monaco in 1956, it seemed a very real possibility that the actress would still make an occasional film while carrying out her duties as princess. Alfred Hitchcock purchased the rights to Winston Graham's novel *Marnie*, with the idea that it would be Grace's return to the screen. There were two problems. One was that MGM had allowed Grace to retire before she fulfilled her contract, and another film would need to be done for them. But the hurdle that could not be overcome was that the people of Monaco did

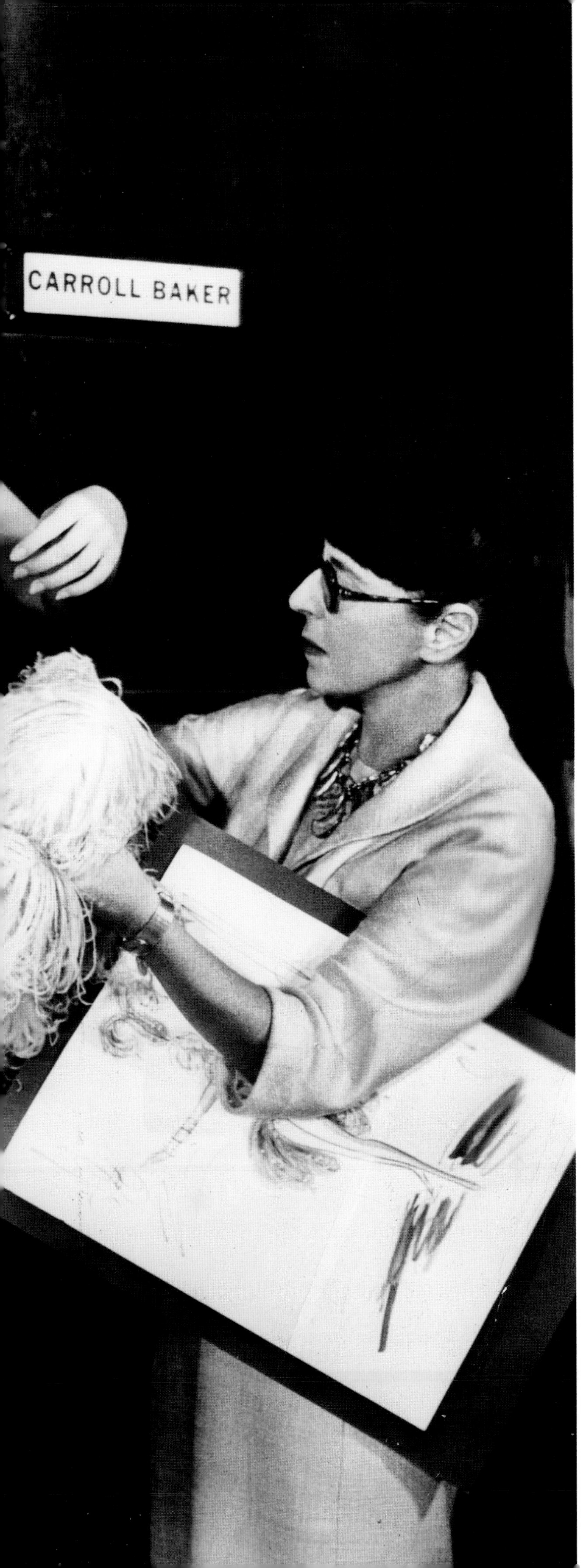

Caroll Baker (with Edith, left, and with George Peppard, above) helped to usher in a frank new sexuality in films like *The Carpetbaggers.*

This page and opposite: **Shirley MacLaine plays a multi-time widow, whose wardrobe keeps getting more outlandish as she becomes wealthier in *What a Way to Go!***

#21

LADIES
WARDROBE
PICTURE A857
TITLE What a Way
DIRECTOR J Lee Thompson
ACTRESS S MacLaine
PART OF Louisa
CHANGE No. 40
INT BEDR
SCENE No. 218
Designer E HEAD 8x10

not want their princess appearing in a film about a compulsive thief. Hitchcock shelved the project while he made *The Birds*.

Working with actress Tippi Hedren on *The Birds*, Hitchcock realized that he already had the perfect actress for *Marnie* (1964), and offered the role to her. In the film, Marnie Edgar is a beautiful woman who uses her charms to attain bookkeeping positions at companies, only to rob them, change identities and repeat the cycle. She marries Mark Rutland (Sean Connery), who is determined to find the cause of Marnie's compulsion.

Once again, Hitchcock mapped out all the colors he needed in the script. For a Hitchcock film, normally the clothes were to reveal the character as who they were, but in *Marnie's* case, they needed to show someone who she was not. "She didn't want anybody to notice her," Hedren says. "We did discuss color and the importance of color, and how after Marnie is married, the clothes change completely." Hitchcock instructed Edith that he wanted no eye-catching colors that would detract from the action and wanted to use warm colors to demonstrate that Marnie was, in fact, a warm person.

In the same way Hitchcock avoided bright colors that pulled focus, he also embraced them to call attention to something. Marnie's handbag, shown in close-up several times, was purposely bright yellow. As details of the robbery are revealed in the beginning, the viewer realizes, that is where the stolen money is located. "We discussed color a lot," Hedren says of working with Hitchcock. "For instance, if someone is running in a crowd, that person wears something that can be noticed, so that you can follow them. The best example of Hitch's use of color was in *Dial M for Murder* (1954) for Grace Kelly. In the opening, she's in bright red, and then after the murder, her clothes become more subdued, and then finally she's wearing gray. That added to her performance because it was drab and she was pretty defeated."

Edith met with art director Robert Boyle before presenting any sketches to Hitchcock to make sure that her designs were in keeping with the cool or warm colors used on the sets. Various colors signified various emotions that the character could be having. A brighter color could mean the wearer was happy or more open, blue could mean the wearer was cool, or passive.

Edith chose a bright yellow dress for a key scene, where Marnie is at her most joyful. Marnie is in a cocktail dress when her husband brings her beloved horse that she has missed so much. Marnie runs straight out the door, jumps on the horse and races off. "There are color codes that everyone could live by. If you're in authority, it's very powerful to wear a bright pink or red. I believe all that," Hedren says.

Marnie's nightgowns are decidedly almost airtight. There is nothing seductive about them. They are constructed to keep people out. The clothes helped Hedren resist the charms of the handsome Connery. Hedren says she told Hitchcock "here I am playing this frigid woman who screams every time a man comes near her and you have chosen an actor who could melt the iciest of blondes. How am I supposed to do that? And he said, 'It's called acting, my dear,' and that was the end of that."

For the character of Lil, Edith developed a totally separate color palette for actress Diane Baker. Though Hitchcock also had very clear ideas about her character, Edith did not have a handle on what Baker should wear. Edith asked the actress to bring in some of her own wardrobe that she thought flattered her, to use as inspiration. Rita Riggs and James Linn were assigned to costume the remaining cast.

"She knew so clearly what she wanted. I think she had a wonderful life because she was so, so opinionated and very sure of herself and her talent," Tippi says of Edith. "We were very good friends. And her husband was charming. And we had dinner every now and then. She was such a fun woman. She was really, really interesting. So up, with a wonderful ability to charm you."

In *Roustabout* (1964), Elvis Presley, plays a tough, leather-jacketed singer, who performs at a carnival so that he can pay to have

Director Alfred Hitchcock (left) embraces Edith on the set of *Marnie*.

FOR A HITCHCOCK FILM, NORMALLY THE CLOTHES WERE TO REVEAL THE CHARACTER AS WHO THEY WERE, BUT IN MARNIE'S CASE, THEY NEEDED TO SHOW SOMEONE WHO SHE WAS NOT.

This page and opposite: **The evolution of Tippi Hedren's character in *Marnie* was helped along by the wardrobe as well as the script.**

his motorcycle repaired. Producer Hal Wallis persuaded Barbara Stanwyck to accept a role in the film as the carnival owner. Stanwyck, now 54, seemed an unlikely co-star for Elvis, but it brought audiences of two generations into the theater. The combination also brought Elvis more respect as an actor, and introduced Stanwyck to a younger generation of fans, soon to get to know her better on television in *The Big Valley.* To create the carnival atmosphere, the three main stages at Paramount were opened and combined for the first time in the history of the studio. Stanwyck, as the owner of the carnival, was a tough hands-on kind of woman, and Edith dressed her in blue jeans, combined with a bright red Western shirt and mid-calf black boots. The jeans were not bought off-the-rack or brought from stock, but were specially designed and fitted for Barbara. Long before the overall acceptance of blue jeans as casual wear, Stanwyck wearing them was considered big fashion news.

By 1965, Edith was making $1,0000 per week at Paramount, not including her additional payments for the radio programs. Adjusting for inflation, she was still making less than Travis Banton had in the 1930's during the Depression. The wardrobe department was struggling to meet producers' demands for creating costumes faster and cheaper. Personally, Edith had been shocked by the sudden death of her sketch artist Grace Sprague in a car accident.

Since 1958, skirt lengths had been getting shorter and shorter, until finally the mini-skirt became one of the most defining fashions of the mid-1960's. The epicenter of change was King's Road in London, where designer Mary Quant had a shop called Bazaar. Fashion magazines were full of trends happening in Swinging London, but Edith had a different problems with minis than she had with the New Look when it was introduced. "The miniskirt was a terrible shock to us because we didn't know how long it would last," she said. The problem wasn't the introduction of the mini itself, but anticipating the timing of when it could fall out of favor, making movies featuring the mini look dated.

HOLLYWOOD STRUGGLES TO REDEFINE ITSELF

Harlow (1965) was part of a wave of nostalgic cinema-related movies that would continue into the mid-1970s. Actress Jean Harlow was given two screen biographies in the same year by different studios. Paramount's *Harlow* starred Carroll Baker as the blonde sex symbol, with Angela Lansbury as her mother. Both films were spurred into production because of interest in Irving Schulman's semi-authentic biography of the late star, and neither film bore much resemblance to the real life of the actress. For dramatic effect, the screenwriters portrayed a boozy Harlow, being consumed by her career. When, by most accounts, the real Jean Harlow was a consummate professional with a great sense of humor. Because of potential lawsuits from Harlow's fiancee William Powell, the love interest played by Mike Connors was tailored to not resemble Powell at all.

Edith knew the Harlow mystique well, having taken credit for some of it with her designs for Jean in *The Saturday Night Kid*. Baker's silk gowns were cut on the bias, in which the fabric is placed on a forty-five-degree angle to the straight of the grain, causing it to shape itself to the body. Edith added plenty of rhinestones and marabou feathers to give audiences the illusion of the way they thought movie stars should dress. But Edith hated that producers wanted to bare more of Baker's flesh than was customary in American films. Edith believed strongly that covering up an actress actually created more drama and mystery. But it was a sign of the times. Nudity was the one area where movies could compete with television.

When Baker returned from a trip to England, she presented her friends, including Edith, with antique ivory disks that had been used in the 1800s as a theatre tickets. Edith liked the disk so much that she began to collect them on her trips to England. Some of them bore the name of the person who had the seats on a specific evening including The Duke of Leeds, Box 21, some just had names of theatres including King's Theatre, Her Majesty's Theatre, and Covent Garden with Thurs-

Edith helped Natalie Wood shape her image as a young woman in films like *Sex and the Single Girl*.

This page and opposite page: **Though the film bore little resemblance to the actress' life, Edith captured the mystique of Jean Harlow for Carroll Baker's costumes in *Harlow*.**

day spelled out on it. Edith had them made into a necklace and it became her most recognized piece of jewelry.

Blake Edwards' *The Great Race* (1965) provided Edith with another chance to do some show-stopping costumes. Set against the backdrop of the first around-the-world automobile race in 1908, the film starred Tony Curtis as The Great Leslie, Jack Lemmon as Professor Fate and Natalie Wood as Maggie Dubois. Edith's elaborate costumes for Wood were done for comedic effect. When Dubois' car breaks down she is given rides by The Great Leslie and others, and despite having limited luggage, she never appears in the same outfit twice. "That was the most fun because it made no sense at all," Edith said. Edwards intention was to make "the funniest comedy ever," but critics panned his use of slapstick and double-entendres. However, audiences disagreed and were willing to put their money where their mouth was. The film became one of the top 10 grossing films of 1965.

Love Has Many Faces (1965) cast Lana Turner as Kit Jordan, a rich playgirl on vacation in Acapulco, where police are investigating the death of one of her husband's friends. "We deliberately avoided making anything for her that resembles either the Acapulco or Mexican look," Edith said. "There's nothing indigenous about Lana's clothes at all. People who live in Acapulco dress one way. Tourists who visit there dress another. And, as Kit, Lana dresses her own way. She makes her own fashion rules."

Edith designed a lounging outfit of a one-piece black bathing suit and a robe of dramatic zebra stripes that showed off Lana's figure and was used on all the advertising art. Of the funeral scene, Edith said "It's the kind of funeral where she knows it would be in very bad taste for her to wear black. So she instinctively goes to the other side of the spectrum and wears white over beige, as they do in the Orient. But her head is covered, of course. She's lived all over the world enough to know that at a ceremony like that, the head must be covered."

Edith said she dressed Lana in heavily jeweled play clothes for a cocktail party scene because Kit "wouldn't dream of conforming. She always has to be different. It amuses her to shock people. The minute

EDITH HATED THAT PRODUCERS WANTED TO BARE MORE OF BAKER'S FLESH THAN WAS CUSTOMARY IN AMERICAN FILMS. EDITH BELIEVED STRONGLY THAT COVERING UP AN ACTRESS ACTUALLY CREATED MORE DRAMA AND MYSTERY.

Lana walks onto the screen, you know what kind of woman she is," Edith said. "And through the rest of the picture, she reflects the same sort of person. Because no matter what happens to her in the story, she hasn't changed a bit."

Alfred Hitchcock originally wanted to cast Eva Marie Saint and Cary Grant in *Torn Curtain* (1965). Cary Grant was in the process of announcing his retirement from making films, so Hitchcock cast Paul Newman as an American physicist who may be defecting to East Berlin. Universal forced Hitchcock to cast Julie Andrews as Newman's fiancée and assistant. The actress had just scored a major triumph the previous year with *The Sound of Music* (1965). The production was plagued with problems including Newman's constant questioning of his motivations in the script, financial problems, delays in shooting and what critics saw as a lack of chemistry between the two main stars.

Edith didn't have much to do in the way of clothes. Andrews' wardrobe was kept to a simple trench coat, a red nightgown and dresses and coats of soft wools in muted colors. But while working on *Torn Curtain,* Alfred Hitchcock, who became a major shareholder at Universal, asked Edith if she would come to work at the studio. She met with Universal chief Lew Wasserman, whose wife Edie was a personal client of Edith's, about the possibility. She declined the offer at the time, but kept the door open, just in case.

Edith was nominated for an Oscar for color costume design for dressing Natalie Wood in *Inside Daisy Clover* (1965), along with Bill Thomas, who did the men's wardrobe. There were no exceptional designs for Anne Bancroft as a suicidal woman in *The Slender Thread*, but Edith's nomination for best black-and-white costume design for that film showed how much her name could generate interest in film. She lost in both categories to Phyllis Dalton for *Doctor Zhivago* (1965) and Julie Harris for *Darling* (1965), respectively.

MGM had been the one studio that had a consistent design staff, and had never asked for Edith's services. It nearly happened once on *North by Northwest* (1959), when Helen Rose was unable to be on set as much as Hitchcock had expected, but the director's solution was to

Occasionally an outfit is so striking that it is used extensively in the advertising art for a film, as was the case with this ensemble for Lana Turner in *Love Has Many Faces.*

Lana Turner's wardrobe had to convey that her character was a rich playgirl in *Love Has Many Faces*, and Edith accomplished the task beautifully.

Edith's costumes for Natalie Wood in *Inside Daisy Clover* earned the designer an Oscar nomination.

buy the clothes instead. When Natalie Wood went to MGM to make *Penelope* (1966), Edith went along with her. Natalie starred as the title character, a young married woman who feels neglected by her husband and begins robbing businesses to get attention. Edith broke her costumes into two groups. One was high-style, comprising beautiful furs, discreet suits, svelte cocktail dresses and sophisticated evening gowns, all expressing financial wealth. The second was more casual and included the first mini-dress that Edith designed for a film. One yellow suit that Natalie wears is actually by Givenchy.

The studio decided to use the wardrobe Edith had designed for Natalie Wood as a marketing tool in a fifteen-minute color promotional film, shown on television. Edith appeared in the trailer with a book on schizophrenia, applying the definition to all the women who just didn't know what to wear. Edith used her own script-analyzing techniques to walk women through the morning fashion choices of the average woman. "Now when she gets up in the morning, is she gay, is she depressed, is she happy, does she think her husband loves her, or is she so emotionally disturbed that she forgets to put on her shoes?" Edith asked. The studio interspersed Wood's actual wardrobe tests with clips from the film to show the full outfits including a sexy candy-striped nightie that emphasized Wood's legs, and the distinctive knee-length wedding dress with an overlay of criss-crossed imported French lace.

Above and opposite page: **Part of the humor in *The Great Race* came from the numerous and elaborate changes of wardrobe for Natalie Wood.**

From the standpoint of understanding what a designer goes through with a script, the short film was very effective. Natalie's character was a woman who stole jewelry to get her husband's attention, but she ultimately wasn't a villain, and Edith couldn't dress her as such. In fact, quite the opposite was true. Penelope had to remain charming and vivacious, or else the audience would have no empathy for her.

The wedding dress that Edith designed for Natalie was so successful and received so much coverage in the press that requests poured in by the thousands from women wanting a pattern for it. Critics were less enthusiastic about the movie, however. Jeanne Miller of the San Francisco Examiner said "George Wells' witless and inane script is so thin, tedious and unfunny that nothing dazzles the imagination except Miss Wood's glorious high-style looks."

In The Swinger (1966), Ann-Margret was all grown up and playing a woman trying to convince the editor of *Girl-lure* magazine (Anthony Franciosa) that she knows enough about swinging to write a magazine article on the subject. To costume Ann-Margret's nice girl playing bad, Edith was given a wardrobe budget of over $150,000 for costumes and over $100,000 in jewelry. Edith designed over two dozen outfits ranging from mink and sable coats to a beaded mini-bikini. One coat had fourteen-karat gold buttons that had once belonged to Napoleon, and were assessed at $1,000 each.

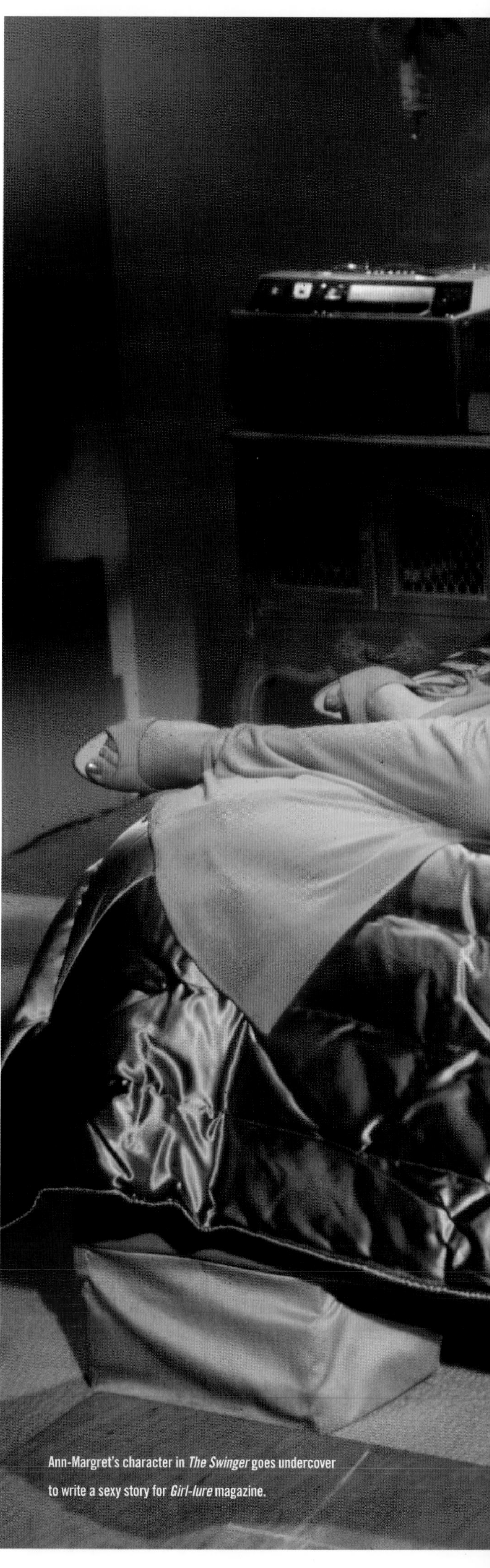

Ann-Margret's character in *The Swinger* goes undercover to write a sexy story for *Girl-lure* magazine.

THE WEDDING DRESS THAT EDITH DESIGNED FOR NATALIE WAS SO SUCCESSFUL AND RECEIVED SO MUCH COVERAGE IN THE PRESS THAT REQUESTS POURED IN BY THE THOUSANDS FROM WOMEN WANTING A PATTERN FOR IT.

As sex comedies became more prevalent, Hollywood decided that European actresses could offer an added exotic sensuality lacking in some American actresses. Claudia Cardinale, Sylva Koscina, and Elke Sommer were among some of the sought-after beauties of the era. Virna Lisi was brought to the United States as a successor to Marilyn Monroe. *In Not With My Wife You Don't!* (1966) Lisi played an Italian nurse who falls in love with two American fliers. Edith designed crisp uniforms, clinging gowns and a sexy black negligee for the actress. Lisi designed her own bathing suit for the film, an op-art one piece with horizontal wavy stripes, virtually backless, worn in a Riviera Beach scene. Lisi extolled Edith's virtues to the press when she was making the film, saying "she is fantastic at creating breathtaking clothes that are also easy to wear."

The decline in theatre attendance was taking its toll on all the major film studios. In 1965, a group of dissident Paramount shareholders led by Broadway producers Ernest Martin and Cy Feuer and chemical manufacturer Herbert Siegel were making plans to unseat the management at the studio. Charles Bludhorn, owner of Gulf & Western Industries made an offer of eighty-three dollars per share to buy Paramount, which was almost ten-dollars over market share. The deal went into effect on October 19, 1966.

Edith attends the premiere of *Sweet Charity,* one of her best designing efforts of the late 1960's

CHAPTER SEVEN

THE UNIVERSAL YEARS

Edith oversees the wardrobe test for Shirley MacLaine in ***Sweet Charity.***

Edith discusses a sketch with actress Katharine Ross for the film *Tell Them Willie Boy Is Here.*

WHEN EDITH REALIZED THAT HER CONTRACT WOULD MOST LIKELY NOT BE RENEWED BY GULF & WESTERN, SHE BEGAN NEGOTIATING WITH LEW WASSERMAN FOR HER SERVICES TO WORK IN THE COSTUME DEPARTMENT AT UNIVERSAL UNDER VINCENT DEE. EDITH HAD HEARD THAT NO ONE WOULD BE ALLOWED TO STAY AT PARAMOUNT THAT WAS OVER SIXTY-FIVE-YEARS-OLD, AND EDITH WAS ALMOST SEVENTY. SHE HAD ALREADY GOTTEN TO THE POINT WHERE SHE WOULD LIE ABOUT HER AGE IN INTERVIEWS BECAUSE SHE FELT AGE WAS NOT VIEWED AS AN ASSET IN THE FILM INDUSTRY. "THE PHRASE 'OVER THE HILL' CHILLS ME," SHE SAID. WITH VERY LITTLE FANFARE, EDITH HEAD LEFT THE BUILDING

Her arrival at Universal, on the other hand, was well-publicized and celebrated with flowers and phone calls from well-wishers. Universal's contract with Edith gave the studio first call on Edith's services, for which they paid her $80,000 per year. They also provided Edith with offices and a car. "Edith knew it was who you knew, who your connections were, that gave you the power," Theadora Van Runkle said. "And so she collected, like she collected her famous necklace of miniature Oscars, she collected people of power."

"She liked a steady life. She liked to know she had peace in her work environment, and that she didn't have to worry where her next job or picture was coming from," Shirley MacLaine said. Life at Universal was very different from Paramount. Instead of an office in the wardrobe building, Edith was given her own bungalow, with signage including a metal cut-out of a dress form and her signature, to announce who was inside. The Oscars were installed, and Edith was given a secretary and a space for her sketch artist Richard Hopper, who had followed her from Paramount. The studio also had a golf cart made with Edith's name emblazoned on it, for her to get around the lot and to the wardrobe building with ease.

Because Edith would only be working on an average of five films a year for the studio, generating publicity and meeting the trams of tourists on the Universal Studios tour became part of the order of the day. The tour had recently been created to shore up the finances of the studio, as movie ticket sales lagged. "I believe in publicity," Edith said. "I like the press. I like to talk. I do a great many lectures. I do a great many fashion shows. I think that one of my great assets is the ability to express myself and I've done a great deal to help myself by my publicity."

The face of fashion changed dramatically with the introduction of hippie culture. Unstructured looks came into vogue with the advent of the shift, a long dress made straight up and down. Tie-dying, in which a shirt is literally tied up and dunked in various dyes became de rigeur for young people. And patterns, which Edith rarely used, became the rage, including big squares, circles and large zigzags, that were influenced by the pop art movement of the period.

Edith's first year at Universal gave her little opportunity to create memorable designs. Edith selected a wardrobe of jeans and poorly draped clothing for Mary Tyler Moore in *What's So Bad About Feeling Good?* (1968). Her designs for Sylva Koscina in *The Secret War of Harry Frigg* (1968), Anjanette Comer in *In Enemy Country* (1968), and Eva Renzi in *The Pink Jungle* (1968) are all but forgotten, as the films themselves have become relatively obscure.

Edith did finally get to design for Joan Crawford for a film. She created a black leotard with a red ringmaster's coat of tails, black gloves, earrings and a top hat, for Joan to wear in the movie *Berserk* (1967). But by this point the actress' career had slipped into acting in these kinds of B-horror films, and Edith chose not to receive a credit on the film.

But one film did set fashion trend for 1967. It was called *Bonnie and Clyde*, designed by Theadora Van Runkle, a talented sketch artist on her first designing assignment. Van Runkle tells a story of running into Edith while she was shopping for fabrics while making the film. "Just use chiffon, you'll have no problem," Edith told the young designer. But Van Runkle's approach to the character was far more radical and based

Elke Sommer's character is employed by Edith in *The Oscar,* and the designer made a cameo appearance as herself in the film.

Life imitates art with Richard Hopper's sketch for Elke Sommer in *The Oscar*. The actress played the role of Edith Head's sketch artist in the film

DESPITE ITS ALL-STAR CAST, *THE OSCAR* RECEIVED NO PRAISE FROM CRITICS. *TIME* MAGAZINE WROTE "EVEN AT ITS AWFUL BEST, THIS MINDLESS JOSEPH E. LEVINE EPIC WILL HARDLY WIN ANYTHING BUT BOOBY PRIZES."

in fact, dressing Faye Dunaway in berets, long cardigans, soft sweaters and midi-skirts. Van Runkle created a global fashion craze and had young girls raiding attics and thrift stores, to create depression-era chic ensembles. Hemlines were lowered from mini- to midi-length, and milliners started working again to appease the demands for berets.

The Oscar (1967) is one of those late 1960's films that Hollywood made about itself that has become an unintentional camp classic. One would think by now that producers would realize that the portrayal of the town's seedy underbelly, unhappy movie stars and hilltop pads never elicits the drama or empathy they expect.

Told in flashback, *The Oscar* follows the career of Frankie Fane (Stephen Boyd), a handsome scoundrel, who alienates everyone close to him on his road to success and eventual downfall. This includes his best friend (Tony Bennett), his pregnant girlfriend Laurel (Jill St. John), a theatre producer (Eleanor Parker) and his wife (Elke Sommer). There are some A-list cameos in the film too, including Frank Sinatra, Merle Oberon, Hedda Hopper, and even Edith, who plays Elke Sommer's employer.

"For the earlier scenes since both Elke and Eleanor play business women roles, we chose tailored costumes—beautifully fitted, three-piece suits-with-sweaters or skirt-blouse-and-jacket ensembles," Edith said. "Elke wears a revealing black lace nightie because at this point in the movie she's a desperate woman, convinced she's losing her husband; this is her weapon."

Despite its all-star cast, *The Oscar* received no praise from critics. Time Magazine wrote "Even at its awful best, this mindless Joseph E. Levine epic will hardly win anything but booby prizes. One can easily imagine the scene next year at the famous ceremonies in Santa Monica: the pit orchestra bravely muddling through Percy Faith's flail-it-with-music themes from *The Oscar* while an Academy spokesman announces that all categories have been hastily revised to permit a few special awards." The article went on to name a host of dubious made-up award categories, and the "winners" from the film. Edith fared the best, winning in the "Least Tedious Performance by a Supporting Actress" category.

Along with Joe Hyams, then husband of Elke Sommer, Edith wrote the book *How to Dress For Success*, which was published in 1967. Edith made it a strictly "how-to" guide and didn't offer any Hollywood tidbits. The reader was given Edith's good sensible advice on how to look younger, but still age-appropriate; how not to over-accessorize; how to dress to get a man and how to keep him; and how to know what's best for your figure. Edith's sketch artist Richard Hopper did the illustrations. The combination of changing attitudes toward fashion, and the fact that Edith couldn't devote as much time and energy to its promotion, left the book sagging in sales compared to Edith's previous book, *The Dress Doctor.*

An elaborate headdress for a dancer in *Sweet Charity.* Opposite: (left to right) Chita Rivera, Shirley MacLaine and Paula Kelly dream of something better in *Sweet Charity.*

Lucille Ball brought Edith on to design her formal clothes for her television special *The Lucille Ball Comedy Hour* (1967). Ball appeared with Bob Hope in an evening dress of white tie and tails, and Edith designed five more outfits for the "Mr. and Mrs." segment including a gold-beaded evening suit, two basic black costumes—one trimmed in lynx fur, an apricot negligee with dyed-to-match fox trim and a maternity dress. As they had done before, Edith shared duties with Ball's longtime designer Edward Stevenson. Along with Della Fox, he created the costumes for the comic numbers.

Hotel (1967) was adapted from the novel by Alex Hailey. Howard Shoup was brought on to the project to design the majority of the cast, and Edith was brought in to design for Merle Oberon. The actress was playing the Duchess of Croydon, who is hiding out with her husband in the hotel after a hit-and-run accident. Oberon had asked director Richard Quine if she could wear pieces from her own legendary jewelry collection in the film. Quine agreed and Edith designed her gowns around them, including a $75,000 brooch.

EDITH FINDS HER WAY

In 1969, Universal renewed Edith's contract for another two years. Edith had begun to take a proactive approach and was actively lobbying producers for work at Universal. In 1968, she designed a film called *Hellfighters* with John Wayne, Vera Miles and Katharine Ross for producer Robert Arthur. The following year, Arthur used Edith on his adaptation of the Broadway musical *Sweet Charity* (1969). It was the first film directed by Bob Fosse, who had directed the original Broadway production, and it reunited Edith Head with Shirley MacLaine.

To work with MacLaine again was a happy coincidence. It had been written that both MacLaine and Natalie Wood specifically put Edith into their contracts after Edith left Paramount, but that was not the case. "It never mattered to me because there were wonderful

Wardrobe tests for the hip nightclub scene in *Sweet Charity*

costume designers," MacLaine says. "Helen Rose was over at Metro, Orry-Kelly was independent. I loved Edith, I must say, she was at the top of my list of the ones I admired and liked the most, but I wouldn't request her. I didn't want to do that. The studios had their own people, and they paid them, and I didn't want to insult whoever was under contract."

In the film, MacLaine played Charity, a hostess in dance hall, who still maintains optimism in spite of her bad choices in careers and men. Chita Rivera and Paula Kelly play her co-workers at the dance hall, and are introduced to the audience in the number *Hey Big Spender*, in which the dancers wear slinky mini-skirts embellished with fringe, tassels and sequins to convey a sense of seediness. Kelly's costume is a standout, totally backless and covered in gold disks.

Edith got on very well with director Bob Fosse, who told her that he didn't want to radically change the look of the costumes from the Broadway production. The sleeveless black dress that Gwen Verdon wore on the original Broadway poster was a look so identified with the production, it needed only to be recreated. For the *Rich Man's Frug* dance number, Edith turned to Richard Hopper for ideas to dress the impossibly chic mod celebrities in the nightclub dance sequence. Hopper created sequined and jeweled black mini-skirts, elaborate wigs, hairpieces and headdresses for the specialized Fosse dance numbers *The Aloof, The Heavyweight*, and *The Big Finish*.

Against the muted grays and blues of a New York rooftop, Edith chose contrasting but effective colors for the song *There's got to Be Something Better than this*. MacLaine wore a red dress trimmed in red sequins, Rivera wore yellow accented with yellow sequins and orange feathers, and Kelly wore lilac with a shocking pink flower and yellow bracelets. The characters are so far removed from the fashion world, that even when they fantasize of the better life to which they are going to escape, Rivera sings that she'll be wearing a "copy of a copy of a copy of Dior." Edith was nominated for an Oscar for Best Costume Design for *Sweet Charity*, but lost to Margaret Furse for *Anne of the Thousand Days* (1969).

Topaz (1969) was another of Hitchcock's spy thrillers set against an International background. The production seemed doomed from the start. Universal executives forced the movie on Hitchcock, and he later said it was one of his unhappiest directing jobs. Hitchcock assembled a cast of respected international actors, but with no standout stars. This time Hitchcock also used colors such as red, yellow and white as the plot was revealed. It was an experiment Hitchcock ultimately felt was not successful. The film did, however, create a tie-in with a manufacturer for Edith to design ready-to-wear clothing. The company Trevira, which owned the label The Trevira Era, commissioned Edith to design a collection called *The Topaz Look*.

Butch Cassidy and the Sundance Kid (1969) starring Paul Newman, Robert Redford, and Katharine Ross, put Edith back on the map with a solid hit with the public. Though some critics were not completely forthcoming in their praise, it was the top grossing film of 1969. Paul Newman and Steve McQueen were originally slated to star in the film, but the actors couldn't reach an agreement on billing. The film was loosely based on the lives of bank robbers Butch Cassidy and his partner The Sundance Kid, and their crime spree in the United States and Bolivia. Edith was loaned to Twentieth-Century Fox for the production.

The wardrobe for Newman and Redford was pulled out of stock at Universal and Western Costume Company. Edith's period clothes for Ross included a group of day suits, an evening gown of cascading ribbons down the shoulders and a swimsuit to be worn in a sepia-toned photo montage. One of the most indelible images of the film had Ross in a cotton print dress with small flowers, riding on the front of Paul Newman's bicycle to the tune of *Raindrops Keep Fallin' on my Head*, beautifully photographed by Conrad Hall.

With fewer films to design, Edith began increasing the number of fashion shows that were staged by her and her friend and business

One of Edith's few ventures in ready-to-wear clothing resulted in disappointing sales when the film on which the clothes were based was not a hit

538 INT SHOOTING GALLERY
(NEW YORK)

ooting gallery
(also arrival)

The popularity of *Butch Cassidy and the Sundance Kid* put the Edith back on the map with a solid hit

partner, June Van Dyke. On tour, local models in each city were cast, and Edith would coach each model in performing in the persona of the star whose gown they were wearing. Long before the days of home video, most audience members couldn't remember what each star wore in each scene of a film, and Edith paraded a bevy of dresses down the runway whose attributions were sometimes slightly inaccurate or completely made up. A pale pink chiffon gown with heavy crystal beading designed by Travis Banton for Carole Lombard in *The Princess Comes Across* (1936) that Lombard had given to Edith, became a gown Edith claimed was designed for Marlene Dietrich in *A Foreign Affair*. Some gowns were remade, such as Olivia de Havilland's gown from *The Heiress* and Grace Kelly's gold ballgown from *To Catch a Thief* (which now had large, clumsy fake bodies of birds spray-painted and attached it to it, rather than the stylized fabric birds on the original).

If Edith wanted to theme a show based on famous lovers, an extra costume from *A New Kind of Love* might be billed as the gown Ava Gardner was wearing the night she met Frank Sinatra. The fact that the dress design would be from the completely wrong period didn't matter, audiences still ate it up. But many dresses were original, such as Natalie Wood's bridal gown from Penelope, and had been purchased from Paramount and Universal, by Edith and June for the fashion shows.

The publicity generated by these shows helped Edith make up for the lack of press generated by the low number of films for which she was designing. Universal was thrilled with the additional exposure, as Edith always plugged her latest projects when doing interviews in each city in which the fashion show appeared. Generally, it was department stores and fundraising councils that would bring the shows to their local cities. And Edith loved the attention, the applause, the contact with fans, and the appreciation that the shows generated for her work, even after so many years.

Personal commissions came from two of Edith's most beloved stars in 1969. Edith designed a gown of periwinkle-blue and violet for Elizabeth Taylor to wear to the Oscar ceremony, as she introduced the Best Picture nominee *Midnight Cowboy* (1969). The dress was auctioned by Christie's in 1999 to raise money for AIDS research. It sold for $167,500 and was purchased by Mattel, Inc.

Edith designed Natalie Wood's wedding gown for her marriage to Richard Gregson on May 30, 1969. Wood was originally born Natalia Zacharenko to Russian immigrant parents, and the wedding ceremony was Russian Orthodox. Edith based Natalie's gown on a costume worn by an 18th-Century Russian princess—white and pale yellow silk and cotton Jacquard fabric in a delicate antique pattern. The under dress was slim and over it Natalie wore a tabard with collar and cuffs of tiny white flowers, gold and pearls. Her headdress was a small flower tiara with pale yellow and white ribbons.

In 1969, *Art Linkletter's House Party* went off the air. Edith had been with the show since it first began on the radio. The show had launched careers of musical artists, given a forum for guest speakers of all walks of life and entertained people with interviews of school children on a variety of topics. Over the years, Edith had counseled thousands of women to simplify their style, and inspired millions of women at home to think about and appreciate what they put on their bodies.

Edith wasn't the only former Paramount employee to find a home at Universal. Hal Wallis began producing films for the studio including *Anne of the Thousand Days* (1969). However, his productions were done out of Great Britain and labor laws precluded Edith working on them. Director George Seaton was another Universal convert, who was setting about bringing the successful book *Airport* by Arthur Hailey to the screen.

The film version of *Airport* (1970) boasted an all-star cast including Burt Lancaster, Dean Martin, Jean Seberg and Jacqueline Bisset, and told the story of a fictional Chicago airport struggling to stay open during a snowstorm. Edith said she saw her main challenge to be figuring what exactly it was that people wore while traveling. Older pas-

Edith's designs for a fictional airline in *Airport* helped her win a contract to design for a real airline

EDITH SAID SHE SAW HER MAIN CHALLENGE TO BE FIGURING WHAT EXACTLY IT WAS THAT PEOPLE WORE WHILE TRAVELING.

Above left: **A wardrobe test for Helen Hayes for *Airport*.** Above: **Edith with actress Dana Wynter on the set of *Airport*.** Right: **Edith with Dean Martin and Jacqueline Bisset at the wrap party for *Airport*.**

G.S.
design for

EDITH CREDITED BISSET WITH HAVING "ONE OF THE GREATEST BODIES I'VE EVER WORKED WITH."

A sketch for a dress for the personal wardrobe of actress Joan Crawford.

sengers would remember the days when people really "dressed" to take a commercial flight. Younger people would dress for comfort.

For Jacqueline Bisset, Edith designed a stewardess uniform for the fictional Trans-Global Airways of orange and gray, made in a polyester-knit fabric. At the time, airline uniforms were short and sexy. But since Bisset was going to meet with a disaster, the uniform was kept on the conservative side. In an interview seven years later, Edith credited Bisset with having "one of the greatest bodies I've ever worked with. But besides that she is rather the opposite, because she is so damned intelligent. It's a strange combination, almost a double personality." Helen Hayes won an Oscar for her role as Ada Quonsett, the perpetual stowaway, whom Edith costumed in a black wool coat and black pillbox hat adorned with a feather.

Edith also designed a line of clothes for Trevira based on her Airport designs, and called it *The Airport Collection*, but the clothing did not sell well and was withdrawn a short time later. However, the film was wildly successful. With a budget of $10 million, it went on to earn over $100 million. Even though the disaster happens very close to the end of the film, *Airport* was credited with laying the groundwork for the disaster film genre of the 1970s, including *The Poseidon Adventure* (1972) and *The Towering Inferno* (1974). Edith was nominated for an Oscar for best costume design for *Airport*, losing to Vittorio Nino Novarese for *Cromwell* (1970).

STORM CLOUDS AHEAD

When Gore Vidal's *Myra Breckenridge* was published in 1968, it was considered a subversive satire on perceived norms of gender and sexuality. Many people of Edith's generation, including Edith herself, found the story to be pornographic. It was, therefore, with some trepidation that Edith agreed to be loaned to Twentieth Century-Fox as a personal favor to Mae West, who had accepted a role in the film version. Theadora Van Runkle designed the costumes for Raquel Welch as Myra.

Long after the advent of color in films and television, Mae still preferred to dress in black-and-white because she felt that the dramatic

Edith only costumed Mae West in *Myra Breckenrige*, and the designer did what she could to maximize the 77-year-old star's assets with underpinnings

"WHITE IS A NON-COLOR, AND BLACK IS A NON-COLOR, AND NO ONE IS ALLOWED TO WEAR NON-COLORS BUT MAE."

–Robert Fryer

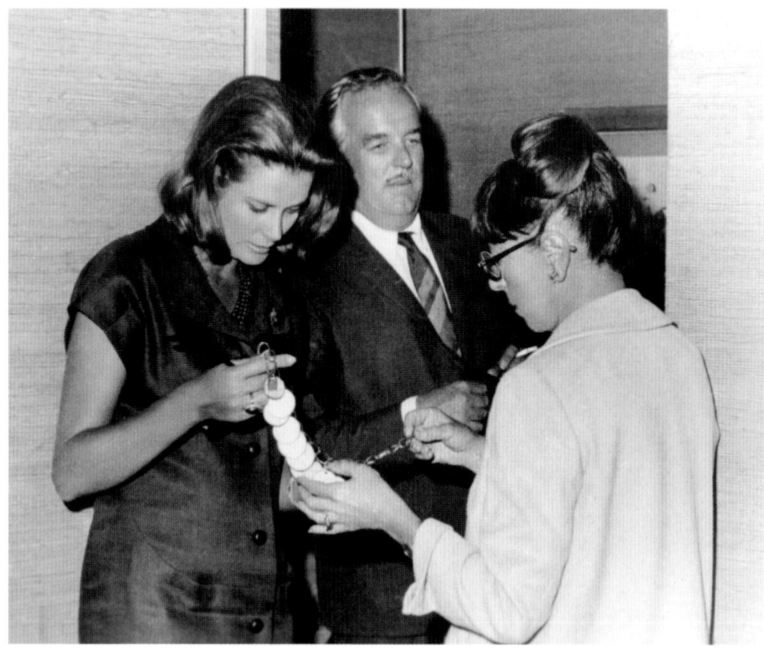

look pulled attention to her. Producer Robert Fryer suggested that in any scene in which she appeared, she should be the only actress wearing black-and-white.

This piece of information was never conveyed to Van Runkle, who designed a black dress with a large white ruffle for Raquel to wear in a scene in which she appeared with Mae. Up until that point, West had worn almost exclusively white ensembles, so Van Runkle felt safe designing a black dress for Welch. When Raquel got to her dressing room the morning the scene was to be shot, the dress was gone. Welch phoned producer Robert Fryer, who informed her that the dress had been confiscated. Fryer told Welch that "white is a non-color, and black is a non-color, and no one is allowed to wear non-colors but Mae." Welch was furious, and went home telling him, "when the dress reappears, so will I." The dress reappeared later that day.

The scuffles between Raquel and Mae were only part of the behind-the-scenes intrigue on the set including breakdowns in communication between the producers and director and the film going way over budget. Gore Vidal disowned the film, and asked that his name be removed from it. *Time* magazine said "*Myra Breckenridge* is about as funny as a child molester. It is an insult to intelligence, an affront to sensibility and an abomination to the eye." Edith's instincts had been right.

When Elizabeth Taylor and Richard Burton, then the most famous couple in the world, approached Lucille Ball at a party with the idea of being guests onTV's *The Lucy Show*, the producers jumped at the chance. Bob Carroll and Madelyn Davis, longtime writers for Lucille Ball, rushed a script into production in which Lucy gets Elizabeth Taylor's ring stuck on her finger minutes before it is to be presented at a press party. Taylor requested that Edith design the two outfits she would wear in the episode. Edith designed a blouse with a large pink and purple paisley design with matching headband and purple slacks, which Taylor wore as she tried to pull the ring from Lucy's finger.

At the show's fictional press reception, as a who's-who of real-life journalists of the day parade by the Burtons, Elizabeth wears a shimmering gold and silver brocade Kaftan, large enough that Lucy could stick her arm through the back. Lucy stands behind a curtain and thrusts

This page: A portrait of Edith by her long-time friend, the photographer John Engstead. Opposite: Princess Grace and Prince Rainier of Monaco visit Edith at her bungalow at Universal, and the Princess admires Edith's famous necklace of antique ivory theatre tokens

Elizabeth Taylor plays a woman trying to regain the interest of her husband (Henry Fonda, seen over Taylor's shoulder) in *Ash Wednesday.*

her hand out, so that guests think it is Elizabeth's hand they're admiring. That episode was the highest-rated program on any network that week, but all was not smooth sailing for Ball and the Burtons. When Lucy suggested that Richard say his lines a bit stronger, the great Welsh actor took umbrage, and shouted his lines all through rehearsal.

Both Taylor and Bette Davis kept Edith working in the early years of the 1970s. Edith designed costumes for Bette Davis in *Madame Sin* (1972) in which Davis appeared as a half-Chinese woman intent on controlling a Polaris submarine. Bette was surprised when Ralph Edwards broke into the middle of her costume consultation with Edith to film a segment of *This is Your Life* in tribute to her. For Taylor, Edith designed her wardrobe in *Hammersmith is Out* (1972) a retelling of the Faust legend co-starring Richard Burton. Based on the success of her designs for *Airport*, Edith also signed a contract with the company Career Apparel to design uniforms for Pan Am. The deal generated a great deal of publicity for both the designer and the airline.

Staying busy at this time was important to Edith. She had been diagnosed with Myelofibrosis, caused by the uncontrolled growth of a blood cell precursor, which results in the accumulation of scar tissue in bone marrow. There is no cure, and treatment options are really just supportive. The average survival rate of patients diagnosed with Myelofibrosis is five years. Frequent blood transfusions became the solution for Edith, to help battle the anemia caused by the disease.

Usually, Edith wouldn't accept television assignments, but work had been so slow, she agreed to design Olivia de Havilland's wardrobe for a TV film titled *The Screaming Woman* (1972). Olivia played Laura Wynant, a wealthy former mental patient who hears the screams of a woman buried alive, only to have her family use the opportunity to try to take control of her estate. The experience in television opened up a new avenue for Edith, and she went on to design TV specials for Raquel Welch and Debby Boone in the 1970's, as well as a television version of The *Little Women* in 1978.

The Life and Times of Judge Roy Bean (1972) cast Paul Newman as Judge Roy Bean, who dispenses his own brand of law in a story set in the Old West. As often had been the case in the past, Edith looked to others for inspiration for the 1920s period clothes required by the script. Director John Huston had requested Edith as costume designer, so there was no doubt that Edith would get credit on the film. But Edith brought on designer Yvonne Wood to essentially design the film for her. Richard Hopper created the pink dress that Ava Gardner wore for her role as Lily Langtry. This was not entirely unusual in the industry. When a designer is in great demand, they may bring another designer on to a project who is between jobs. Generally, credits are discussed up front, and sometimes the secondary designer may receive credit for work done, but sometimes they do not.

"In any one building on New York's Seventh Avenue, there are

"The Sting"

Paul Newman

1936

Edith Head –

The Sting!

Robert Redford
1936

Edith Head

The Sting provided Edith with her last Oscar, though she contributed little to the actual design of the clothing

Above: **Eileen Brennan in a dress that was selected by women's costumer Andrea Weaver from stock for *The Sting*.** Right: **Paul Newman and Robert Redford in wardrobe designed by Vincent Dee.**

20 designers better than I. But they wouldn't last a day in Hollywood," Edith once said. Diplomacy was one of the traits that helped sustain Edith's long career in the business. But Edith's desire for publicity and her territorial instincts, especially in the Oscar arena, caused a fissure with her co-workers that never quite healed when working on *The Sting* (1973).

Director Rob Cohen was working as a script reader for Mike Meadavoy when he read the script for *The Sting*. He wrote in his coverage of it that it was "the great American screenplay and . . . will make an award-winning, major-cast, major-director film." Based on the coverage, Meadavoy sold it that afternoon to Universal. Paul Newman and Robert Redford were brought on to the project as two professional grifters who set up an elaborate scheme to con a mob boss (Robert Shaw) out of a substantial amount of money, in retaliation for the murder of a mutual friend.

Director George Roy Hill wanted the film to be shot on location in Chicago, but Art Director Henry Bumstead decided it would be easier to create the period feel right on the Universal back lot. The men's wardrobe responsibilities fell to Peter Saldutti, working as the men's costume supervisor and Vincent Dee, head of the Universal Costume Department. Andrea Weaver, who worked as the women's costumer on the film, remembers "there were three people's (Newman, Redford, and Robert Shaw) clothes made and those were designed by Vincent Dee. Vincent worked up the sketches and showed the actors, and Vincent and the actors picked the clothes. And Vincent put the clothes into the workroom to be made."

Weaver pulled the vintage clothes that actress Eileen Brennan wore in the movie from stock at Western Costume. "Edith came to the fitting with Eileen. It was just a matter of Edith showing up and selling the goods. That was her expertise. There was one woman's outfit made and that was for the stripper (Sally Kirkland). That costume was designed by Richard Hopper. He designed that costume and he and I put it into the workroom," Weaver said.

Essentially Edith had no real design responsibilities on *The Sting*, though she received singular design credit. Edith's real job was to make sure that everyone was satisfied with the costumes overall, and sell the film to the press. Edith told stories about how Newman and Redford got in some good-natured sparring at each other because each wanted a blue shirt or a blue tie that would help to bring out their eyes, and how Edith alternated blue between them in each scene. In fact, Redford is the only one of them to wear any blue. Newman alternates between white and brown-striped shirts, finally ending in a dinner jacket with a white shirt. Most likely, these stories were just another example of Edith stoking the press.

"A lot of producers were very happy to have Edith's name on a film because then you automatically get press because everybody knew who Edith was. She got more press out of *The Sting* than anything she ever did, and she didn't even do it," Bob Mackie said. The film was a huge box office success bringing in $160 million. It won seven Academy Awards, including Best Picture, Best Director and Best Costume Design for Edith.

People in the costume industry were shocked when Edith offered no acknowledgement of the contributions of Dee, Saldutti, or Weaver in her speech. "She thanked Robert Redford and Paul Newman," Weaver says. "When we work with designers, it's very much a team effort and usually the designer acknowledges everybody's contribution. They lead the way and the look is theirs and they instruct as to what they want. That was just not the case in this instance." To control the damage, Edith took out an ad in the Costume Designer Guild's newsletter to thank the costumers, but the wounds never healed. When Paddy Calistro was writing *Edith Head's Hollywood*, Saldutti declined to be interviewed for the book. "Her Academy Awards were her children," Tippi Hedren says. Indeed, they seemed to be the area in which Edith was most territorial.

Edith's work on *The Sting* was to ensure that all parties (including Robert Redford, pictured here with Edith) were happy with the clothes and to a lend hand in the tremendous publicity push given to the film

"SHE GOT MORE PRESS OUT OF *THE STING* THAN ANYTHING SHE EVER DID, AND SHE DIDN'T EVEN DO IT."

–Bob Mackie

WOMEN'S WARDROBE

CHARACTER ____________

CHARACTER ____________

SCENES ____________

Dress

Hat

Coat

Shoes

Stockings

Purse

Gloves

Fur

Jewelry earrings turquoise center w/diamond surrounding & setting

Hand Props

Miscellaneous

Gold wedding band

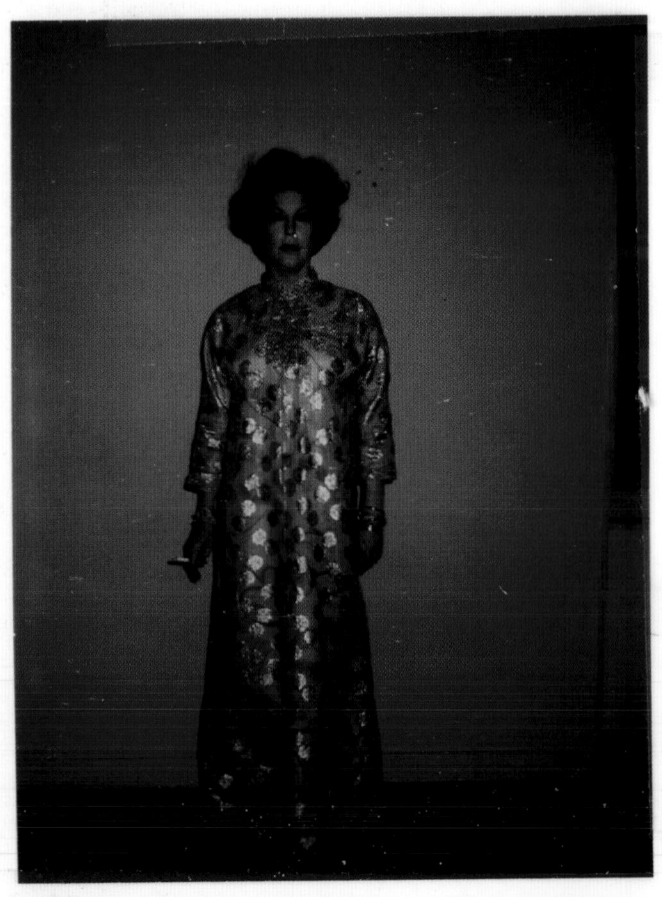

CHARACTER ____________

SCENES ____________

Dress

Hat

Coat

Shoes

Stockings

Purse

Gloves

Fur

Jewelry

Hand Props

Miscellaneous necklace worn as bracelet RH

Same earrings

This page and opposite page: **Wardrobe department test Polaroids of Ava Gardner in *Earthquake*.**

BACK ON TRACK

Edith said she was approached "every hour on the hour" to create a ready to wear line, but always refused. "Suppose I made a line of clothes and nobody bought them? What would I do?" she asked. Edith was very insecure about her designing ability outside of tailoring a garment for a script and having it approved by an actress or director. However, Edith had always had success with home-sewing patterns. Vogue Patterns, who marketed Edith's designs from 1973-1979 would make up sketches of designs that they thought would sell, and then Edith would make changes according to what she felt was true to her style. Edith and June Van Dyke toured their fashion show to help promote the patterns. That, coupled with the tremendous amount of publicity generated by *The Sting*, helped the patterns to become some of the company's most successful offerings.

In 1973, Edith appeared in an episode of the Peter Falk TV series *Columbo*. Edith played a costume designer opposite Anne Baxter as a film star accused of killing her secretary. Edith's friendship with Anne Baxter was one of the few close relationships she established with an actress. Melissa Galt, daughter of Anne Baxter, says "my mother had three personas, there was mom, which was the side that we knew, then there was Anne Baxter, the actress and there was Anne, the private person. And the part that Edith trusted, was Anne, the private person. Mother, as gracious as she was as an actress, did not participate in all the Hollywood gossip and all the Hollywood doodah. She kept herself and us very far out of that. Edith was very similar to that. She had her public persona and she had her private persona, and they were actually quite separate. But they each had that in common.

"I think Edith was at least as private as mother, if not even more so. In order to be themselves, they associated with a completely separate group of people, who were much more real, much more grounded. They didn't go in for all the gossip and back stabbing. They talked about cultural things, travel, adventures that they'd had. That gave them a lot of common ground to talk about, especially since her mother had spent at least three years in New Mexico, and Edie was very big on the Southwest, and all things Native American. I don't think my mother had quite the kinship for the Native American pieces that Edith did, but she had an appreciation for all the arts."

Edith liked being Edith Head, says David Chierichetti. "She liked being important and being famous and known everywhere. But she generally, as much as she could, enjoyed the friendships that she had. She kept in touch with people she'd known in high school and as a child."

Edith worked again for Paramount on *Ash Wednesday* (1973). Elizabeth Taylor played Barbara Sawyer, a woman who has plastic surgery in an attempt to save her marriage. When Barbara checks into a ski resort to wait for her husband (Henry Fonda), the script gave Edith a chance to dress Taylor in furs and a turban dripping with pearls. Roger Ebert wrote "The whole movie, indeed, feels longer than it is. It's fifteen minutes short of two hours, and still it takes forever to be over. The problem is that not enough happens; she waits at the resort, she drinks, she eats, she meets her daughter for a tearful lunch, she talks with a friendly fashion photographer, she waits, she has the affair, she waits, sighs, telephones, looks at herself and models the Edith Head wardrobe. It's all so slight."

The Burtons' marriage was unraveling as *Ash Wednesday* was being made. Richard Burton wrote to an employee that that Taylor's "singular acceptance of this film is because she wants to remain a famous film star. What the stupid (occasionally) maniac doesn't realize is that she is already immortalized (as a film person) forever." In June, Elizabeth Taylor and her daughter Maria moved in with Edith and Wiard after her separation was announced from Richard Burton.

When Ava Gardner committed to film *Earthquake* (1974), she requested Edith's services for her clothes. Burton Miller designed the remainder of the film, and received credit for the costumes. When Edith was addressing a symposium about some of the problems costume designers face, she cited the necessity of sometimes having to design for a star that isn't there. "Ava Gardner arrived on a Saturday, and was filming on Monday," Edith said. Gardner had flown in from her home in London just as filming began, and last minute adjustments needed to be made on the weekend. In the Paramount days, Edith had to give up her weekends very often. Now she was becoming more guarded with them, to ensure she was getting enough rest.

There were often plenty of distractions at home, though. As part of her publicity blitz, Edith would occasionally be photographed at Casa Ladera on weekends, if it was required for a newspaper or magazine story. Photographer Michael Childers was one of the photographers who photographed Edith at her home and on the Universal lot. "The first time I shot Edith Head, it was for an article about famous Hollywood swimming pools," says Childers. "I got an introduction to Edith Head through George Cukor, so we set it up for me to come up to the house in Coldwater Canyon. The house was dazzling. Her level of taste was extraordinary, and she had a great collection of Mexican art. She was quite a stern lady, but she was everything I thought Edith Head was going to be. I asked her to smile and she said 'I don't do that.' These people created a persona and a style for themselves that was so incredible. Her skin was quite white, with white make-up and black hair. But once she warmed up, she couldn't have been more charming.

"I started talking to her about the '30s and the '40s, working with Mae West, and she opened up. She was like a tough, old walnut when I arrived, but she melted. She originally told me that she was only giving me ten minutes, but it turned out to be two hours. She said 'you must come out to Universal to photograph me with my Oscars.' So about six months later, when she was in full-production for a film and her office was open with her staff, I went out there and photographed her with all

"NOBODY LOOKS SOIGNÉE ON THOSE TRIPS– I'VE BEEN ON PLENTY, AND I'VE SEEN WHAT WRECKS PEOPLE ARE."

–Edith Head

The cast of *Airport '75* included Charlton Heston, Karen Black, Myrna Loy and Gloria Swanson

"I LET HIM DECIDE WHICH IS BEST FOR HIM. USUALLY HE WILL PICK THE ONE THAT IS MOST MASCULINE."
–Edith Head

The great wave of nostalgic films of the 1970's included Robert Redford and Susan Sarandon in *The Great Waldo Pepper.*

the Oscars. She suggested we go out to the fitting rooms where there must have been mannequins of twenty-five stars with their names on them. When we walked back to her office, the Universal tour bus went by and all the people yelled 'There's Edith Head! There's the Edith Head!' and she waved at them."

In 1974, Edith was awarded a star on Hollywood's Walk of Fame at 6504 Hollywood Boulevard. In a bid to make sure that photo editors at newspapers and magazines took note, Edith knelt down at the star and pretended to wipe it with her Gucci scarf, as photographers clicked away. The photo ran in hundreds of publications.

The script for *Airport 1975* (1975) was originally written as a TV movie, but executive producer Jennings Lang saw the wisdom of creating an Airport sequel. Karen Black starred as a stewardess who must take the controls of a Boeing 747 after the flight crew is killed in a mid-air collision. Gloria Swanson made a return to the screen after a twenty-two-year absence, and the film also starred Charlton Heston, George Kennedy and Myrna Loy. Of Karen Black, Edith said "she had always played a tough, kooky character before, but she made the transition to a very smart-looking senior stewardess who wore clothes beautifully. The clothes, plus her own talent, of course, have changed her image."

As she had with *Airport*, Edith had to figure out what typical airline travelers were wearing to pull clothes for the extras. "Nobody looks soignée on those trips- I've been on plenty, and I've seen what wrecks people are," Edith said. Swanson, on the other hand, was playing herself and had to look elegant. Edith dressed her in a black and white coat and a white cloche hat.

The Great Waldo Pepper (1975) was a George Roy Hill film about a biplane pilot who takes up barnstorming to relive his glory days of World War I. Susan Sarandon played Mary Beth, a young woman who is introduced into Pepper's air shows as a wing walker to attract bigger crowds.

69-37

The film takes place in the time between 1926 and1931. It was made on location in Egin, Texas and the aerial sequences were filmed at Zuehl Airfield near San Antonio. George Roy Hill had been a marine pilot, and often flew the airplane pictured in the film while directing the action. On working with Hill, Edith said "he's a perfectionist. I had to show him all the fabrics. This doesn't happen very often, but he has a tremendous interest in everything, and I like to work with someone like that." Redford was a little easier. "I go to Redford and I show him three sketches, telling him 'this one will make you seem more sensitive, this one is more aggressive, and this one is more romantic.' I let him decide which is best for him. Usually he will pick the one that is most masculine," Edith said. The Great Waldo Pepper is one of the films credited with revitalizing the interest in leather bomber jackets, which were also called barnstormer jackets.

Edith was finally reunited again with producer Hal Wallis on *Rooster Cogburn* (1975). Actually, she was reunited with both Mr. and Mrs. Wallis—as Martha Hyer had co-written the screenplay under the name Martin Julien. The sequel to the 1969 film *True Grit* teamed original cast member John Wayne as Rooster Cogburn opposite Katharine Hepburn as Eula Goodnight. Goodnight enlists Cogburn to rid her town of a band of marauding thugs.

Katharine Hepburn had collected all kinds of scarves and samples of fabrics, which she brought to show Edith in their initial meeting. Edith called their costume consultation "one of shortest and most business-like" of her career. "What she showed me was exactly right and perfect for the film," Edith said. She matched the fabrics and designed around them, and then Hepburn experimented with a saddle on a saw-horse to make sure that she could properly ride on a horse in the dresses. Wayne and Hepburn both had physically demanding roles that tested their limits. Wayne had a cancerous lung removed ten years before and had to breathe through an oxygen mask between takes, and Hepburn had recently recovered from hip surgery.

Katharine Hepburn (opposite, and below with John Wayne) brought scraps of fabric to her costume consultation with Edith for *Rooster Cogburn.*

Opposite page: **Elizabeth Taylor played the Queen of Light in the ill-fated production of *The Blue Bird*.** Below: **Sean Connery and Michael Caine in *The Man Who Would Be King*.**

Making the film had been a bit of a stretch. When *True Grit* was first made by Paramount, a sequel had been conceived. The idea was abandoned as westerns fell out of favor, and producers weren't sure that Wayne could still carry a film. Even with the addition of Hepburn, the film still couldn't reel in audiences. But a weak script may bear more of the responsibility than the drawing power of the two leads. Audiences turned out in droves to see Hepburn again in *On Golden Pond* (1981). Rooster Cogburn was to be Hal Wallis' last film.

The Man Who Would Be King (1975) was based on a short story by Rudyard Kipling. John Huston directed Sean Connery as Daniel Dravot and Michael Caine as Peachy Carnehan, two British soldiers who, after their tour of duty in India, begin taking over villages in Kafristan. Huston had wanted to make this film since the 1950s and had originally considered casting Humphrey Bogart and Clark Gable.

The film was shot on location in Morocco and boasted the largest number of costumes Edith had ever done for a film, totaling 15,000 people to dress. This included hordes of warriors, nomads, shepherds, horsemen, plus uniforms of the British army in the 1880s in India and brightly-clad desert warriors crossing the Khyber Pass. Everything had to be brought in to make the costumes. Wardrobe supervisor John Wilson-Apperson and wardrobe supervisor Paul Vachon set up a workshop in a warehouse and hired locals to dye the fabric and sew the costumes to Edith's specifications.

Of the numerous local extras used, Edith said "we were shooting in the Atlas Mountains, and they were supposed to be a race of people who had never been seen. We were using these people from way up in these little tiny mountain resorts. Some of them had never taken a bath. They'd come down in these funny costumes, and we'd put these others on. And the next morning we couldn't find them. They'd disappeared with the clothes." Edith's tales of the making of this film varied depending on whom she was telling. Sometimes in her stories, the tribesmen did come back with the clothes. Edith was nominated for an Oscar for Best Costume Design, losing to Ula-Britt Söderlund and Milena Canonero for *Barry Lyndon* (1975).

"THE ONLY THING IN THE PICTURE THAT LOOKS REALLY PERIOD ARE THE 'PLUS FOURS' (KNICKERS) ON GABLE. WE JUST ACCIDENTALLY HIT A PERIOD THAT LOOKS LIKE OUR PERIOD."

–Edith Head

Universal wanted to show its appreciation to The United States Coast Guard for their help during the filming of the enormously successful movie *Jaws* (1975). The studio asked officials if there was anything that could be done for them, and reply came saying "the women of the Coast Guard have not had a new uniform for forty years." Edith's answer was to design an entire line of uniforms, employing both skirts and slacks. The previous uniform had only been available with a skirt and a jacket tailored in the men's style. Touches that were typical of Edith's design sensibility included a belted back that allowed women to adjust their uniform for an individualized fit and a neckerchief. Edith's only faux pas was not sticking to her philosophy predicting trends: the slacks of the uniforms were designed as bell bottoms, which fell out of favor within a few years.

Edith traveled between the Marrakech location of *The Man Who Would Be King* and Russia to oversee the costuming of *The Blue Bird* (1976). If blue birds are supposed to represent happiness, there was very little to be found on the set of this film. It was the first American-Soviet co-production, created to foster better relations between the nuclear superpowers. Since it was deemed best that the subject of the film be non-political, it was decided to adapt Maurice Maeterlinck's children's theater play *The Blue Bird*. Producing company Twentieth-Century Fox already owned the rights to the property, having made it with Shirley Temple in 1940.

In the film, two peasant children are led by the human embodiments of a cat, light, fire, night and other entities as they search for the Blue Bird of Happiness. "Every character was expressed in color," Edith said. "Water (Valentina Gonilce Ganibalovain) in pale shades of blue green, Fire (Yevgeni Shcherbakov) in flaming red and orange, Cat (Cicely Tyson) in soft brown and beige, Night (Jane Fonda) in black leather and silver, and Luxury (Ava Gardner) in gold, crimson with rubies and emeralds."

There were numerous technical difficulties at Lenfim Studios due to inferior equipment, as well as infighting among the producers and director George Cukor. Elizabeth Taylor came down with amoebic dysentery and needed medical care in London. Cukor accused Cicely Tyson of practicing voodoo to doom him and the production. Even with a budget of $12 million dollars, the production still had a Third World feel, with mismatched shots and poor sets.

Gable and Lombard (1976) gave Edith a chance to return to some of the glamorous techniques used in the 1930s, such as heavy beading and trimming gowns in fur. Edith discussed the clothing with film historian Tony Macklin. "It's almost contemporary," Edith said. "We had a complete cycle, from '36 to '76. It's never, ever happened to me that I did a period film that looked contemporary. Because usually you say 'oh, the shoulders are very broad, I know it's the '40s. The only thing in the picture that looks really period are the "plus fours"

Edith toured the country moderating fashion shows with examples of costumes from her legendary career.

Edith looks over the costume in her final fitting with Jill Clayburgh for *Gable and Lombard*.

Carole Lombar
white satin
"fox -
Edith Head -

(knickers) on Gable. We just accidentally hit a period that looks like our period."

But the glamour ended there for Edith, who saw very little of the two stars that she knew personally in their film counterparts, played by James Brolin and Jill Clayburgh. Director Sidney J. Furie and screenwriter Barry Sandler, perhaps to make a film accessible to modern audiences, took dramatic license with the characters behaving more in a style akin to the liberated 1970s. The Carole Lombard who had been such a support to Travis Banton and Edith herself, knew the place for her ribald sense of humor, and Edith didn't care for the crass way she was portrayed.

When Edith was asked to create designs for *Airport '77* (1977), it made her one of the few people (including George Kennedy) to have stayed with the *Airport* franchise from the beginning. When producers offered the part of Emily Livingston to Joan Crawford, the actress refused, later saying "they actually asked me to fly out there with only one week's notice! Why, that is hardly enough time for makeup tests or rehearsals. And when I asked about costume fittings, they said they wanted me to wear my own clothes!" This may not be entirely accurate since Edith was already working on the film, designing the stewardess uniform for Brenda Vaccaro to wear. Burton Miller was also assigned to the production.

When Olivia De Havilland accepted the role, she did get Edith's services to design the one outfit she would wear - a slimming black dress with a matching coat. Olivia had originally wanted to wear purple, but Edith thought black would be more flattering. The storyline involved the plane being submerged in water, and eventually flooding, and dressing Olivia in black ensured that the fabric would not turn transparent. De Havilland told an interviewer that the secret to Edith's success was that "she knows when the lionesses need to be fed. Surely one of the reasons she has all her limbs, no scars and all those Oscars is that she knows just the right moment to produce a

The original sketch (left) and white satin gown trimmed in fur (above) for Jill Clayburgh in *Gable and Lombard*.

Though Edith didn't do her own presentation sketches at this point in her career, she could still sketch out an idea to give to her sketch artist Richard Hopper to complete, such as this one for Mae West in *Sextette*

chicken sandwich." Edith received her final Oscar nomination for *Airport '77*, but lost to John Mollo's innovative designs created for *Star Wars* (1977).

THE LEGEND IN DECLINE

Hallmark Hall of Fame provided Edith her last opportunity to work with Bette Davis in *The Disappearance of Aimee* (1976). Two years later, the same series would provide the last project with which Edith would work with Elizabeth Taylor. *Return Engagement* (1978) cast Taylor as a college professor, hiding the secret that she was once a famous Vaudeville performer. The film was made during a difficult period in Taylor's life, when she felt isolated during her marriage to Senator John Warner, and her alcohol dependency had increased. Taylor was only 5' 2" and even with slight weight variations, she could appear heavier on screen. As much as Edith tried, she simply couldn't hide the fact that Taylor was at the heaviest point in her life.

The Big Fix (1978) was a rare chance for Edith to do a project that was not associated with one of the actresses with whom she had worked during Hollywood's Golden Age. The film starred Richard Dreyfuss as a detective and co-starred Susan Anspach and Bonnie Bedelia. Dreyfuss had his own costumer on the film, and Edith was assigned to dress the female leads. This was Edith's first assignment that was entirely shopped, with nothing designed. The trend had become the norm now in filmmaking, and continues to this day.

"The young actresses today are not nearly as easy to work with," Edith said at one of the many question-and-answer appearances she was doing at the time. "They are concerned with what they like. I have a few of them, which I never had with a great star, ever. You have an actress who says 'I don't like pink.' Well, who the hell cares? I get so mad at them."

Edith praised the director of *The Big Fix*, as she often did with the people who employed her. "If a person comes on the set and they do not look right, they say that translates itself not into the actress, but into the director and everybody else," she said. "Now with Jeremy Kagan, we get the things, and even if it's late at night, he stays and he looks at the clothes. He never shoots anything unless he has seen and approved it. He seems to know fabric. He seems to know color. He must have studied the script thoroughly because he seems to know ahead of time what kind of clothing will help motivate a scene."

Edith was stunned when Mae West announced she would be returning to the screen at eighty-four in *Sextette* (1978), based on West's own play Sextet. Though the film was produced by Crown International Pictures, it was shot on the Paramount lot. Mae played Marlo Manners, a still vital and appealing film star on her honeymoon, which is constantly interrupted by a string of photo sessions, dress fittings, meetings with muscle men, interviews and one ex-husband, desperate for a last fling. The movie co-starred Timothy Dalton as Marlo's new husband, and contained a procession of improbable cameos of stars including Tony Curtis, Alice Cooper, Ringo Starr, and George Hamilton.

The script was set up for Mae to deliver strings of her one-liners including "I'm the girl who works for Paramount all day, and Fox all night" and "Marriage is like a book. The whole story takes place between the covers." Edith put Mae in a powder blue negligee trimmed in blue marabou feathers for a scene where Dalton says to her, "I told the world about the real Marlo Manners." Mae waved her hands around her breasts and said "it's real honey, it's all real." Keith Moon played Roger, Marlo's dress designer, in a scene offering up some of Edith's best designs for the film. When Marlo appears in a white gown, covered entirely in brilliants, Roger squeals "that dress is so fantastic, even I would wear it. In fact, I have."

The film looks like it could have been nothing but a vanity piece for an aging actress trying desperately to cling to a notion of an adoring public that still finds her sexually attractive. That would have been the case maybe for anyone but Mae West. When *Sextette* premiered in Hollywood and San Francisco, thousands of adoring fans swarmed the actress, like nothing Marlo Manners had ever seen.

Universal had considered laying Edith off in the mid-1970s. She managed to keep her job, but at a much lower salary, though Universal did continue to supply her with the bungalow, a secretary and a car. Even though she wasn't always busy doing actual design work, she was as busy as ever with personal appearances and interviews. The Ihnens would attend industry functions in the evenings, or entertain friends at home.

Late in 1978, Wiard was diagnosed with cancer of the prostate, and lost a lot of weight. Edith had just undergone a facelift the year before, and although she looked well, she was also fatigued from the blood transfusions required to fight the Myelofibrosis. She kept her condition hidden from almost everyone. She relied on her friend David Chierichetti to help with sketching and photo research when needed. Elois Jenssen, one of the few other designers with whom Edith was close, would drive Edith to her transfusion appointments.

On some weekends, Anne Baxter would bring her daughters Melissa and Maginal Galt to Casa Ladera for a swim and lunch. "I knew Edith differently than most people," Melissa says. "I saw her only once or twice at the studio, otherwise I knew her at home. The 'Aunt Edie' I remember is not the one that is always pictured in her little gray suit with all her Oscars. I remember her better dressed in very colorful Mexican garb, kind of bohemian looking, at her casa. My mother would take my sister and me to the pool, which was above the house in the back, and we would play in the pool, and then have a little time with 'Aunt Edie.'"

On June 22, 1979, Wiard lost his battle with prostate cancer. The man who had quietly been "Mr. Edith Head," who had helped Edith realize her full potential both as a designer and as a woman was gone. Edith held the service at Forest Lawn. David Chierichetti says Edith was never the same after losing Wiard. If Edith ever needed work as a distraction, this was the time. June Van Dyke arranged more fashion shows and Edith continued to promote her patterns. She appeared in a documentary about herself done for West German television.

Edith attended the American Film Institute tribute to Alfred Hitchcock, held in 1979. Within a year, the director would be gone. Mae West also died in 1980. More than 100 mourners attended her funeral at the Old North Church at Forest Lawn in the Hollywood Hills. Mae was laid out in one of Edith's gowns from *Sextette*. And though no one could imagine it at the time, Natalie Wood would also be gone just two years later.

The Last Married Couple in America (1980) was Natalie's last completed theatrical release. She played Mari Thompson, a woman who begins to doubt her own marriage to Jeff (George Segal), when all of her friends' marriages start breaking apart. All of the men's clothes were to be bought, and Edith was given a budget of $12,000 to design Natalie clothes. In the end, Natalie opted to shop for her own wardrobe, only wearing one of Edith's designs for the film. The movie was not a financial or critical success, though critics thought Natalie gave the script better than it deserved. Valerie Harper's performance as Mari's newly-divorced friend, who gets a new lease on life when she undergoes a vaginoplasty, was singled out by critics.

Probably one of the best investments Edith ever made was what came to be known as *The Edith Head Collection*, the collection of gowns (some from her films, some from other sources) that Edith used in her fashion shows with June Van Dyke. They continued to pay off in publicity for her over and over again. In June, 1980, Edith appeared with the collection on an episode of the television series *Omnibus*. Popular actresses of the day modeled the gowns, including Cindy Williams in Audrey Hepburn's black *Sabrina* dress, Carol Lynley in Grace Kelly's gold ball gown from *To Catch a Thief*, and Victoria Principal in the white tulle gown Elizabeth Taylor wore in *A Place in the Sun*. An exhibition of Edith's gowns and costume sketches titled

Edith's last film was *Dead Men Don't Wear Plaid* starring Rachel Ward and Steve Martin.

Reflections of Edith Head opened at the California Museum of Science and Industry in August, 1981.

Though the film didn't have a large budget, director Carl Reiner opted to use Edith's services for his film *Dead Men Don' t Wear Plaid* (1982). The film was a comic homage to classic film noir detective films, and starred Steve Martin and Rachel Ward. Edith's challenge was to recreate classic costumes from classic films, some that she had originally designed and some that she had not, for new scenes with actors that would be intercut with scenes from the original movies. Edith took particular delight in re-doing a dress that she had designed for Barbara Stanwyck in *Double Indemnity* (1944), only now it was to be worn by Steve Martin for comedic effect.

Martin played Rigby Reardon, a private investigator, hired by beautiful Juliet Forrest (Rachel Ward) to investigate the death of her father. Along the way, Rigby encounters some of filmdom's most famous faces, including Humphrey Bogart in *The Big Sleep* and Burt Lancaster in *The Killers*. "When Edith said she wanted to do it, it was like a stamp of approval," Reiner said. "We knew we had a good script, but when somebody like Edith Head or John DeCuir comes in and they say they want to be a part of it, and they say 'this is original and funny and wonderful, can we help?' You feel pretty good about that. Edith Head was like the stamp of approval of the almighty people up there."

In his biography of Edith, David Chierichetti told how she called him to Casa Ladera one day, and asked him to bring any costume research he might have from the 1940s. Since Edith wasn't being paid enough to hire a sketch artist for the film, David helped Edith do the drawings. At first Edith was filled with self-doubt, but as she sketched, her confidence grew. "I had never seen such virtuosity," Chirechetti wrote "at that moment, I knew what she had never known: Edith Head was a great designer."

Edith showed up on the set every day, but no one working with her on the film realized how sick she was. Reiner told author Paddy Calistro that one day, a fatigued Edith fell asleep on a couch on a part of a set that wasn't being used. Within two weeks of the wrapping of the film, Edith was in Good Samaritan Hospital. Upon her release, she began calling friends, and in her cryptic way, said her goodbyes. Edith had to be taken back to the hospital when, during a violent coughing spell one night, she ruptured her esophagus. She never left the hospital. On the evening of October 24, 1981, Edith Head passed away.

WITHIN TWO WEEKS OF THE WRAPPING OF THE FILM, EDITH WAS IN GOOD SAMARITAN HOSPITAL. UPON HER RELEASE, SHE BEGAN CALLING FRIENDS, AND IN HER CRYPTIC WAY, SAID HER GOODBYES.

Edith outside her bungalow on the Universal lot.

"A QUEEN HAS LEFT US, THE QUEEN OF HER PROFESSION. SHE WILL NEVER BE REPLACED." –Bette Davis

It seemed an appropriate end that on Edith's last film, she should work again with Ingrid Bergman, Bette Davis, Ava Gardner, Veronica Lake, Barbara Stanwyck, and Lana Turner, even if they were just shadows. *Dead Men Don't Wear Plaid* was dedicated to Edith Head.

A memorial service was attended by many of the luminaries that Edith had dressed including Elizabeth Taylor, Paul Newman, Loretta Young and Jane Wyman. Bette Davis eulogized Edith saying "a queen has left us, the queen of her profession. She will never be replaced. Her contribution to our industry in her field of design, her contribution to the taste of our town of Hollywood, her elegance as a person, her charms as a woman—none of us who worked with her will ever forget."

Bette Davis probably understood Edith's struggle through life better than anyone. As a young contract player at Warner Brothers, Bette was nearly dropped by the studio early on after a string of uninteresting pictures in which she failed to make an impact. When George Arliss cast her in 1932's *The Man Who Played God*, it was the break she needed to show the world her acting capabilities. Across town, Edith, another woman full of potential, was struggling to make an impression on her employers in the costume department. Both Edith and Bette struggled nearly daily to stay at the top of their professions and both showed the world what dogged determination can produce - a career spanning decades of quality work that will awe and inspire for many generations to come.

EPILOGUE

SHORTLY BEFORE HER DEATH, Edith began a series of interviews with writer Norma Lee Browning for a book to be titled *Hollywood Magic*. Those interviews became part of the book *Edith Head's Hollywood* by Paddy Calistro, published in 1983. David Chierichetti published a biography about Edith, including his personal reminiscences, titled *Edith Head: The Life and Times of Hollywood's Celebrated Costume Designer*, in 2003.

Casa Ladera was willed to the Motion Picture & Television Fund. It was sold in 1983 to an architect. Actress Carrie Fisher bought the property in 1993.

June Van Dyke died in August 1997. Her collection of over 100 Edith Head gowns was auctioned in March 2004.

A benefit was held at Cipriani in New York, April 23, 1998, for The Motion Picture & Television Fund and for The Design Industries Foundation Fighting AIDS. Actress Debi Mazar impersonated Edith in clothes by Isabel Toledo. The evening acknowledged the effect Edith had on contemporary designers like Ms. Toledo.

On February 25, 2003, The United States Postal Service issued a 37-cent stamp bearing Edith's likeness honoring costume design as part of their series celebrating "American Filmmaking: Behind the Scenes."

Both Paramount and Universal studios named their wardrobe buildings after her.

In 2006, Edith was honored with a Rodeo Drive Walk of Style Award in Beverly Hills, California, along with James Acheson and Milena Canonero.

In 2008, actress Susan Classen and author Paddy Calistro collaborated on a one-woman show about Edith called *A Conversation with Edith Head*, which Classen performed in the United States and England.

A younger generation was introduced to the Edith Head mystique indirectly. On their 2001 album *Mink Car,* alternative rock band *They Might Be Giants* included a song called "She Thinks She's Edith Head." Toronto neo-swing band Atomic 7 released an album called *Gowns by Edith Head* in 2002. For the 2004 animated feature *The Incredibles*, director Brad Bird created the character of a designer named Edna Mode. Some speculate she is based on a hybrid of several designers that could include Mary Quant, Una Jones, and Edith Head.

ACKNOWLEDGEMENTS

IT IS VERY IMPORTANT TO FIRST ACKNOWLEDGE THE WRITERS who have come before me that have helped shape the perception of Edith Head's career. The first were Jane Kesner Ardmore and Joe Hyams, who collaborated on *The Dress Doctor* and *How to Dress for Success with Edith*, respectively. Paddy Calistro was the first to give a thorough career overview and put Edith's work in historical perspective in her book *Edith Head's Hollywood*. David Chierechetti shared his vast first-hand knowledge of the costume industry and Edith herself in his biography Edith Head, and was a tireless help to me on this book.

I am very grateful to the associates of Edith, who allowed me to interview them, including: Shirley MacLaine, Tippi Hedren, Joan Fontaine, Rhonda Fleming, Arlene Dahl, Ronald Neame, Patricia Morison, Melissa Galt, Patricia Crowley, and Michael Childers. I would also like to thank Stephen Rebello for allowing me to quote extensively from his interview with Kim Novak.

The late Robert Cushman of the Academy of Motion Pictures and Sciences was an indispensible help in guiding me through the vast wealth of visual material related to Edith Head. My gratitude also extends to his colleagues Jenny Romero, Barbara Hall and the staff at The Margaret Herrick Library, who assisted me with my research. Others who generously shared their collections of photographs include Manoah Bowman, Michael Childers, Matt Tunia, Tom Wilson, Jim Avey, and David Chierechetti. Costume historian Greg Schreiner allowed access to his Edith Head originals, and James Jaeger photographed them beautifully.

I am in awe that Sandy Powell, a woman whose talent I greatly respect, has written the Foreword for this book. I also must thank Cindy De La Hoz of Running Press and Jacqueline Grace and Jamie Locher of LifeTime Media for their guidance, and Roger Gorman for his beautiful design work.

I am very lucky to have supportive friends who contributed in many ways to the completion of this book. They include Robert Mycroft, Michael Giammarese, Mark Mayes, Will Meister, James Radford, Grant Taylor, Mark Biberstine, Stephen Nye, James D. Rieker, Valerie and Bill Mayes, Tim Jenkins, Lisa Malec, and the Albrecht and Salinas families. This book is dedicated to the memory of Walter Albrecht, who never saw a movie he didn't love.

INDEX

PHOTO CREDITS

Cover: Photofest; Pages 2, 4, 7, 9: Photofest; Pages 10-11, 12, 14-15: Courtesy of the Academy of Motion Picture Arts and Sciences; Pages 17, 19, 20-21, 23: Photofest; Page 24: Author's Collection; Pages 25, 26, 27, 28, 30, 31, 32, 33, 36, 38, 40, 43, 44, 47, 48-49, 51, 52-53, 55, 56-57, 58, 60, 61, 62-63, 64, 65, 66, 68, 70, 73, 74-75, 76, 77, 78, 79, 80, 81, 82, 83, 84, 85, 86, 87, 89: Photofest; Page 90: James Jaeger; Pages 91, 92-93, 94, 95, 96, 97, 99, 100-101, 102-103, 105, 106-107, 108, 109, 110: Photofest; Page 111: James Jaeger; Pages 112, 113, 115, 116, 117, 119, 120, 121, 122, 123, 124, 125, 127, 128, 131, 132: Photofest; Page 134: James Jaeger; Page 136, 139, 141, 142, 143, 144, 145, 146-147, 149, 150, 151, 152-153, 154, 156-157: Photofest; Page 158: James Jaeger; Page 159, 160, 161, 162, 163, 164, 165, 166, 167, 168, 169, 170, 171, 172-173, 175, 177, 178: Photofest; Page 179: Courtesy of the Academy of Motion Picture Arts and Sciences; Page 180, top: Photofest; Page 180, bottom, and Page 181: Michael Childers; Pages 182-183, 185, 188, 190, 191, 193, 194, 196-197, 199, 200, 202, 203, 205, 206-207, 208, 209, 210, 211, 212, 213, 215, 216, 217, 218, 219, 220, 221, 223, 224, 225, 226, 227, 228, 229, 230: Photofest; Page 231: James Jaeger; Pages 232, 233, 234, 235, 237, 238-239, 240, 243, 244, 247, 248, 250-251, 252, 253, 254, 255, 256-257, 258, 259, 260, 261, 263, 264, 265, 266, 268, 270-271; 272, 274, 275, 276: Photofest; Page 277: James Jaeger; Pages 279, 280, 281, 282, 284, 285,286-287, 289, 290, 291, 292, 294, 296, 297, 298, 299, 301, 302-303, 304, 305, 306, 307, 309, 310, 311, 312, left: Photofest; 312, right: James Jaeger; Pages 313, 315, 316, 317, 319, 320, 321, 323, 324, 325, 326, 327, 328-329, 331, 332-333, 334, 336-337, 338, 340, 341, 342, 343, 345, 346, 347, 349, 350, 351, 352, 354, 355, 356, 357, 358, 360, 361, 362, 363, 365: Photofest; 366-367: Jim Avey Collection; Pages 369, 371, 372, 373, 374, 375, 377, 378-379, 380: Photofest; Page 381: James Jaeger; Pages 383, 385, 387: Photofest; Page 388: Michael Childers.